Ecological Communication and Ecoliteracy

Bloomsbury Advances in Ecolinguistics

Series Editors:
Arran Stibbe and Mariana Roccia

Advisory Board:
Nadine Andrews (Lancaster University, UK)
Maria Bortoluzzi (University of Udine, Italy)
Martin Döring (University of Hamburg, Germany)
Sue Edney (University of Bristol, UK)
Alwin Fill (University of Graz, Austria)
Diego Forte (University of Buenos Aires, Argentina)
Amir Ghorbanpour (Tarbiat Modares University, Iran)
Nataliia Goshylyk (Vasyl Stefanyk Precarpathian National University, Ukraine)
Huang Guowen (South China Agricultural University, China)
George Jacobs (Independent Scholar)
Kyoohoon Kim (Daegu University, South Korea)
Katerina Kosta (Oxford Brookes University, UK)
Mira Lieberman-Boyd (University of Sheffield, UK)
Keith Moser (Mississippi State University, USA)
Douglas Ponton (University of Catania, Italy)
Robert Poole (University of Alabama, USA)
Alison Sealey (University of Lancaster, UK)
Nina Venkataraman (National University of Singapore, Singapore)
Daniela Francesca Virdis (University of Cagliari, Italy)
Sune Vork Steffensen (University of Southern Denmark, Denmark)

Bloomsbury Advances in Ecolinguistics emerges at a time when businesses, universities, national governments and many other organizations are declaring an ecological emergency. With climate change and biodiversity loss diminishing the ability of the Earth to support life, business leaders, politicians and academics are asking how their work can contribute to efforts to preserve the ecosystems that life depends on.

This book series explores the role that linguistics can play in addressing the great challenges faced by humanity and countless other species. Although significant advances have been made in addressing social issues such as racism, sexism and social justice, linguistics has typically focused on oppression in human communities and overlooked other species and the wider ecosystems that support life. This is despite the disproportionate impact of ecological destruction on oppressed groups. In contrast, this book series treats language as an intrinsic part of both human societies and wider ecosystems. It explores the role that different areas of linguistic enquiry, such as discourse analysis, corpus linguistics, language diversity and cognitive linguistics, can play at a time of ecological emergency.

The titles explore themes such as the stories that underpin unequal and unsustainable industrial societies; language contact and how linguistic imperialism threatens the ecological wisdom embedded in endangered languages; the use of linguistic analysis in ecocriticism, ecopsychology and other ecological humanities and social sciences; and emerging theoretical frameworks such as Harmonious Discourse Analysis. The titles also look to cultures around the world for inspirational forms of language that can lead to new stories to live by. In this way, the series contributes to linguistic theory by placing language fully in its social and ecological context and to practical action by describing the role that linguistics can play in addressing ecological issues.

Titles published in the series:
Corpus-Assisted Ecolinguistics, Robert Poole
Language and Ecology in Southern and Eastern Arabia, edited by Janet C. E. Watson, Jon C. Lovett and Roberta Morano
Storytelling and Ecology, Anthony Nanson
TESOL and Sustainability, edited by Jason Goulah and John Katunich

Ecological Communication and Ecoliteracy

Discourses of Awareness and Action for the Lifescape

Edited by
Maria Bortoluzzi and Elisabetta Zurru

BLOOMSBURY ACADEMIC
LONDON • NEW YORK • OXFORD • NEW DELHI • SYDNEY

BLOOMSBURY ACADEMIC

Bloomsbury Publishing Plc, 50 Bedford Square, London, WC1B 3DP, UK
Bloomsbury Publishing Inc, 1359 Broadway, New York, NY 10018, USA
Bloomsbury Publishing Ireland, 29 Earlsfort Terrace, Dublin 2, D02 AY28, Ireland

BLOOMSBURY, BLOOMSBURY ACADEMIC and the Diana logo are trademarks of Bloomsbury Publishing Plc

First published in Great Britain 2024
Paperback edition published 2026

Copyright © Maria Bortoluzzi, Elisabetta Zurru and Contributors, 2024, 2025

Maria Bortoluzzi, Elisabetta Zurru and Contributors have asserted their right under the Copyright, Designs and Patents Act, 1988, to be identified as Authors of this work.

For legal purposes the Acknowledgements on p. xvi constitute an extension of this copyright page.

Cover design: Elena Durey

This work is published open access subject to a Creative Commons Attribution-NonCommercial-NoDerivatives 4.0 International licence (CC BY-NC-ND 4.0, https://creativecommons.org/licenses/by-nc-nd/4.0/). You may re-use, distribute, and reproduce this work in any medium for non-commercial purposes, provided you give attribution to the copyright holder and the publisher and provide a link to the Creative Commons licence.

Bloomsbury Publishing Plc does not have any control over, or responsibility for, any third-party websites referred to or in this book. All internet addresses given in this book were correct at the time of going to press. The author and publisher regret any inconvenience caused if addresses have changed or sites have ceased to exist, but can accept no responsibility for any such changes.

A catalogue record for this book is available from the British Library.

Library of Congress Cataloging-in-Publication Data

Names: Bortoluzzi, Maria, editor. | Zurru, Elisabetta, editor.
Title: Ecological communication and ecoliteracy : discourses of awareness and action for the lifescape / edited by Maria Bortoluzzi and Elisabetta Zurru.
Description: London; New York: Bloomsbury Academic, 2024. | Series: Bloomsbury advances in ecolinguistics | Includes bibliographical references and index. | Summary: "This open access book discusses how the environmental crisis is communicated as an urgent global and local issue in a variety of media, texts and events. Focusing on a wide range of case studies (news articles, institutional websites, artwork installations, signposting, social campaigns, and other) the contributions explore how communicative actions can help meet the challenges of ecologically-oriented change"– Provided by publisher.
Identifiers: LCCN 2023049971 (print) | LCCN 2023049972 (ebook) | ISBN 9781350335820 (hardback) | ISBN 9781350335868 (paperback) | ISBN 9781350335844 (epub) | ISBN 9781350335837 (ebook)
Subjects: LCSH: Ecolinguistics. | Discourse analysis. | Communication in ecology. | LCGFT: Essays.
Classification: LCC P39.5 .E2546 2024 (print) | LCC P39.5 (ebook) | DDC 306.44–dc23/eng/20231212
LC record available at https://lccn.loc.gov/2023049971
LC ebook record available at https://lccn.loc.gov/2023049972

ISBN: HB: 978-1-3503-3582-0
PB: 978-1-3503-3586-8
ePDF: 978-1-3503-3583-7
eBook: 978-1-3503-3584-4

Series: Bloomsbury Advances in Ecolinguistics

Typeset by Deanta Global Publishing Services, Chennai, India

For product safety related questions contact productsafety@bloomsbury.com.

To find out more about our authors and books visit www.bloomsbury.com and sign up for our newsletters.

To Pietro and Flora

To Francesco

Contents

List of Figures	xi
List of Tables	xii
List of Contributors	xiii
Acknowledgements	xvi

Introduction: Ecological Communication for Raising Awareness and
    Ecoliteracy for Taking Action *Maria Bortoluzzi and Elisabetta Zurru* 1

Part I Context Setting

1 Tension in Ecological Communication *Alwin Frank Fill* 25

2 A Corpus-Assisted Ecolinguistic Analysis of *Hurricanes* and
    Wildfires and the Potential for Corpus-Assisted Eco-Pedagogy
    in ELT Classrooms *Robert Poole* 44

Part II Multimodal Discourses for Ecological Action

3 Discourses of Cycling Advocacy and Power amidst Wars, Petro-
    Masculinity and Climate Inaction *M. Cristina Caimotto* 67

4 Communicating the Urgency of the Climate Emergency through
    Verbal and Non-Verbal Metaphors *Elisabetta Zurru* 88

5 Unreliable Narratives and Social-Ecological Memory in Kara
    Walker's *A Subtlety* *Emilio Amideo* 112

6 (Un)welcome Waters for Multispecies Hospitality in the
    Anthropocene *Gavin Lamb* 132

7 Identity Representation of Plants in Relation to Humans and
    the Lifescape *Maria Bortoluzzi*

  152

Part III Ecoliteracy for Citizenship Education 175

8 Promoting Ecoliteracy in Essayistic Media Texts through the Case
    of *The Anthropocene Reviewed* *Andrea Sabine Sedlaczek* 177

9   Picturebook Mediation for Children's Ecoliteracy in English L2
    Elisa Bertoldi 197

10 Communicating In and About the Ocean through SCUBA
    Interaction and Ocean Picturebooks *Grit Alter* 217

11 Positive Multimodal Analysis of EU Learning Materials to Promote
    Ecoliteracy for Young People *Sole Alba Zollo* 235

Conclusion: A Closing and an Opening for Action-Taking through
    Communication *Maria Bortoluzzi and Elisabetta Zurru* 257

Index 261

Figures

3.1	Tweet 'Fight Putin, ride a bike' by @HarryHamishGray	75
3.2	Tweet 'When you drive a car, you drive with Putin' by @no_face	76
5.1	Kara Walker, *A Subtlety, or the Marvelous Sugar Baby, an Homage to the unpaid and overworked Artisans who have refined our Sweet tastes from the cane fields to the Kitchens of the New World on the Occasion of the demolition of the Domino Sugar Refining Plant*, 2014	120
5.2	Kara Walker, *A Subtlety, or the Marvelous Sugar Baby, an Homage to the unpaid and overworked Artisans who have refined our Sweet tastes from the cane fields to the Kitchens of the New World on the Occasion of the demolition of the Domino Sugar Refining Plant*, 2014	121
5.3	Kara Walker, still from *An Audience*, 2014	123
9.1	TMA output: transcription of multimodal ensembles in E. S.'s read-aloud performance	206
10.1	Signal for '*We need to resurface to a depth of 5m to do a 3min safety stop*'	222
10.2	Signals for '*I have problems with my ear*'	222
10.3	Signal for '*How much air do you have?*' and the answer '*I have 100 bar left*'	223
10.4	Signal for '*Ok*'	223
11.1	*MECO – Motivational Eco-Friendly App*	248
11.2	Maps, before and after restoration	249
11.3	Brochure *Why buy it when you can make it?*	250

Tables

2.1	Use trends with the top twenty adjective collocates of [hurricane]	51
2.2	Representations of [hurricane] with strongest use trends	53
2.3	Adjective collocates of [wildfire]	55
2.4	Activity no. 1: Climate change or global warming?	58
6.1	Media sources contained in the two pinniped corpora	137
7.1	Occurrences of generic terms related to plants in RLL2021 and WHF2021	161
7.2	Images in RLL2021	165
11.1	Data set	237
11.2	Main topics of students' projects	246

Contributors

Grit Alter is Professor of Teaching English as a Foreign Language at the University College of Teacher Education in Innsbruck, Austria. Her research focuses on using picture books in English language teaching (ELT), playful learning in primary ELT, diversity education, curriculum studies and critical pedagogy. She is currently involved in projects on critical textbook studies, teaching Canadian studies on the secondary and tertiary levels, and narrative inquiry into teacher education.

Emilio Amideo, PhD in English, is Assistant Professor of English Language and Translation at the University of Naples 'Parthenope', Italy. His research interests include English language and translation studies, cultural and postcolonial studies, gender studies, critical race theory, ecocriticism, multimodality and body studies. He is a member of the editorial board of the *Journal of Gender Studies* and the advisory board of *JAm It! – Journal of American Studies in Italy*. His most recent publications include the monographs *Queer Tidalectics: Linguistic and Sexual Fluidity in Contemporary Black Diasporic Literature* (2021) and *Il Corpo dell'Altro. Articolazioni Queer della Maschilità Nera in Diaspora* (2021).

Elisa Bertoldi is a PhD candidate at the University of Udine, Italy. From 2017 to 2020, she was a full-time research assistant in the Department of Languages, Literatures, Communication, Education and Social Studies. She is a teacher of English as a Foreign Language in Italian primary schools, a teacher educator and developer of teaching resources. She has published articles on technologies applied to language teaching. She co-authored the book *Let's Tell a Tale. Storytelling with Children in English L2* (2019). Her recent research work and publications deal with interactions between storytellers and children in read-aloud sessions in English L2/FL.

Maria Bortoluzzi (PhD, Edinburgh) is Associate Professor of English Language in the Department of Languages, Literatures, Communication, Education and Society of the University of Udine, Italy. Her research interests include critical discourse studies, and multimodal and multiliteracy awareness for language teacher education (English as foreign/additional language). She has published extensively in these fields. Her latest publications deal with identity representation in online communities, critical multimodal discourse for ecological awareness raising, and multimodal approaches for ecoliteracy education.

M. Cristina Caimotto is Associate Professor of English Linguistics and Translation at the University of Turin, Italy. Her research interests include political discourse and environmental discourse, with a focus on ideology. She is the author of *Discourses of Cycling, Road Users and Sustainability: An Ecolinguistic Investigation* (2020), a study that observes how discourses shape cycling and explores how cycling could shape new discourses. Her book offers tools to study the influence of narratives and discourses in resisting change towards more cycling-oriented policies. She is also a cycling advocate.

Alwin Frank Fill (PhD) is Professor Emeritus of English Linguistics at 'Karl-Franzens' University in Graz, Austria. He studied English and Latin at the University of Innsbruck and undertook further studies at Queen's College (University of Oxford, UK) and the University of Michigan (Ann Arbor, USA). His main research interests are ecolinguistics, language and suspense and linguistics for peace. He has published books on all these topics. His books on ecolinguistics include *The Ecolinguistics Reader* (co-edited with P. Mühlhäusler, 2001) and the *Routledge Handbook of Ecolinguistics* (2018, co-edited with H. Penz). His most recent book is *Linguistics for Peace* (2022).

Gavin Lamb is Postdoctoral Fellow in the Center for Multilingualism in Society across the Lifespan, at the University of Oslo, Norway. His research draws on ethnography, ecolinguistics, discourse analysis, nexus analysis and posthumanist methods to examine the sociolinguistics of multilingualism and intercultural communication mediating human relationships with animals and the natural environment. His previous publications have appeared in *Applied Linguistics*, *Applied Linguistic Review*, *Multilingua* and in two recently edited volumes on Intercultural Communication in Tourism and Communicating Endangered Species.

Robert Poole is Assistant Professor of TESOL and Applied Linguistics at the University of Alabama, United States. His research interests include ecolinguistics, corpus-assisted discourse analysis and corpus-aided approaches to language teaching and learning. His most recent book is *Corpus-Assisted Ecolinguistics* (2022).

Andrea Sabine Sedlaczek is a PhD researcher of linguistics at the University of Vienna, Austria. Her research interests lie in multimodal and critical discourse studies, ecolinguistics and semiotics. She has published on discourses about climate change and sustainability with a focus on documentary film and television. Next to her university research, she has also been working on projects promoting critical media literacy for the community media institute COMMIT in Austria.

Sole Alba Zollo is Lecturer of English Linguistics and Translation at the University of Naples 'Federico II', Italy. She holds a PhD in English for Special Purposes (ESP) from the University of Naples 'Federico II'. She has published extensively on her research interests which include human rights discourse, multimodal critical discourse analysis in institutional contexts, rhetoric and visual argumentation, education and social media, the language of tourism and new literacies.

Elisabetta Zurru is Senior Lecturer in English Language and Translation at the University of Genoa in Italy and a member of the Inter-University Centre for Metaphor Research (CIRM) based at the University of Genoa. Her main research interests lie in stylistics, pragmatics, media studies, ecolinguistics and metaphor studies, which she has explored in a number of national and international publications. Her recent publications include *The Stylistics of Landscapes, the Landscapes of Stylistics* (2017), *Language in Place: Stylistic Perspectives on Landscape, Place and Environment* (2021) and *Variations on Metaphor* (2021), which she co-edited.

Acknowledgements

This volume would not exist without the generous work of the authors who contributed to it and shared their research studies as perspectives held together by the belief that communication is crucial for action and can contribute to positive ecological change and climate justice. We are grateful for their thought-provoking contributions and their constant support. We are also deeply grateful to the many colleagues who accepted to discuss the issues stemming from this volume during its various stages of development and gave us insightful comments throughout. Our research and teaching work has been sustained over the years by the vibrant and multidisciplinary community of the International Ecolinguistics Association. Many thanks also to our students who taught us to clarify our reflections and offered us insights during class discussions on climate (in)justice.

This publication became possible thanks to the encouragement and support of the series editors, Arran Stibbe and Mariana Roccia. Arran, in a friendly and forward-looking way, suggested solutions when there did not seem to be one in sight.

The editorial board of Bloomsbury Academic has been ever supportive and professional; we are particularly grateful to Morwenna Scott, Laura Gallon and Sarah MacDonald. Giada Pontoni and Filippo Mucignato (postgraduate students at the University of Udine, Italy, at the time of writing) were an invaluable and caring help at the stage of formatting the volume.

Finally, we wish to thank the following copyright holders for giving their permission to reproduce artwork and images:

Figure 3.1 Tweet 'Fight Putin, ride a bike' by @HarryHamishGray

Figure 3.2 Tweet 'When you drive a car, you drive with Putin' by @no_face

Figure 5.1 Kara Walker, *A Subtlety, or the Marvelous Sugar Baby, an Homage to the unpaid and overworked Artisans who have refined our Sweet tastes from the cane fields to the Kitchens of the New World on the Occasion of the demolition of the Domino Sugar Refining Plant*, 2014. Polystyrene foam, sugar. Approx. 35.5 × 26 × 75.5 feet (10.8 × 7.9 × 23 m). Installation view: Domino Sugar Refinery, A project of Creative Time, Brooklyn, New York, 2014. Photo: Jason Wyche. Artwork © Kara Walker, courtesy of Sikkema Jenkins & Co. and Sprüth Magers

Figure 5.2 Kara Walker, *A Subtlety, or the Marvelous Sugar Baby, an Homage to the unpaid and overworked Artisans who have refined our Sweet tastes from the cane fields to the Kitchens of the New World on the Occasion of the demolition of the Domino Sugar Refining Plant*, 2014. Installation view: Domino Sugar Refinery, A project of Creative Time, Brooklyn, New York, 2014. Photo: Jason Wyche. Artwork © Kara Walker, courtesy of Sikkema Jenkins & Co. and Sprüth Magers

Figure 5.3 Kara Walker, still from *An Audience*, 2014. Digital video with sound, 27:18 minutes. Artwork © Kara Walker, courtesy of Sikkema Jenkins & Co. and Sprüth Magers

Introduction

Ecological Communication for Raising Awareness and Ecoliteracy for Taking Action

Maria Bortoluzzi and Elisabetta Zurru

Interweaving perspectives on the lifescape

This volume offers interweaving and complementary perspectives of verbal and non-verbal communication to make sense of the ecological crisis and promote positive change for restoring a respectful, caring and healthy relation with ecosystems and their delicate, endangered balance. Drawing on ecolinguistics, ecoliteracy and multimodal studies, the contributions in this volume offer multifaceted views of awareness raising and action-taking for the care of the lifescape, namely the complex, delicate and rich systemic relation between all living beings and the con-vironment we belong to (Fill 2001; this volume), that 'home' that is instantiated by the prefix 'eco-' in ecology, ecolinguistics, ecoliteracy and, we also propose in this volume, ecomultimodality.

The plan for this book initiated at a time when social movements such as #FridaysForFuture were gaining influence and strength for effective action worldwide; from 2020, the overpowering urgency of the Covid-19 pandemic overshadowed all other events in the mediasphere and in our lives, while global and local inequalities and sociopolitical tensions have never ceased to exist, as present-day rampant warfare, injustice, poverty and displacing of refugees demonstrate. This volume has the aim of contributing to refocusing attention on the profound impact communication has on events, perceptions and value systems in relation with the greatest impending global issue we are collectively and globally facing, the environmental crisis, and the actions we need to undertake in order to meet the challenges of change (also post-pandemic) to avert this human-inflicted calamity (Figueres and Rivett-Carnac 2021; Lopez 2021; Staid 2022; Milstein, Thomas, Hoffmann and Carr 2023). These situations and their complex outcomes are related to our individual and collective beliefs, values and behaviours vis-à-vis ourselves as humans and the ecosystems that sustain multispecies life on the planet. Systems (ecological, social, cultural, etc.) in their complexity are supported and instantiated by language and other semiotic resources in situated practice (Jewitt, Bezemer and O'Halloran 2016). Communication (verbal and non-verbal) gives shape, texture, potential and relevance to events, participants, features and relations; and it can also background, obfuscate or erase situations, actors, connections and causality relations.

In this volume, communicative situations, events and their discourse practices are viewed as an integral part of the ecosystems: through them we construe ourselves as humans in relation with the more-than-human world and as part of the 'lifescapes' we belong to. We use the overarching term 'communication' to address the interplay and co-deployment of a variety of modes in situated discourse practices in which linguistic features are intrinsically related and intertwined with other semiotic modes (still and moving images, graphic features, sounds, music, gestures, facial expressions, proxemics, space layout, etc.). This volume takes its moves from ecolinguistics and the focus on verbal discourse in context, and explores other interconnected areas such as ecoliteracy and ecomultimodality in order to analyse and interpret socioculturally situated discourses and texts in present-day society through an ecological lens. Verbal discourse is the focus of all contributions, while most contributions also include the analysis and discussion of other semiotic repertoires which contribute to meaning through the co-deployment of modes in interaction (Parts II and III).

Thus, the perspectives offered in this book create interwoven networks that investigate discourses, question conventions and rethink the way we experience, endorse, convey, assess, resist and reframe socioculturally construed events, norms and texts. This draws on the wide-ranging and interdisciplinary field of Critical Discourse Studies (among many other seminal studies: Fairclough 2003, 2010, 2014 [1989]; van Dijk 2009; Wodak and Meyer 2016; Wodak 2013; Stibbe 2014). Wodak defines this area of research (in the quote, CDA is the acronym for Critical Discourse Analysis) as follows:

> In general, CDA is characterised by a number of principles [. . .]: for example, all approaches are problem oriented, and thus necessarily interdisciplinary and eclectic. Moreover, CDA is characterised by the common interests in demystifying ideologies and power through the systematic and retroductable investigation of semiotic data (written, spoken or visual). CDA researchers also attempt to make their own positions and interests explicit while retaining their respective scientific methodologies and while remaining self-reflective of their own research process. (Wodak 2013: xxi)

In 2004, Martin theorized and promoted Positive Discourse Analysis (adopted by many scholars: among them, Macgilchrist 2007; Bartlett 2012; Stibbe 2018) which posited the need to go beyond critiquing by focusing on positive discourses; this stems from the agenda of Critical Discourse Studies which also includes offering alternative views through the study of language and communication.

A common key feature of the contributions in the present volume is the focus on the potential of communication as positive ecological action in society and education since 'learning is the inevitable outcome of any and every engagement with the (socially made) world' (Bezemer and Kress 2016: 37). Learning is change, and change is needed to face the climate crisis we are experiencing. Positive action starts from self and collective reflections on the complexity (and contradictions) of 'ecological communication' and acts upon them. In this volume, 'ecological communication' means both communication about ecological issues (which include communication itself) and the ecology of communication, that is, a reflective, critical and positive view of how verbal and non-verbal communication instantiates our world view and influences our values and behaviour towards it. The themes dealt with in the volume investigate diverse communicative contexts that have contributed to the present Anthropocene crisis or increased its scope at global level through injustice and exploitation grounded on the value principle of continuous 'growth' (Halliday 2001 [1990]; Shiva 2015; Eisler and Fry 2019; Figueres and Rivett-Carnac 2021; Staid 2022).

Notions about human-influenced climate change were already known at the beginning of the twentieth century, as a recently gone viral post[1] reminded us. The post contains a picture of a 1912 newspaper article entitled 'Coal consumption affecting climate', which is in turn based on the report 'Remarkable Weather of 1911: The Effect of the Combustion of Coal on the Climate – What Scientists Predict for the Future' (Molena 1912). This text discusses early data of human-generated impact on climate, celebrating it as an accomplishment of the human mind rather than questioning it as a cause for concern. On the one hand, it underlines that coal consumption 'tends to make the air a more effective *blanket* for the earth and to raise its temperature' and that the effects of this trend 'may be considerable in a few centuries' (Molena 1912: 341; (emphasis is ours)). On the other, it glorifies the ability of human inventions to 'reach beyond the near at hand and the immediate present and modify the cosmic processes themselves' and stresses that the human-caused addition of carbon dioxide to the atmosphere of our planet will allow 'men in generations to come [to] enjoy milder breezes and live under sunnier skies' (Molena 1912: 342). This text represents a telling example of what Halliday (2001 [1990]: 196) called 'growthism': a strongly anthropocentric mentality celebratory of humans' domination over the environment based on such ideas as the continuous growth and accumulation in every aspect of human life, and a top-down approach to the relationship with the ecosystems humans are but a part of. The very idea that humans are to 'protect' earth's ecosystems – or lifescapes (see definition later) – stems from this approach and is a sign of the widely shared anthropocentric narrative that puts humans at the centre of the human–nonhuman relation. This narrative is grounded in the notion that humans are the actors and main agents in this relation, and it is thus up to them to be the 'protectors' of nature; in fact, humans should simply respect ecosystems and coexist with other living beings without actively harming them: humans find themselves in need to actively 'protect earth's ecosystems' now, because they damaged them in the first place. In other words, rather than viewing the planet as con-vironment (see later in the text), this system of beliefs, attitudes and behaviours construes it as the background to human existence and activity. In turn, this kind of anthropocentric mentality is entrenched in deep-seated Western cultural and religious beliefs which celebrate humans as the most prized among divine creations and assign to every other aspect of life on earth an ancillary status, as exemplified by the central role that the notion of 'The Great Chain of Being' held in Western thought for centuries (Nee 2005). Many cultures and religions, other than the dominant ones in Western affluent societies, have been and are still based on very different views on the relation between human and other-than-human. Native tribes in what are now the United States, for instance, did not conceive the land as an individual commodity, and this became transparent when the first contracts for their land enclosure in reservations were written after the colonization of their territory by the Europeans.[2] By the same token, several cultures (based on religions such as Hinduism and Buddhism, among others) revolve around the idea that all living and non-living creatures on earth are interconnected, and humans need to live in harmony with nature rather than lording over it. This explains, at least in part, why very little has been done since the publication of Molena's article (1912) in order to prevent human activities from further negatively impacting on the atmosphere, while much has been done to add to the damage. Among the twenty countries with the highest yearly CO_2 emissions in the world, many are Western affluent countries which have done little to nothing to curb their carbon footprints since 1990 (UNEP 2021). At the same time, massive extensions of territories from the southern and eastern areas of the globe (such as India, Mexico and China) have experienced a surge in industrial, technological and economic development from the last decades of the twentieth century. The general result is that CO_2 emissions have globally ramped up in the past thirty years.[3]

Against this backdrop, all the voices in this volume envisage global and local transformative actions as urgent and possible and give complementary and alternative insights into how communication and citizenship education can contribute to respecting and preserving the living ecosystems adopting principles of deep ecology as posited by Næss: 'Ecologically responsible policies are concerned only in part with pollution and resource depletion. There are deeper concerns which touch upon principles of diversity, complexity, autonomy, decentralization, symbiosis, egalitarianism, and classlessness' (Næss 1973: 95; Næss 1995, 2021).

The volume builds on the overarching definition of ecolinguistics by Steffensen and Fill (2014: 21):

> Ecolinguistics is (1) the study of the processes and activities through which human beings – at individual, group, population and species levels – exploit their environment in order to create an extended, sense-saturated ecology that supports their existential trajectories, as well as (2) the study of the organismic, societal and ecosystemic limits of such processes and activities, i.e. the carrying capacities for upholding a sound and healthy existence for both human and non-human life on all levels.

As Alexander and Stibbe (2014) mention, ecolinguistics does not only include the investigation of texts and discourses specifically about the environment, but it also explores a variety of text typologies and interactions which represent and instantiate values, beliefs and behaviours that have an impact on our world and influence our actions. As Fill (2018: 5) mentions, Halliday was among the first to ask the question that is now central in ecolinguistics: 'Do linguistic patterns, literally, affect the survival of the human species as well as other species on Earth?' (see Halliday 2001 and his 1990 speech in which this issue was first raised; Steffensen and Fill 2014: 9; Goatly 2018; Stibbe 2018, 2021).

Döring (2018: 297) writes that 'language is not estimated to represent a self-contained element processing the outer world, but it is an integrated and socially interlinked entity'. As Fill and Mühlhäusler (2001b: 3) highlight, communication emphasizes the interconnectedness of social and natural aspects of the environment and its inhabitants. To underline that all living beings are an integral part of their ecosystems, Fill (2001; this volume) uses the term con-vironment, rather than 'environment'[4]: the latter evokes and etymologically derives from 'surroundings' and linguistically represents the natural world as surrounding humans rather than including them (see OED online 2022). Steffensen and Fill (2014: 17) and Steffensen (2018) write that language is not just *about* nature but is *of* nature. Thus, this volume sets out to show the impact that language in situated communicative contexts and in relation with other semiotic systems can have in acting in, with and towards the living environment or, as Stibbe calls it, 'the ecosystems that life depends on' (Stibbe 2021: 42).

The prefix 'eco-' reminds us of housekeeping (Fill and Mühlhäusler 2001b: 3) since it draws its origins from 'oikos', in Ancient Greek 'house, dwelling place' (OED online 2022). Stibbe (2021: 8) views the 'eco' of ecolinguistics as referring 'to the life-sustaining interactions of humans with other humans, other organisms and the physical environment, with some kind of normative orientation to protecting the flourishing of life'. Along these lines, in this volume, ecolinguistics, ecoliteracy and ecomultimodality are understood as the study of 'situated' communication dealing with 'our home', where local events impact on the global and vice versa in the short- and the long-term, representing ecosystems in their complexity and including human communication and its contexts of action and interaction. Quoting Stibbe, '[t]he link between ecology and language is that how humans treat each other and the natural world is influenced by our thoughts, concepts, ideas, ideologies and worldviews, and these in turn are shaped through language' (Stibbe 2021: 1; see also Fill and Mühlhäusler 2001a; Steffensen and Fill 2014; Stibbe 2018; Fill and Penz 2018).

This volume encompasses also the multimodal perspective of situated communication to account for its semiotic complexity, since communicative events are never monomodal but relational interaction and co-deployment of various modes on the basis of sociocultural conventions and affordances. As Kress and van Leeuwen wrote (2001: 1): 'we see the multimodal resources which are available in a culture used to make meanings in any and every sign, at every level and in any mode.' Jewitt (2017b: 15) remarks:

> Multimodality [. . .] proceeds on the assumption that representation and communication always draw on a multiplicity of modes, all of which have the potential to contribute equally to meaning. The basis assumption that runs through multimodality is that meanings are made, distributed, received, interpreted and remade in interpretation through many representational and communicative modes – not just language – whether as speech or as writing.

Communication is therefore an orchestration of modes which orient the co-construction of meaning, and language, in its diverse realizations, is co-deployed with other semiotic systems according to conventions and available repertoires. This profoundly influences our perception and interpretation of the world, including human and more-than-human identities.

Thus, in this volume we complement ecolinguistics with ecomultimodality which we define as the multimodal perspective applied to communication instantiating the lifescape(s) (see later in the text). What is not surprising is that the definition of ecolinguistics by Steffensen and Fill (2014) quoted earlier can also apply, and be extended, to multimodality, or, within our perspective, 'ecomultimodality'. Several seminal studies in ecolinguistics have already dealt with many aspects of multimodal communication: see, among others, some of the contributions included in Fill and Mühlhäusler (2001a) and Fill and Penz (2018), as well as other seminal works such as Stibbe (2012, 2021). Even the opening towards the analysis of modes (including language) for ecology is not new: see, among many others, Bortoluzzi (2009, 2010); Sedlaczek (2016, 2017); Hansen and Machin (2013); Hansen (2018); Caimotto (2020); Zurru (2021, 2022); and Dancygier (2023). The present volume gives explicit salience to this 'ecomultimodal turn' which, in fact, started a long time ago. The 'eco' prefix reminds us of our abode, the earth, the irreplaceable home we belong to, and is metonymically related to the multimodal affordances of space, sound, texture we inhabit, see, listen to and embody.

In our view, multimodality for ecological communication remains a wide-ranging field still to be explored which offers the potential of cross-fertilization between the principles of deep ecology and different strands and developments of multimodality (see Jewitt 2017a, 2017b). We only mention here the issue of 'design' as developed by Kress and van Leeuwen (2001: 5 *et passim*): 'Designs are means to realise discourses in the context of a given communication situation. [...T]hey realise the communication situation which changes socially constructed knowledge into social (inter-) action' (see also Kress and Selander 2012). This brings us beyond critiquing and raising awareness towards 'social action'. Focusing on the notion of 'design', Adami, Diamantopoulou and Lim (2022: 8) underline 'its potential for changing paradigms in our respective fields, challenging how we conceive learning and communication and, more generally, the agents of semiotic knowledge production towards social change'. In their view, the perspective of design promotes transformative social change recognising 'the agentive, creative and transformative roles of sign-makers and meaning-makers in learning and teaching'.

The perspective of transformative discoursal roles through awareness raising, co-construction of meaning and the relevance of agentivity contributes to action-taking through language and multimodal communication for the lifescapes we are part of. In education and pedagogy, the recent decades have seen a progressive move from the emphasis on verbal literacy (oracy, reading and writing) towards the more complex set of evolving and intertwining 'literacies' combining critical reflection and active use of affordances encompassing those potentially found in still and moving images, sound and music, movement in space, gestures, graphic features, which nowadays intermesh embodied, contextual and digital features (see Vasta and Baldry 2020). Multiliteracies pedagogies view the participants as actively involved in their individual and collective change through the process of learning: 'meaning making is an active, transformative process', whereby 'all forms of representation, including language, should be regarded as dynamic processes of transformation rather than processes of reproduction' (Cope and Kalantzis 2009: 175). Discovery and transformative action through learning brings us to the next step: ecoliteracy as viewed and enacted through language, multimodal discourse and multiliteracies.

In the present volume, ecoliteracy is based on the perspective initiated by Orr (1992) and continued by Capra (1997) who coined the term 'ecoliteracy' in his seminal book *The Web of Life*. Capra connected the educational fields of humanities and scientific disciplines by establishing a profound contact between these traditions and showing how they can cross-fertilise and expand perspectives in wider educational areas.

McBride et al. (2013) identify and compare three main strands of education and the environment: environmental literacy, ecological literacy and ecoliteracy. They identify 'environmental literacy' as focused on scientific disciplines and comprising 'an awareness of and concern about the environment and its associated problems, as well as the knowledge, skills, and motivations to work toward solutions of current problems and the prevention of new ones' (McBride et al. 2013: 3). 'Ecological literacy' focuses 'on the key ecological knowledge necessary for informed decision-making, acquired through scientific inquiry and systems thinking' (McBride et al. 2013: 3). Ecoliteracy (addressed in Part III in this volume) is a third strand inspired by the groundbreaking work by Orr (1992) and Capra (1997): it encompasses the perspectives of hard and applied sciences, social and cultural humanities to offer a broad transdisciplinary view of knowledge and education. McBride et al. (2013: 14) summarise Capra's view of ecoliteracy

> as an understanding of the principles of the organization of ecosystems and the application of those principles for creating sustainable human communities and societies. [. . .] An ecoliterate person is prepared to be an effective member of

sustainable society, with well-rounded abilities of head, heart, hands, and spirit, comprising an organic understanding of the world and participatory action within and with the environment. (see Capra 1997, 2013)

In 1995 the Center for Ecoliteracy was co-founded by Fritjof Capra, Peter Buckley and Zenobia Barlow in Berkeley, California. Its mission is 'cultivating education for the sustainability of people and the planet'. Over the years, 'the Center for Ecoliteracy has identified vital practices' that integrate emotional, social and ecological intelligence in order to strengthen and extend our 'capacity to live sustainably' (Goleman, Bennett and Barlow 2012: 30–1). In the volume *Ecoliterate*, Goleman, Bennett and Barlow (2012: 21) write: '"Ecoliterate" is our shorthand for the end goal, while "socially and emotionally engaged ecoliteracy" is the process that we have identified for getting there.'

Their work is based on the recognition of systemic networks of relations: 'The complexity of the web of connections that characterize our global society has created a vast collective blind spot about the effects of human behavior on natural systems' (2012: 21). They believe that 'ecological intelligence' is collective and based on 'nurturing communities'.

In this systemic vision of ecoliteracy, research studies in science, technology, social science and humanities converge and inform action on education and through education. Along these lines, Stibbe (2009) offers a multifaceted, interdisciplinary and transdisciplinary perspective on sustainability literacy. In the introductory chapter of the volume, Stibbe and Luna (2009) remark:

> The ability to take steps towards building a more sustainable self and society requires far more than knowledge about sustainability – it requires sustainability literacy. This book uses the term sustainability literacy to indicate the skills, attitudes, competencies, dispositions and values that are necessary for surviving and thriving in the declining conditions of the world in ways which slow down that decline as far as possible. Gaining practical skills requires a form of learning which goes beyond memorising and repeating facts. It requires active learning, a broad term used to refer to self-reflection, self-directed enquiry, learning by doing, engagement with real life issues, and learning within communities of practice. (Stibbe and Luna 2009: 10–11)

Communication (verbal and non-verbal) is also action through and on learning since it influences the perception of and the impact on ecosystems. Van Lier states that '[i]n addition to the multisensory nature of language perception, we must tie perception to the realm of action. [. . .L]anguage perception occurs in a context of activity and interactivity' (van Lier 2008: 55). Thus, the reflection on ecological communication has the power of raising awareness, and ecoliteracy (encompassing verbal and non-verbal aspects) has the aim to promote a more positive relation of respect and care for the lifescape(s). Learning is viewed as an embodied experience that involves all human participants throughout their life in natural and sociocultural contexts: discoursal, multimodal and multiliteracies studies meet ecoliteracy to promote individual and collective action at the cognitive, emotional, practical, embodied level. The inevitability of linguistic anthropocentrism (Heuberger 2018; Steffensen 2018) can be thus balanced and complemented by the reflection on an orchestration of modes in local and global communication which includes and recognizes ecosystems as life-sustaining (lifescapes).

The contributions in this volume deconstruct what appears to be 'normalized' texts and representations, reveal neglect and backgrounding, give salience to respectful, equalitarian and fruitful communicative solutions for taking action in constantly changing scenarios while endorsing positive awareness raising about the major emergency the world is experiencing. Each contribution presents and discusses both theoretical and practical aspects of ecological communication: (1) reflecting on how we humans position and represent ourselves and our behaviour in relation with the ecosystem we are part of (lifescapes); (2) taking positive action through communication: how communicative strategies can challenge anti-ecological discourse, and can imagine and co-construct the future of our ecosystems, looking at the past and moving beyond the present.

To overcome the limits posed by language itself in order to perceive and represent the earth's ecosystems as a 'living entity' (see Halliday 2001; Mühlhäusler 2001), this volume investigates ecological communication in a variety of contexts to reveal, instantiate and offer 'embodied' evidence of the relevance of 'lifescape(s)'. The term 'lifescape' is intended not as limited to encompass 'living creatures' but includes the immersive complex ecosystems existing globally and locally on earth. 'Lifescape' is based on Fill's concept of 'con-vironment': human animals are part of nature, and we act on our common home through our sociocultural constructs which include communication. The term 'lifescape' is inspired by the 'Gaia' hypothesis developed as early as 1972 by Lovelock (1972). Lovelock and Margulis (1974: 3) posited the hypothesis 'that the total ensemble of living organisms which constitute the biosphere can act as a single entity' and is 'an active adaptive control system able to maintain the Earth in homeostasis'. Through the term 'lifescape(s)' we want to echo the knowledge and the wisdom of native peoples who perceive themselves in profound connection with the natural world (Fabiano and Mangiameli 2019;

Borgnino 2022). We were also inspired by the work and writing of Vandana Shiva against 'fragmentation and separation', for a holistic sense-making of the world we inhabit: 'Life and its vitality in nature and society is based on cycles of renewal and regeneration of mutuality, respect and human solidarity. The relationship between soil and society is a relationship based on reciprocity, on the Law of Return, of giving back' (Shiva 2015: 5).

Through imagination and creativity, literary voices are capable to reaching and bridging the gap created by Western linguistic and sociocultural conventions between humans and the more-than-human world (see Riem and Hughes-d'Aeth 2022; Zapf 2016). Nan Shepherd's *The Living Mountain* (2011; written during the Second World War and first published in 1977) is profoundly inspirational in this sense. Shepherd's words are guided by her deep connection with the con-vironment she feels part of: air, rock, water, animal, plant and human body blend into an encompassing awe-inspiring vision. Shepherd's view can be related to Næss's (1995, 2021) principles of deep ecology and the realization of a profound and radical respect for the ecosystems that sustain us within an ecocentric (ecology-centred, rather than an anthropocentric) world view. The biosphere and its network of life (Capra 1997, 2007) become the main focus of concern for humans narrating lifescapes as the realm of 'cobecoming': van Dooren, Kirksey and Münster (2016: 2) write that '[t]his cobecoming involves the exchange and emergence of meanings, immersion in webs of signification that might be linguistic, gestural, biochemical, and more'.

The notion of 'lifescape(s)' incapsulates the value system we advocate for in the present volume as care, respect, equality, justice, attentiveness and responsibility for the earth system in its multiple perspectives and strands.

The tapestry of the volume

The volume is organized in three interrelated parts: their different strands of issues, methodological solutions and reflections form patterns across the sections and chapters creating a rich interconnecting tapestry. The contributions offer insights across topics, methodologies and research interests which complement one another, highlight innovative approaches and demonstrate how verbal and non-verbal communication is an integral part of lifescapes and our actions.

Part I, Context Setting, opens the whole volume with two contributions that set the context of ecological communication and offer theoretical and methodological advances through the investigation of 'tension' as a communicative phenomenon (Fill, Chapter 1), the exploration of corpus-assisted ecolinguistics as a powerful and innovative research area, and corpus-aided eco-pedagogy for language education (Poole, Chapter 2). In **Chapter 1**, 'Tension in Ecological Communication', **Alwin Frank Fill** offers a theoretical framework of 'tension' that connects several linguistic and communicative phenomena: he shows how ecological communication has both the potential to identify problems and can also contribute to solving them through revealing and defusing communicative 'tension' among humans and between humans and the con-vironment. Fill uses the term 'con-vironment' to re-conceptualize the notion of 'environment' as togetherness, whereby all elements and processes are closely interrelated in a web of mutual connection informed and supported by verbal and non-verbal communication. This contribution anticipates many of the themes of the volume, reaches out to the research area of Part II (which focuses on multimodal studies) and lays the foundations of its ethical principles: 'tension' can potentially become open conflict but it can be also defused through humour, argumentation and respect, thus demonstrating the power of communication as action and in action. A reflection on 'tension', writes Fill, 'should make us think and act more moderately, so that the present values and resources are retained, but perhaps distributed more equally – a development through which peace is promoted' (see also the book *Linguistics for Peace*, Fill 2022).

In **Chapter 2**, **Robert Poole** offers insights into the advances of corpus-assisted ecolinguistics and eco-pedagogy (see also Poole 2022). Poole interrogates and compares diachronically data sets from the Corpus of Contemporary American English to reveal and discuss the evolving representation of the terms *hurricane/s* and *wildfire/s* in US American discourse from 1990 to 2019. The comparison of adjectives and collocates of the two terms demonstrates the increased severity and strength of the two phenomena over the three decades. This study shows the methodological potentialities of corpus-assisted analysis in its diachronic perspective, as it gives evidence for 'the dynamic nature of meaning and representation' and provides 'an impetus in the potential cultivation of more ecologically sustainable language use' (Poole, this volume). Through the evidence of language use, corpus-assisted ecolinguistics can challenge popular notions or beliefs of language use and contribute to promoting 'emergent more sustainable construals'. The chapter also explores the advantages of 'corpus-assisted eco-pedagogy' for education, thus anticipating the main theme of Part III (ecoliteracy). As shown in this study, corpus-assisted eco-pedagogy can raise students' awareness on prevailing language uses, reflect on how these influence and potentially inform our behaviour and give students agency through ecolinguistics discovery learning.

Part II, Multimodal Discourses for Ecological Action, expands the field of ecolinguistics to include multimodal discourse, and investigates the influence and impact of a variety of discourses and texts in relation with the construal of ourselves as part of the lifescape. The potential themes and methodologies of this wide-ranging research field are countless. This part of the volume offers some insights into a variety of areas (mobility discourse, creative art installations, visual and verbal metaphors, media and social media communication, etc.) and shows how multimodal communication instantiates and influences the action we take on the ecosystems. Ecolinguistics has frequently explored multimodal contexts of verbal interaction, but the emphasis (as the name itself suggests) has been on language. In this volume we give relevance to communication as multimodal interaction in context; thus we propose the term 'ecomultimodality' to give relevance to this 'multimodal turn' in (ecolinguistic) research studies.

In **Chapter 3**, 'Discourses of Cycling Advocacy and Power Amidst Wars, Petro-Masculinity and Climate Inaction', **M. Cristina Caimotto** looks at active mobility discourses as key aspect in our lives in relation with climate change, pollution, health issues and 'fossil fuel lifestyle'. Her contribution establishes a clear connection between ecolinguistics and mobility justice: 'automentality' is shown to be a pervasive hegemonic discourse that instantiates and perpetuates inequality, promotes pollution, exploitation and, ultimately, social conflict and 'fossil wars' (see also Caimotto 2020). Caimotto analyses verbal and visual discourses that promote active mobility through everyday cycling; she shows how some of these policymaking discourses would need to be reframed to prevent reproducing the problematic consumeristic mindset that has brought us to 'environmental hypocognition'. Caimotto powerfully advocates for a reframing of the stories we live by regarding cycling and mobility in order to better promote positive change in life quality and equality.

Elisabetta Zurru also reflects on the notion of environmental hypocognition and frames in 'Communicating the Urgency of the Climate Emergency through Verbal and Non-Verbal Metaphors'. **Chapter 4** investigates the communicated urgency of acting against climate change through verbal and non-verbal instantiations of the powerful metaphor of the TICKING CLOCK. By combining ecolinguistics and studies on verbal, conceptual, visual and multimodal metaphors, the author analyses case studies drawn from artivism, news reports and social media, in order to explore the communicative purposes and potential effectiveness of the TICKING CLOCK metaphor in the current debate on the environmental crisis. Drawing the conclusion from the data analysed that the TICKING CLOCK metaphor seems to be mainly used to frame the environmental crisis within an apocalyptic narrative, the study suggests a reframing of the metaphor itself as a means to move away from doomsday scenarios and towards a communication able to frame in more encouraging terms the need to act swiftly to counteract anthropocenic climate change.

Human artefacts as contemporary artistic installations are the focus of **Emilio Amideo**'s study 'Unreliable Narratives and Social-Ecological Memory in Kara Walker's *A Subtlety*'. In **Chapter 5**, Amideo adopts Multimodal Critical Discourse Analysis to present and discuss the emergence of a social-ecological memory in Kara Walker's monumental installation *A Subtlety* (2014, USA). He writes that 'recognizing the political imbrication of history, race, and gender with the environment (not only in terms of representation but also in terms of materiality), points to a different understanding of the human relationship with the "con-vironment"' (Fill 2001; this volume). The orchestration of different semiotic modes in the installations (images, videos, sounds, music, materials, written and spoken language, etc.) encourages the audience to reflect on social-ecological memory and the impact of colonial and neocolonial practices and mindset on ecological matters, while actively interacting with the installations.

In **Chapter 6**, '(Un)welcome Waters for Multispecies Hospitality in the Anthropocene', **Gavin Lamb** takes two highly mediatized events (which happened in August 2022) involving the relation between humans and pinnipeds in two distant parts of the globe (monk seals in Hawai'i and a walrus in Norway) to investigate and critique discourses of hospitality. Analysing media and social media texts, Lamb discusses the positioning of participants as '(human) "hosts" and (un)welcome guests'. The study shows the necessity to interrogate the underlying 'appropriative' and hegemonic human world views as instantiated in discourses about encounters between humans and wildlife in Anthropocene.

In **Chapter 7** 'Identity Representation of Plants in Relation to Humans and the Lifescape', **Maria Bortoluzzi** looks at the representation of plants as a crucial and often neglected part of ecosystems which tends to be portrayed and perceived through the lens of human-animal identities. The chapter analyses written multimodal institutional reports and two short videos which recognize the value of plants and promote environmental protection; their aim is investigating the representation of plants in relation with the ecosystems they contribute to creating and maintaining for themselves and animals. The study discusses some discoursal and social roles of plant identities as instantiated in the data and shows the need for further studies to identify frameworks of analysis which can better capture the roles of plants in human discourses. These living beings are often misrepresented as passive and inactive due to the underlying bias of human communication (and cognition) on 'animal' and 'human' characteristics and values.

Part III, Ecoliteracy for Citizenship Education, is closely related to Part II in terms of its focus on multimodal communication and interaction. Here, however, the perspective shifts to educational aspects related to ecological communication and ecoliteracy for citizenship education. Ecoliteracy (see Section 0.1) is viewed as one of the most powerful sets of learning actions that can be adopted to restore and heal the human relationship with and within the lifescape. Ecoliteracy is intended as a catalyst for transformative and creative changes in society through different sociocultural target groups (the studies focus on adults, young adults and children).

The opening contribution of this section offers the theoretical contextualization for the notion of 'ecoliteracy' and related areas of educational investigation. In 'Promoting Ecoliteracy in Essayistic Media Texts through the Case of *The Anthropocene Reviewed*' (**Chapter 8**), **Andrea Sabine Sedlaczek** theoretically analyses and then methodologically expands on the scope and practice of ecoliteracy for adult and young adult learners. Drawing on the holistic semiotic theory by C. S. Peirce, Sedlaczek adopts an ecosemiotic perspective to ecoliteracy and applies it as a theoretical and methodological framework for her ecolinguistic multimodal and Critical Discourse Analysis. The study focuses on two essayistic media texts – the podcast and book project *The Anthropocene Reviewed* – and shows how, by co-deploying multimodal resources, they combine different generic patterns such as narration, argumentation, explication and description. Sedlaczek's primary purpose is to demonstrate 'the potential of a concept of ecoliteracy that goes beyond ecological awareness and a narrow view of field-specific skills', towards 'a more dynamic and holistic perspective on (eco)literacy practices'. This perspective aims at positively influencing individual and collective values and behaviours towards the environment.

In **Chapter 9**, 'Picturebook Mediation for Children's Ecoliteracy in English L2', **Elisa Bertoldi** shows that caring attitudes and behaviours towards different features of the lifescape can be potentially fostered in children through storytelling events. Her data were gathered during the events Telling and Listening to Ecosustainable Stories (TALES) organized in collaboration with the local Natural History Museum in her university town and the local university course of primary teacher education (Udine, Italy). During the events, ecological communication became alive for children through informative (non-fiction) stories told in English as L2 in informal read-aloud events. By adopting a multimodal perspective on interaction, the study looks at the process of picturebook mediation by volunteer storytellers: the analysis focuses on multimodal aspects that allow storytellers to give salience to natural elements during read-aloud sessions and promote respect for nature and ecosustainable ways of living.

Ecoliteracy for adults and children is also the focus of **Chapter 10**, 'Communicating In and About the Ocean through SCUBA Interaction and Ocean Picturebooks', by **Grit Alter**. The study consists of two complementary sections. In the first, the author shows how limited communicative repertoires taking place in the extreme conditions of underwater interactions (SCUBA diving sessions) can become an exemplary case study for multimodal ecoliteracy. The second part of the chapter uses the multimodal text *The Brilliant Deep* (Messner 2018), a children picturebook on coral restoration, to show how the intricate interplay of verbal and visual text can raise children's awareness about the critical condition of the ocean and what scientists are doing to improve it. Alter demonstrates how communicating *in* and *about* the ocean can contribute to ecoliteracy for children and adults.

In **Chapter 11,** 'Positive Multimodal Analysis of EU Learning Materials to Promote Ecoliteracy for Young People' **Sole Alba Zollo** combines the frameworks of social-semiotic multimodal analysis and Positive Discourse Analysis to investigate how groups of university students respond to online resources of the European Union (EU) created to sensitize young citizens towards environmental sustainability. The context of the study is a class of undergraduate university students; after discussing and identifying with them the most significant verbal and visual strategies promoting positive ecological discourses, Zollo conducts an empirical study to observe the students' response to the EU resources and their ability to propose alternative local actions and sustainable events through text typologies similar to those analysed. The task gives agency to the students to imagine future good practices for their communities through learning by design.

The different threads of the volume converge as a tapestry of communication for ecological commitment to the lifescape(s) through ecosystemic relations of justice and mutual care. New research perspectives suggested by the contributions conclude the volume opening it towards future studies.[5]

Notes

1. https://twitter.com/Mykejv1137/status/1553824690317283333?s=20&t=w8AEGPo8YWvidYHKbl_USQ.
2. https://americanindian.si.edu/nk360/manhattan/different-views-land/different-views-land.cshtml.
3. https://ieep.eu/news/more-than-half-of-all-co2-emissions-since-1751-emitted-in-the-last-30-years
4. 'environment, n.'. OED Online. December 2022:

   '**Etymology:** Originally < Middle French *environnement* (French *environnement*: see below) action of surrounding something (1487; earlier in senses "proximity" (first half of the 12th cent. in Anglo-Norman as *avirounement*) and "surroundings, periphery" (*c*1200 in Anglo-Norman as *envirunement*)) < *environner*, *envirunner* environ *v.* + *-ment* -ment *suffix*.'
5. This contribution was jointly written and edited by both authors.

References

Adami, E., S. Diamantopoulou, and F. V. Lim (2022), 'Design in Gunther Kress's Social Semihotics', *London Review of Education*, 20 (1): 41. https://doi.org/10.14324/LRE.20.1.41.

Alexander, R. and A. Stibbe (2014), 'From the Analysis of Ecological Discourse to the Ecological Analysis of Discourse', *Language Sciences*, 41: 104–10.

Bartlett, T. (2012), *Hybrid Voices and Collaborative Change Contextualising Positive Discourse Analysis*, London: Routledge.

Bezemer, J. and G. Kress (2016), *Multimodality, Learning and Communication*, London: Routledge.

Borgnino, E. (2022), *Ecologie Native*, Milan: Elèuthera.

Bortoluzzi, M. (2009), 'Towards a Framework of Critical Multimodal Analysis: Emotion in a Film Trailer', in A. Esposito and R. Vich (eds), *Cross-Modal Analysis of Speech, Gestures, Gaze and Facial Expressions, LNAI,* 5641, 50–62, Berlin: Springer Verlag.

Bortoluzzi, M. (2010), 'Energy and Its Double: A Case-Study in Critical Multimodal Analysis', in E. A. Swain (ed), *Thresholds and Potentialities of Systemic Functional Linguistics: Applications to Other Disciplines, Specialised Discourses and Language Other Than English*, 158–81, Trieste: Edizioni Universitarie.

Caimotto, M. C. (2020), *Discourses of Cycling, Road Users and Sustainability. An Ecolinguistic Investigation*, Cham: Palgrave Macmillan.

Capra, F. (1997), *The Web of Life*, New York: HarperCollins.

Capra, F. (2007), 'Sustainable Living, Ecological Literacy, and the Breath of Life', *Canadian Journal of Environmental Education*, 12 (1): 9–18.

Capra, F. (2013), 'Deep Ecology: Educational Possibilities for the Twenty-First Century', *NAMTA Journal*, 38 (1): 201–16.
Center for Ecoliteracy. Available online: https://www.ecoliteracy.org (accessed 21 March 2021).
Cope, B. and M. Kalantzis (2009), 'Multiliteracies: New Literacies, New Learning', *Pedagogies: An International Journal*, 4: 164–95.
Dancygier, B. (2023), 'Multimodal Media: Framing Climate Change', *Discourse Studies*, 25 (2). https://doi.org/10.1177/14614456231154724.
Döring, M. (2018), 'Media Reports about Natural Disasters: An Ecolinguistics Perspective', in A. F. Fill and H. Penz (eds), *The Routledge Handbook of Ecolinguistics*, 293–308, London: Routledge.
Eisler, R. and D. P. Fry (2019), *Nurturing Our Humanity*, Oxford: Oxford University Press.
Fabiano, E. and G. Mangiameli, eds (2019), *Dialogo con i non umani*, Milano: Mimesis.
Fairclough, N. (2003), *Analysing Discourse*, London: Routledge.
Fairclough, N. (2010), *Critical Discourse Analysis: The Critical Study of Language*, London: Longman.
Fairclough, N. (2014 [1989]), *Language and Power*, New York: Longman.
Figueres, C. and T. Rivett-Carnac (2021 [2020]), *The Future We Choose*, New York: Vintage Books.
Fill, A. (2001), 'Ecolinguistics: State of the Art 1998', in A. Fill and P. Mühlhäusler (eds), *The Ecolinguistics Reader: Language, Ecology and Environment*, 43–53, London: Continuum.
Fill, A. (2018), 'Introduction', in A. F. Fill and H. Penz (eds), *The Routledge Handbook of Ecolinguistics*, 1–7, London: Routledge.
Fill, A. (2022), *Linguistics for Peace*, Würzburg: Königshausen & Neumann.
Fill, A. and P. Mühlhäusler, eds (2001a), *The Ecolinguistics Reader: Language, Ecology and Environment*, London, New York: Continuum.
Fill, A. and P. Mühlhäusler (2001b), 'Introduction', in A. Fill and P. Mühlhäusler (eds), *The Ecolinguistics Reader: Language, Ecology and Environment*, 1–9, London, New York: Continuum.
Fill, A. and H. Penz, eds (2018), *The Routledge Handbook of Ecolinguistics*, London: Routledge.
Goatly, A. (2018), 'Lexicogrammar and Ecolinguistics', in A. F. Fill and H. Penz (eds), *The Routledge Handbook of Ecolinguistics*, 227–48, London: Routledge.
Goleman, D., L. Bennett, and Z. Barlow (2012), *Ecoliterate. How Educators are Cultivating Emotional, Social and Ecological Intelligence*, San Francisco: Wiley (Kindle edition).
Halliday, M. A. K. (2001 [1990]), 'New Ways of Meaning: The Challenge to Applied Linguistics', in A. Fill and P. Mühlhäusler (eds), *The Ecolinguistics Reader: Language, Ecology and Environment*, 175–202, London, New York: Continuum.

Hansen, A. (2018), 'Using Visual Images to Show Environmental Problems', in A. F. Fill and H. Penz (eds), *The Routledge Handbook of Ecolinguistics*, 179–95, London: Routledge.

Hansen, A. and D. Machin (2013), 'Researching Visual Environmental Communication', *Environmental Communication: A Journal of Nature and Culture*, 7 (2): 151–68.

Heuberger, R. (2018), 'Overcoming Anthropocentrism with Anthropomorphic and Physiocentric Uses of Language?', in A. F. Fill and H. Penz (eds), *The Routledge Handbook of Ecolinguistics*, 342–54, London: Routledge.

Jewitt, C., ed (2017a), *The Routledge handbook of Multimodal Analysis*, London: Routledge.

Jewitt, C. (2017b), 'Different Approaches to Multimodality', in C. Jewitt (ed), *The Routledge Handbook of Multimodal Analysis*, 31–43, London: Routledge.

Jewitt, C., J. Bezemer, and K. O'Halloran (2016), *Introducing Multimodality*, London: Routledge.

Kress, G. and S. Selander (2012), 'Multimodal Design, Learning and Cultures of Recognition', *Internet and Higher Education*, 15 (4): 265–8.

Kress, G. and T. van Leeuwen (2001), *Multimodal Discourse: The Modes and Media of Contemporary Communication*, London: Routledge.

Lopez, A. (2021), *Ecomedia Literacy: Integrating Ecology into Media Education*, New York, London: Routledge.

Lovelock, J. E. (1972), 'Gaia as Seen from the Atmosphere', *Atmospheric Environment*, 6 (8): 579–80.

Lovelock, J. E. and L. M. Margulis (1974), 'Atmospheric Homeostasis by and for the Biosphere: The Gaia Hypothesis', *Tellus*, 26 (1–2): 2–10.

Martin, J. R. (2004), 'Positive Discourse Analysis: Solidarity and Change', *Revista Canaria de Estudios Ingleses*, 49: 179–200.

Macgilchrist, F. (2007), 'Positive Discourse Analysis: Contesting Dominant Discourses by Reframing the Issues', *Critical Approaches to Discourse Analysis Across Disciplines*, 1 (1): 74–94.

McBride, B. B., C. A. Brewer, A. R. Berkowitz, and W. T. Borrie (2013), 'Environmental Literacy, Ecological Literacy, Ecoliteracy: What Do We Mean and How Did We Get Here?', *Ecosphere*, 4 (5): 1–20.

Messner, K. (2018), *The Brilliant Deep: Rebuilding the World's Coral Reefs*, San Francisco: Chronicle Books.

Milstein, T., M. O. Thomas, J. Hoffmann, and J. Carr (2023), "Even I Am a Part of Nature': Unraveling the Human/Nature Binary to Enable Systems Change', *Environmental Communication*, 17 (4): 421–36.

Molena, F. (1912), 'Remarkable Weather of 1911: The Effect of the Combustion of Coal on the Climate – What Scientists Predict for the Future', *Popular Mechanics*: 339–42. Available online: https://books.google.it/books?id=Tt4DAAAAMBAJ&pg =PA341&lpg=PA341&dq=this+tends+to+make+the+air+a+more+effective+blanket +for+the+earth&source=bl&ots=QvdH-SgFLl&sig=WiPUNOIzM6udOSTBm2V

XzRQB9K8&hl=en&sa=X&redir_esc=y#v=onepage&q&f=false (accessed 29 March 2023).

Mühlhäusler, P. (2001), 'Talking About Environmental Issues', in A. Fill and P. Mühlhäusler (eds), *The Ecolinguistics Reader. Language, Ecology and Environment*, 31–42, London, New York: Continuum.

Næss, A. (1973), 'The Shallow and the Deep Long-Range Ecology Movement: A Summary', *Inquiry*, 16 (1): 95–100.

Næss, A. (1995), 'The Shallow and the Long Range, Deep Ecology Movement', in A. Drengson and Y. Inoue (eds), *The Deep Ecology Movement: An Introductory Anthology*, 3–19, Berkeley: North Atlantic Books.

Næss, A. (2021), *Siamo l'aria che respiriamo. Saggi di ecologia profonda*, Prato: Piano B edizioni.

Nee, S. (2005), 'The Great Chain of Being', *Nature*, 435: 429. https://doi.org/10.1038/435429a.

OED Online. December 2022. 'Environment', Oxford University Press. Available online: https://www-oed-com.altais.uniud.it/view/Entry/63089?redirectedFrom=environment (accessed 9 February 2023).

OED Online. December 2022. 'Ecology, n', Oxford University Press. Available online: https://www-oed-com.altais.uniud.it/view/Entry/59380?redirectedFrom=ecology (accessed 9 February 2023).

Orr, D. W. (1992), *Ecological Literacy: Education and the Transition to a Postmodern World*, New York: SUNY Press.

Poole, R. (2022), *Corpus-Assisted Ecolinguistics*, London: Bloomsbury Academic.

Riem, A. and T. Hughes-d'Aeth, eds (2022), *Ecosustainable Narratives and Partnership Relationship in World Literatures in English*, Newcastle-upon-Tyne: Cambridge Scholars.

Sedlaczek, A. S. (2016), 'Representations of Climate Change in Documentary Television. Integrating an Ecolinguistic and Ecosemiotic Perspective into a Multimodal Critical Discourse Analysis', *Language and Ecology*. Available online: http://ecolinguistics-association.org/journal (accessed 1 July 2022).

Sedlaczek, A. S. (2017), 'The Field-specific Representation of Climate Change in Factual Television: A Multimodal Critical Discourse Analysis', *Critical Discourse Studies*, 14 (5): 480–96.

Shepherd, N. (2011 [1970]), *The Living Mountain. A Celebration of the Cairngorm Mountains of Scotland*, Edinburgh: Canongate.

Shiva, V. (2015), 'Terra Viva', *Our Soil, Our Commons, Our Future*. Available online: https://seedfreedom.info/campaign/terra-viva-our-soil-our-commonsour-future (accessed 21 March 2023).

Staid, A. (2022), *Essere Natura*, Milan: UTET.

Steffensen, S. V. (2018), 'The Microecological Grounding of Language', in A. F. Fill and H. Penz (eds), *The Routledge Handbook of Ecolinguistics*, 393–405, London: Routledge.

Steffensen, S. V. and A. Fill (2014), 'Ecolinguistics: The State of the Art and Future Horizons', *Language Sciences*, 41: 6–25.
Stibbe, A., ed (2009), *The Handbook of Sustainability Literacy*, UIT Cambridge Ltd. (kindle edition).
Stibbe, A. (2012), *Animals Erased*, Middleton: Wesleyan University Press (kindle edition).
Stibbe, A. (2014), 'An Ecolinguistic Approach to Critical Discourse Studies', *Critical Discourse Studies*, 11 (1): 117–28.
Stibbe, A. (2018), 'Positive Discourse Analysis. Rethinking Human Ecological Relationships', in A. F. Fill and H. Penz (eds), *The Routledge Handbook of Ecolinguistics*, 165–78, London: Routledge.
Stibbe, A., (2021 [2015]), *Ecolinguistics: Language, Ecology and Stories We Live By*, New York, London: Routledge.
Stibbe, A. and H. Luna (2009), 'Introduction', in A. Stibbe (ed), *The Handbook of Sustainability Literacy*, 10–15, UIT Cambridge Ltd. (kindle edition).
UNEP (2021), 'State of the Climate'. Available online: https://www.unep.org/explore-topics/climate-action/what-we-do/climate-action-note/state-of-climate.html?gclid=Cj0KCQjwyt-ZBhCNARIsAKH1177Za-ofsWWVspOhjJRjJX0a5RQbaTdOymYszhylNOzn7CGJq_-v6cMaAmfVEALw_wcB (accessed 29 March 2023).
van Dijk, T. (2009), *Society and Discourse: How Social Contexts Influence Text and Talk*, Cambridge: Cambridge University Press.
van Dooren, T., E. Kirksey, and U. Münster (2016), 'Multispecies Studies: Cultivating Arts of Attentiveness', *Environmental Humanities*, 8 (1). http://doi.org/10.1215/22011919-3527695
van Lier, L. (2008), 'The Ecology of Language Learning and Sociocultural Theory', in A. Creese, P. Martin, and N. H. Hornberger (eds), *Encyclopedia of Language and Education*, Vol. 9: Ecology of Language, 53–65, Berlin: Springer Science Business Media LLC.
Vasta, N. and A. Baldry, eds (2020), *Multiliteracy Advances and Multimodal Challenges in ELT Environments*, Udine: Forum Editrice.
Wodak, R. (2013), 'Editor's Introduction: Critical Discourse Analysis – Challenges and Perspectives', in R. Wodak (ed), *Critical Discourse Analysis*, Vol. 1, xix–xliii, London: Sage.
Wodak, R. and M. Meyer, eds (2016), *Methods for Critical Discourse Analysis*, London: Sage.
Zapf, H. (2016), *Literature as Cultural Ecology: Sustainable Texts*, London: Bloomsbury.
Zurru, E. (2021), '"Your Planet Needs You": An Ecostylistic Analysis of an Ecology-Oriented Interactive Exhibition', in J. Douthwaite, D. F. Virdis, and E. Zurru (eds), *The Stylistics of Landscapes, the Landscapes of Stylistics*, 210–27, Amsterdam, Philadelphia: John Benjamins Publishing Company.
Zurru, E. (2022), 'Social Movements and Metaphor: The Case of #FridaysForFuture', in M. Prandi and M. Rossi (eds), *Researching Metaphors. Towards a Comprehensive Account*, 224–44, London, New York: Routledge.

Part I

Context Setting

1

Tension in Ecological Communication

Alwin Frank Fill

Introduction

Ecological communication can first of all be defined as the use of language about environmental problems. With language, environmental problems can be described, but our languages can also be responsible for increasing these problems, in so far as our languages are anthropocentric and represent the world from the point of view of the use humans make of the 'environment' (Mühlhäusler 2003). An example of this is the way animals are treated in our languages and in texts about them. They are shown as objects which are useful to us, and frequently they are even 'erased' (cf. Stibbe 2012, 2021).

Language is like a musical instrument, with which we can cause pleasure to ourselves and to others, but it is also a tool, with which we can achieve something or even provoke something. In traditional linguistics, four main syntactic functions of language were distinguished: statement, question, command and exclamation (Quirk, Greenbaum and Leech 1972: 50–8). Halliday and Matthiessen (2004) mention three meta-functions of language, namely the ideational, the interpersonal and the textual functions. Jakobson (1980) distinguishes six functions: among these are also the meta-function (using language to talk about language), the poetic and the phatic function – the latter meaning that language can create a feeling of togetherness, without expressing a great deal of meaning (e.g. talking about the weather). Bühler (1999) wrote of the representative, the expressive and the appellative functions.

In this chapter, one function of language will be dealt with that was not identified by any of the authors mentioned: the **tensional function**, that is, the possibility of creating tension (and suspense) not only within texts but also between language and other media. Both tensions will be dealt with in this chapter. The next section will, however, be about the tension which language creates between humans and their natural environment (e.g. animals). One could distinguish between positive (eu-tension) and negative tension (dys-tension). These two types of tension, however, are not polar contrasts, but there are certain degrees between eu-tension and dys-tension. The tension discussed in Section 1.1 is certainly negative – whereas tension between different media is mostly positive. This is also true of 'suspense', for instance, in a novel, which is resolved at the end of the text (see Section 1.2).

1.1 Language creates tension between humans and their natural environment

The tension dealt with in this section was already described by Michael Halliday (2001), although he did not call it 'tension' but 'discontinuity'. According to Halliday, language creates discontinuity between ourselves and the rest of creation, because many words are reserved for humans, such as *think*, *act* and *do*. Through this, Nature appears as passive (cf. Halliday 2001: 194–5). Language 'imposes a strict discontinuity between ourselves and the rest of creation, with "ourselves" including a select band of other creatures that are in some semantic contexts allowed in' (2001: 195).

This discontinuity (or 'negative tension') shows itself for instance in what is called 'distancing' (Fill 1993: 107–9), namely the fact that for the same process or quality, different words are used for humans and animals. Humans 'eat', animals 'graze' or 'feed', women are 'pregnant', female animals 'gravid'. Words like 'father', 'mother', 'brother' and 'sister' are reserved for humans. 'Son' and 'daughter', with animals, are called 'offspring', and for each animal species, a different word for their offspring is used, for example, *cow – calf, goose – gosling, horse – foal* and *sheep – lamb*. Human 'flesh' becomes 'meat', when it is the flesh of animals which is eaten. The 'meat' of certain animals is named in such a way that the name of the animal is not contained in it:

Thus, the meat of calves is called *veal*
' of cows, oxen etc. *beef*
' of pigs   *pork*
' of sheep   *mutton*
' of deer   *venison.*

The same is true of furs, which are mostly not named after the animal from which the skin is taken but have 'refined' names to hide the animal which had to be killed, for example:

Animal: dog	fur: sobaki
Animal: squirrel	fur: feh [dozens of squirrels for one feh!]
Animal: seal	fur: greenlander
Animal: Bengal cat	fur: lipiskin

The German ecolinguist Wilhelm Trampe (2001: 237) has collected numerous passages from texts about animals, in which the animal is described like a thing which can be used. Here are a few examples: animals are *meat producers, livestock, slaughter stock, pork and piglet material* and so on. Trampe writes (2001: 238): 'Living beings are treated in accordance with the economic-technological ideology like objects that are *produced, managed, optimized* and *utilized.*'

In many dictionary definitions of animals, the human use of the animal is the most important part. Here are two examples given by Heuberger (2003: 96–7):

Trout: a fish that lives in rivers, lakes etc. and is good to eat (OALD[1])

Chicken: a domestic fowl bred for its flesh or eggs, esp. a young one (CED[2])

It has to be mentioned, however, that the probably now most frequently used 'dictionary', namely the *Wikipedia*, is much less anthropocentric and more 'neutral' and scientific than traditional dictionaries. Thus, in the entry *trout*, the first section deals with the species of this animal (**'Trout** are a species of freshwater fish belonging to the genera Oncorhynchus, Salmo and Salvelinus, all of the subfamily Salmoninae'). Only after the presentation of the anatomy, the habitat and the diet of this animal is there a section 'as food',[3] in which the preparation of the animal for meals is shown.

A particular kind of tension between humans and animals is created by the special language of hunters, also called hunters' jargon. This jargon names animals and their body parts in a specific way which is on the one hand euphemistic and on the other hand meant to put the hunters onto a specific refined level. Thus, *the quarry* means the animals to be hunted, *the bag* are the animals killed, which have been *harvested*. *Mask* means the head of a dead animal, *brush* the tail of a fox and *slots* the feet of deer or their footprints (cf. Wikipedia 'Hunting terms').

A specific kind of tension is created by the use of **euphemisms**. Euphemisms present facts, for example, the killing of animals, as 'innocuous' events which have nothing to do with the death of 'living' beings. For example, animal experiments are palliatively called 'toxicological tests', and a specific experiment, in which half the animals involved die, is harmlessly called 'LD-50-Test', LD-50 standing for 'lethal doses for 50 %'! In Brazil, where the breeding of bovine animals is of particular economic importance, a farm where this is done is called 'Spa Bovino' (apparently a wellness resort for cows and bulls!), and the owner of the farm says, 'The animals die happily and in dignity, because they know that you enjoy eating them' (Hartmann 2018: 159). The 'pseudonyms' for furs have already been mentioned. Words like *Greenlander, blueback, beater, ranger* and *square flipper* are nominations which sound innocent but which hide the fact that they name furs for whose 'production' seals had to die.

The use of animals (mostly the killing of them) is frequently described with words like 'biological', 'ecological', 'natural' and even 'sustainable'. 'The animals [whose meat we eat] were kept sustainably' is a frequent phrase in advertisements for *pork* and *beef*. 'Slaughter-feast' (in German *Schlachtfest*), in some cultures, is even presented as a kind of cultural event. When we read 'you will be eating meat "without any feeling of guilt"', 'feeling of guilt' is not meant concerning the animals but concerning one's own body, which will not put on more weight. *Grass-fed meat, green beef* and *happy meat* are also euphemistic expressions which create tension between language (surface structure) and reality (cf. Cole 2011).

Most of the types of tension discussed in this section can be resolved by using the term 'con-vironment', a term which puts humans and nature on the same level.

1.1.1 Animal idioms and animal stereotypes

Perhaps we should not talk only about negative tension in the language about animals. There are also positive relations between language and animals. Many inns and pubs are named after animals (e.g. the famous *Weißes Rössl* in Austria), and many idioms and phrases use animal names not negatively, for example, 'to get the lion's share' or 'straight from the horse's mouth'. Counterexamples are 'it's raining cats and dogs' or 'going at a snail's pace' (animal stereotype!). Also, we should not forget the many fables (from Aesop to Lafontaine) in which animals appear like humans. There are also 'heraldic animals' which represent noble families and even whole countries. The heraldic animal of England is the lion, of Austria the eagle.

Many animal stereotypes are positive. The dog, for instance, is seen as 'faithful' and 'man's best friend', and the dove is 'the animal representing peace'. On the internet (Wikipedia: 'animal stereotypes'), we find a very large number of animals to which (to whom!) human qualities are attributed, many of them positive, for example,

The owl is wise
The beaver is hard-working
The elephant has a long memory
The lion is proud, brave and noble ('the king of beasts').

The negative and the positive tension between language and the environment (particularly animals) is an interesting topic which would deserve further investigation. In particular, it could be investigated to what extent the negative tension is more frequent than the positive one – also in different cultures! Another topic worth investigating is to find out whether the definition of 'animal rights' (Precht 2016; Singer 2009) and more precise studies of animals (their 'languages', their 'emotions', etc.; see Goodall 1991) are already contributing to a new image of animals which shows less tension between language/texts and animals.

1.1.2 Ecoliteracy

An initiative which might help to solve the negative tension between human thinking and the environment is the creation of a Center for Ecoliteracy. In the 1990s, David Orr (1992) and Fritjof Capra (1997) created the idea of and the term *ecoliteracy*, which means being literate as far as ecosystems and ecological (also environmental) problems are concerned. In 1995, Capra, who was originally from Austria (born 1939 in Vienna), founded the above-mentioned Center for Ecoliteracy, which is located in the David Brower Center in Berkeley, California. The Center for Ecoliteracy was created to make it possible to teach young people the basics of ecological thinking and further their knowledge about sustainability. The present author would like to suggest that the Center should also teach young people the role of language in ecological (or non-ecological!) thinking, and this should include the topics of ecolinguistics – including its role in bringing about peace (see Section 1.4).

Mühlhäusler (2020: 8) has compiled a list of topics which have so far 'for whatever reasons', as he writes, been excluded from ecolinguistic research. Among these are the following:

1. The negative effects of tourism, including eco-tourism (visiting a country because of its specific animals or trees)
2. Migration of human, plant and animal populations – their negative impact on endemic cultures and natural kinds (see Boschian Bailo 2021)
3. The negative and denigrating views on animals in many of the world's major religions –

4. Military expenditure and conflict.

Topic 4 is one which will be dealt with at the end of this chapter, in Section 1.4.

In the next two sections, different types of tension will be discussed, particularly the tension between text and music and between text and image.

1.2 Intermedial and plurimedial tension

Tension can arise within a medium, say a painting or a symphony, and particularly in a work of literature. The tension within a novel is usually called 'suspense', which arises from uncertainty about the continuing part and particularly the ending of a narration. Suspense can even be seen as the most important quality of a novel. However, discussing suspense would take us into the study of literature – which is not one of the topics to be addressed in this chapter. Thus, this chapter will continue with a discussion of tension not just in one 'medium' (i.e. section of culture) but between two (intermedial) or even three media (plurimedial tension).

1.2.1 Tension between text and music

In the understanding of most people, a song or aria of the best quality is one in which the music is perceived as coherent with the words or even reinforces the contents of the 'lyrics'. It is frequently overlooked that it is the differing messages or rather the tension between two works of art which make them outstanding.

The 'cooperation' of two media is called 'intermediality'. *The Musicalization of Fiction* (Wolf 1999) is an example of this but also the combination of text and image. In what follows, the tension between language and music is highlighted by the investigation of lyrics set to 'a specific music' which is in tension with the lyrics.

A good example of this is the German lyrics to Giovanni Gastoldi's madrigal *Amor vittorioso* (cf. Fill 2007: 152–3). The Italian original begins with an invocation to armed soldiers: 'Tutti venite armati, o forti miei soldati!' [Come all armed, o my strong soldiers]. Corresponding to this, the music is very rhythmical, and it tries to imitate the marching of soldiers. Alexander Pope's sentence 'the sound must seem an echo to the sense' (1711/1963) is here transferred into reality. However, the music of the madrigal was used by a German poet of the nineteenth century (Peter Cornelius) whose lyrics to the music are about a couple who sit together in a boat and are having a good time: 'Fahren wir froh im Nachen / Himmel und Erde lachen' [Let us ride happily in the boat, while heaven and earth are laughing]. The tension between lyrics and music leads to the wish to solve this tension by interpreting the song as meaning 'love may also imitate war' or rather 'love is stronger than war' (cf. Fill 2007: 153).

A well-known and more recent example of tension between words and music is the song *The Highway Code* of the Master Singers (The Master Singers, Horrex/ Keating. E.M.I. Records 1966). The words are taken from the totally prosaic Part I of the Highway Code:

> Walking alone, where there is a pavement or adequate footpath, use it. On a pavement or footpath, do not walk next to the kerb with your back to the traffic. Do not step into the road without first looking.

The music, however, sounds like a psalm sung by a quartet of four men. However, as we listen to it, we realize that the syntax of the text in some way resembles that of the *Ten Commandments* in the Bible ('Do not . . .', etc.). The conclusion we unconsciously draw from this is that an instruction to behaving correctly in modern traffic has certain features of the *Ten Commandments*, because it keeps all persons involved safe and is thus indispensable for survival (see Fill 2007: 155–6).

We have seen that tension between language and music is a phenomenon which creates additional meaning and increases the effect of the work of art. Consciously or unconsciously, the listener looks for solutions of the tension and finds additional meanings. This kind of intermedial tension brings about a certain creativity within our listening and thinking.

1.2.2 Tension between text and picture

In contrast to texts, which use an arbitrary system of signs, namely language, a picture conveys its meaning iconically, that is, the picture shows its motif not in an arbitrary, unconnected way but (at least traditionally) tries to interpret reality as a two-dimensional representation. Pictures are frequently combined with text, for example, in book illustrations, in newspapers, in advertising and in comics, and also when paintings or photographs are being described to make it easier to interpret them.

As concerns the relation between text and picture, the following degrees of repetition or tension can be distinguished (cf. Fill 2007: 137):

1. Text and picture give the same information with their respective symbols (repetition)

2. Text and picture complement each other and one of them contains additional information (addition)
3. Text and picture contradict each other (contradiction)
4. Text and picture seem to be disconnected (irrelevance).

In type one, tension arises only through the different codifications of what is presented. Book illustrations and picture postcards are examples of this. Type two is frequent in advertisements, in which a certain degree of tension is used in order to make the reader interested in the product advertised and induce him/her to buy it. Type three is also occasionally used in advertising, in order to make the reader puzzle over the link between text and picture, which may make him/her more interested in the product advertised. An example of this (taken from Mühlhäusler 1999: 174) is given in Fill (2007: 140): a picture of mountains and glaciers has the title: 'Our factory'. Looking at this tensional combination more closely, the reader discovers that the picture and the text are used to advertise a certain mineral water, which obviously is supposed to come from the glaciers in the mountains.

Another example of this contradiction is a picture of a huge congestion of cars in front of the *Brandenburger Tor* in Berlin – with the textual line: 'Berlin is free!' This picture appeared in various newspapers on the day on which the Berlin wall had fallen (in November 1989), and it was possible for the first time after the Second World War to drive from one part of the city to the other. The photographer (Günter Peters) probably wanted to express with this contradiction that *freedom* is only relative: gaining freedom in one area may lead to loss of freedom in another (cf. Fill 2007: 142). A third example of this is a postcard which shows the prison gates of Dartmoor Prison, with the accompanying text 'Wish you were here' (Fill 2007: 146). In this case, the tension between words and picture is only meant to cause humour: the sentence frequently used on postcards, in this case, has a somewhat macabre meaning, which however is immediately understood by the receiver as being ironic.

Type 4 (irrelevance) will make the viewer search for connections between the two media and thus experience tension. Advertising commercial videos in television frequently begin with showing children playing or a young lady on a palm beach – as an attempt to catch the viewer's attention and make him/her curious about the product which is advertised. Television advertising has a great number of possibilities for creating tension, among which the following (cf. Fill 2007: 149):

1. Beginning with the text and showing the relevant video somewhat later;

2. Contrasting the topics of text and video, e.g. talking about industry, but showing a farm;
3. Contrasting image and sound, e.g. showing a waterfall, but playing the sound of a machine;
4. Contrasting fast sequences of pictures with slow talk (or the other way round).

Television and the internet offer new and wide-ranging possibilities of creating tension between visual and auditive presentation – a topic which could bring about new methodologies of research. Here we also have a field in which text, picture and music may be combined – with all kinds of tension arising. Tension between **three** media is something which up to now has not become a topic of research, whereas the research concerning tension has a wide field of theory and application. Thus, it is not just 'intermediality' which should be investigated concerning repetition and tension but also 'plurimediality', which is becoming more and more frequent in television and in the social media and which offers many opportunities for new research.

1.3 Tension in linguistic interaction

Linguistic interaction can occur between several persons but also between only two. In this section, we will mainly deal with the latter type of interaction. The first distinction to be made concerning this is between (1) purpose-oriented and (2) phatic communication. The first type is directed towards giving and exchanging information, while the second one is directed towards social togetherness and 'companionableness' (cf. Fill 2007: 111–12).

Interaction between two speakers can be symmetrical or complementary (Watzlawick, Beavin and Jackson 1982: 68–70). In the first case, hardly any tension will arise, in the second, there can be enough tension to either create comic effects, misunderstanding or even quarrel. The next section (1.3.1) will be about the kind of humour (and laughter) which may be the result of tension.

1.3.1 Comic effects arising from tension

In conversation, comic effects arise from the tension between expected and unexpected utterances (cf. Fill 2007: 113, 115–23). Frequently, the unexpected utterance contains a contradiction or something which is obviously untrue. In the following example, the comic effect is based on contradiction:

1.   A: Do you also have problems with your memory?

   B: Not at all. But what was the question you just asked me?

Speaker B's utterance contains a clear contradiction. But the tension which arises through this creates a humorous effect, which could also be called a case of self-irony. In the following example, the humour arises from the tension between the speech act expected by speaker A (praise, gratitude) and the speech act really produced by speaker B (devaluation of A):

2.   A: I have brought a little present for you.

   B: That's what I was afraid of.

Whether speaker A accepts this as humorous or as an offense depends of course on the relation between the two and their previous conversations, particularly on whether they frequently create tension when talking together.

In the next example, an Austrian politician's speech in Parliament is interrupted by a heckler with a question which is probably meant as an offence. The tension that this creates is resolved by the politician with a surprising answer which by relaxing the tension creates humour (source: Austrian television, November 1990; see also Fill 2007: 117):

> Situation: speech of Heinrich Neisser in the Austrian Parliament (November 1990)
>
> Heckler interrupts: Do you know Machiavelli?
>
> Neisser: Not personally (*continues his speech*).

Creating humour by introducing tension can also avoid conflict and even quarrel. As Radcliffe-Brown (1952: 107) writes: 'It is also fairly evident that a relationship in which insults are exchanged and there is an obligation not to take them seriously, is one which, by means of sham conflicts, avoids real ones.' Radcliffe-Brown (1952: 90) created the term 'joking relationship' for a relation between two persons in which it is permitted to make fun of the other, who is required to take no offense. In this context, it would be of interest whether men make fun of other persons more frequently than women. Helga Kotthoff has edited a book about this, in which Senta Trömel-Plötz writes that women's humour is not usually directed *against* another person but is rather meant to help the other person (foreword to Kotthoff ed. 1988: 7–17).

1.3.2 Eu-tension and dys-tension: Conflict and quarrel

So far, this section of my chapter has been about the positive aspects of tension, particularly about humour arising from communicational tension. However, tension can also lead to conflict and even quarrel. This is why Fill (2007: 9 f.) distinguishes between 'eu-tension', that is, tension leading to positive effects, and 'dys-tension', that is, tension having negative effects. Dys-tension shows itself particularly in conflict or even quarrel arising from it.

In this section, we first of all have to distinguish between conflict and quarrel. Following Dahrendorf (cf. 1972: 41–42), we should see 'conflict' merely as a collision of interests which can be 'handled' and resolved and which has even the potential of a certain creativity. Conflict, however, may also lead to an 'argument', a 'dispute' or even to a quarrel. Thus, while conflict could be seen as a form of 'eu-tension', quarrel is definitely a form of 'dys-tension', which, as most people think, should, if possible, be avoided.

However, several authors see not only conflict but also quarrel as something which has its positive sides. There is even a book (Bach and Wyden 1983) titled *Streiten Verbindet* ('Quarrelling Unites') and another one (Rother 1964) about *Die Kunst des Streitens* ('The Art of Quarrelling'). The point about quarrelling is that it leaves an argument on the verbal side and thus avoids violence.

It could also be argued that quarrelling could bring about a reduction of aggression, in other words a certain diminution of dys-tension. Following Aristotle, we could say that quarrelling may lead to *'catharsis'* (Greek for 'purification'), that is, getting rid of strong negative emotions. The desire of people for tension could be satisfied by having a quarrel with someone. Thus, quarrelling could be called a particularly interesting combination of eu-tension and dys-tension.

The famous Gricean maxims were established in 1975, that is, at a time when tension was not yet seen as something positive in conversation. Grice called his maxims 'the Cooperative Principle', a principle which demands that speakers observe the maxims of quantity, quality, relevance and manner. What follows is a brief discussion first of Grice's maxim of **quantity** and then that of **relevance.** The maxim of quantity says: 'Do not say less, and do not say more than is necessary for the purpose of the conversation.' This has value only in a purpose-oriented conversation but would be completely out of joint in phatic communion, that is, in conversations in which togetherness, humour and joking play the most important part. The maxim of relevance says: 'Say only what is relevant to what is being spoken about.' This maxim is also completely out of place in any kind of conversation which is not directed towards the purpose of communicating facts. Utterances containing irrelevant elements may cause laughter because of the tension between expected and unexpected words. In 1975, the principle of tension (and suspense) had not yet arrived in the discussion of conversation.

We have argued that in personal communication tension and even quarrelling do not lead to violence, since tension in language leaves aggression on the side of language, which prevents violence. However, there are a few linguistic strategies which may lead to violence. Among these are the following:

1. Linguistic devaluation: words like *dreamer, chatterbox, flop, washout* etc. may lead to the aggravation of a quarrel and finally even to violence.
2. Generalization: *you always . . ., you never . . ., you persistently do this* etc. make the addressee look in a negative perspective and acting without deliberation. Remarks like 'I know your habits' make the addressee look like some machine which operates the same all the time.
3. Sarcasm and irony (e.g. 'you are *soooo* reliable and never forget anything') are also negative strategies of this kind.

Perhaps the most dangerous linguistic strategy is making the other person look ridiculous and laughing at him/her. This is a type of aggression, particularly because laughing about someone provides the laughing person with power over the one who is being laughed at. Several acts of violence in recent years have had their cause in the perpetrator having been made to look ridiculous and being laughed at. In many cases, this has happened between wife and husband.

However, the present author is of the opinion that all these devaluing strategies are not examples of tension but rather of 'lack of tension', at least of eu-tension.

1.4 Language, war and peace

This final section will show that an awareness of the dys-tension or rather the lack of tension in some uses of our languages could lead to more peaceful thinking. This awareness should be conveyed to all politicians, leaders and commanders who have power over nations, tribes and other communities which might be involved in war. In the year 2022, awareness of growthism (see later in the text) should have been present not only in the leader of NATO but also in the Russian government, particularly in the mind of its representatives.

1.4.1 Growthism

One author who wrote about this dys-tensional quality of language is Michael Halliday. Following Halliday (2001: 192–3. *et passim*), we should take up the topic of **growthism**, a way of thinking which Halliday criticized in the following way (2001: 192):

> texts repeated daily all around the world contain a simple message: growth is good. Many is better than few, more is better than less, big is better than small, grow is better than shrink, up is better than down, Gross National Products must go up, standards of living must rise, productivity must increase.

Halliday then writes that with this 'growthism' we are using up capital resources, fresh water supplies and agricultural soils. 'And at the same time as we are consuming we are also destroying. We are destroying many of the other species who form part of the planet's life cycle; and we are destroying the planet itself, through global warming' (2001: 192). Notice that Halliday used the term 'global warming', where today we would probably write of 'climate change'.

Halliday's critique of growthism is justified also for the following reason: thinking that everything must grow leads to conflict between tribes and nations, which all want to grow at the expense of their neighbours. Both world wars had their origin in some countries wishing to enlarge their territory and their power. The current conflict between Russia and Ukraine is also due to this thinking – both on the part of NATO and of Russia.

Of course, we have to be aware that growthism is not something created initially by language. It is a very old way of thinking which began in the Stone Age before the 'agricultural revolution', when humans still had to rely on nature (wild animals) to have enough to eat. They *had* to become stronger and faster and also more numerous, in order to defend their area. But this way of thinking consolidated itself in language and still remains there, although the problems of the Stone Age have disappeared (at least for most humans). 'The grammar of "big" is the grammar of "good", while the grammar of "small" is the grammar of "bad". The motif of "bigger and better" is engraved into our consciousness by virtue of their line-up in the grammar' (Halliday 2001: 194).

'*Citius – altius – fortius*' (faster – higher – stronger) is still the motto of the Olympic Games (created by Pierre de Coubertin 1896), although the idea of 'taking part is everything' is getting more and more central in this sports event – as it should! It is also to be hoped that the traditional wish of being victorious will more and more (and in more and more countries!) be restricted to sports events and thus replace the ambition of conquering the territory and the possessions of others. In 2022, unfortunately, this is not te case, as the 'conflict' between Russia and Ukraine proves.

Semper augustus was the slogan of the 'Holy Roman Empire', a slogan which was interpreted to mean 'always increasing the empire' (Latin *augere* means 'increase'), although the meaning intended was 'always sublime'. More peaceful was the slogan of the Habsburg Dynasty: '*Bella gerant alii, tu felix Austria nube*' ('Others may lead wars, you, happy Austria, marry!'), which alluded to the fact that several Habsburg princes and princesses retained or increased (!) the size of the empire by marrying someone from another country.

There are at least two philosophers who also took position against 'growthism': Ernst Friedrich Schumacher, in his book *Small Is Beautiful* (1973), and the Austrian Leopold Kohr, in *Das Ende der Großen* (1986). Schumacher (1973: 29) quotes Mahatma Gandhi, who said that the earth offers enough for our needs but does not satisfy our greed. Growth to a certain limit is possible, but there should not be an unlimited general growth. Kohr (1986: 15) writes that the main problem of our time is not ideological but 'dimensional'. He quotes Shakespeare's Hamlet, who when living today would not say 'to be or not to be' but 'to be small or not to be at all, that is the question'.

The critique of growthism was taken up by Stibbe, who writes (2021: 19–20): 'If inundated by statements that economic growth is good then the message may penetrate deep into people's minds and become a story that they live by. This story, once in their minds, then has an influence on their behaviour and how they treat the systems which support life.' Stibbe (2021: 19–20) speaks of 'appraisal patterns', which are 'clusters of linguistic features which come together to represent an area of life as good or bad'. The present author would call this a type of 'dys-tension' which overlooks the stages or degrees of tension which one has to realize in order to do justice to what exists in the world.

In writing about 'language' (or 'grammar', as Halliday called it), we always have to realize that we are writing about those languages which Whorf (1956) called Standard Average European (SAE) languages. As Whorf has shown, there are indigenous languages (e.g. the Hopi language) in all parts of the world which have features different from the SAE languages. In the rest of this chapter, this author will do justice to these differences and will therefore write about 'our languages'.

1.4.2 Thinking in contrasts

A second point discussed by Halliday is that our languages make us think in contrasts, and we do not even realize that in reality there are transitional values between the 'poles'. 'Small' and 'big', 'good' and 'bad' are extreme simplifications of reality, whose different grades – with a little more thoughtfulness – can even be expressed through language (e.g. *monstrous, huge, big, medium-sized, small* and *tiny*). Particularly contrasts like **friend** and **enemy** are dangerous for peace. Instead of *friend versus enemy*, we could at least use three grades: *like-minded, similar-minded* and *different-minded person*.

'Among the properties construed by the grammar as gradable, most have a negative and a positive pole' (Halliday 2001: 194). Halliday then speaks of a 'binary theory of phenomena [which] has obviously been important for our survival, in the stage of history that is now coming to an end' (2001: 195). Instead, we should adopt a 'graduated' theory of the phenomena in our world, which will give us a much more precise view of these phenomena and will thus prevent our thinking in terms of *large* and *small* or *friend* and *enemy*. Such a theory of the world would make us think more in keeping with reality (not in 'poles'!) and would also avoid construing other people as friends or enemies. Ecolinguistics should show that an awareness of this role of language would make us more peaceful and could even prevent war.

1.5 Summary

Tension is inherent in ecological communication, since 'ecology' itself is something that contains tension. Ernst Haeckel (1866 II, 268), who coined the term, defined ecology as 'the study of reciprocal action between organisms and their living and non-living surroundings'. 'Reciprocal action' (in German '*Wechselwirkung*') is definitely something that brings about tension. Indeed, it could be seen as a dynamic definition of tension. This chapter does not just describe the tension 'between organisms and their living and non-living surroundings', but it also describes the tension that *language* creates when it is used to describe organisms and their surroundings.

In particular, Section 1.1 of this chapter deals with the tension between humans and their 'living surroundings' or 'natural environment', that is, animals and plants, as it arises from our way of using language. This tension is created, for instance, by 'distancing', that is, the use of different words with humans and animals for analogous processes (humans *eat*, animals *feed* or *graze*). Euphemisms also create tension, since they present the killing of animals as a harmless and innocuous event (e.g. *LD-50 test*). Words for furs do not contain the name of the animal killed (e.g. *Greenlander*, in which the animal – a seal – is not contained). The language of hunting also frequently 'erases' (cf. Stibbe 2012) the animals referred to, for example, when *the quarry* is used for the animals hunted. However, there are also positive relations between language and animals, for example, positive 'animal stereotypes', such as 'faithful dog' or 'peaceful dove'.

'Ecoliteracy' (namely being literate as far as ecological problems are concerned) is taught in Capra's Centre for Ecoliteracy (California). In this chapter, it is argued that ecoliteracy should also concern the knowledge about the different kinds of tension which *language* creates between humans and their living environment. To contribute resolving this tension, the term 'con-vironment' has been created, a term which puts humans and nature on the same level.

In Section 1.2, intermedial and plurimedial types of tension are dealt with. It is the author's opinion that in every work of art tension plays an important role; this role is even greater when two media, for example, text and music or language and picture, are united. The tension between text and music is shown using Giovanni Gastoldi's *Amor vittorioso* as an example. The German lyrics to this madrigal (written by Peter Cornelius around 1870) create tension with the music which tries to imitate the marching of soldiers. 'Let us ride happily in the boat' does not seem to fit to the music, but the wish to solve this tension in the listener leads to an interpretation of the song as meaning 'love is stronger than war'.

Tension between text and picture is not particularly frequent, since usually repetition or addition is used. However, there are also examples in which text and picture contradict each other. A few of them are discussed in Section 1.2.2. It is shown that this tension either creates humour or makes the reader/viewer think more profoundly about the meaning of the text. It is argued that in our age of television and the social media, 'intermediality' is being replaced more and more by 'plurimediality', in which more than two media are combined.

In the penultimate Section 1.3, it is shown that in 'linguistic interaction', for example, in everyday conversation, too, tension may arise, which may lead either to comic effects – see Examples 1–3 – or to conflict and quarrel. Conflict can be 'handled' and may even lead to a certain creativity (Dahrendorf 1972), but quarrel also has its positive sides. Quarrelling may for instance lead to '*catharsis*' (Aristotle) and thus make people get rid of negative emotions by fulfilling their wish for tension. It could be argued that quarrelling occurs only on the level of language, but certain linguistic strategies may indeed lead to violence, for example, linguistic devaluation ('you are a dreamer'), generalization ('you keep making this mistake') and particularly making another person look ridiculous and laughing at her/him.

The final Section 1.4 takes up the topic of 'language, war and peace' and shows how 'growthism' (Halliday 2001) may bring about and has frequently brought about war. It is a kind of thinking ('bigger is better') which arose in the Stone Age but is now no longer necessary, although several peoples and nations still stick to it. Thinking in the manner of 'small is beautiful' (Schumacher 1973 and Kohr 1986) is much more up to date and should become a 'story we live by' (Stibbe 2021). This is particularly important in the age of the climate change, which may well have one of its causes in growthism.

A second way of thinking (and speaking) which is out of date in the twenty-first century is thinking in contrasts, which simplifies our perception of the world. *Good* and *bad*, *large* and *small*, *friend* and *foe* are contrasts which hide the many grades in between and make us think in 'poles'. Instead of this 'binary theory of phenomena [which] has obviously been important for our survival, in the stage of history that is now coming to an end' (Halliday 2001: 195), we should adopt a 'graduated' theory, which will give us a much more precise view of the world and will also avoid growthism and imagining the existence of enemies. Heraclitus's sentence 'War is the father of all things' should be replaced by another statement made by him, namely '*panta rhei* – everything flows'.

The *résumé* of this final section can be expressed with the following three sentences: 'Tensional thinking' should help to change the direction of human evolution in such a way that we no longer wish to grow. It should make us think and act more moderately so that the present values and resources are retained but perhaps distributed more equally – a development through which peace is promoted. One of the tasks of ecolinguistics is to take us away from 'thinking in poles' and lead us towards an accentuated and graduated thinking, in which degrees (!) of eu-tension play an important role and dys-tension between poles will disappear.

Notes

1 *Oxford Advanced Learner's Dictionary* (1995).
2 *Collins English Dictionary* (1995).
3 Accessed 14 June 2021.

References

Bach, G. R. and P. Wyden (1983), *Streiten Verbindet*, Frankfurt/M: Fischer tb.
Boschian Bailo, V. (2021), 'Communicating Environmental Migration: Strategic Representations in the Discourse of International Organisations and News Discourse', Udine: As yet unpublished doctoral dissertation (Università degli studi di Udine).
Bühler, K. (1999 [1934]), *Sprachtheorie. Die Darstellungsfunktion der Sprache*, 3rd edn, Stuttgart: G. Fischer.
Capra, F. (1997), *The Web of Life: A New Synthesis of Mind and Matter*, London: Harper Collins.
Cole, M. (2011), 'From "Animal Machines" to "Happy Meat"? Foucault's Ideas of Disciplinary and Pastoral Power Applied to "Animal-Centered" Welfare Discourse', *Animals*, I (1): 83–101.
Dahrendorf, R. (1972), *Konflikt und Freiheit. Auf dem Weg zur Dienstklassengesellschaft*, München: Piper.
Fill, A. (1993), *Ökolinguistik. Eine Einführung*, Tübingen: Gunter Narr Verlag.
Fill, A. (2007), *Das Prinzip Spannung*, 2nd edn, Tübingen: Gunter Narr Verlag.
Goodall, J. (1991), *Through a Window: My Thirty Years with the Chimpanzees of Gombe*, Reinbek: Rowohlt.
Grice, H. P. (1975), 'Logic and Conversation', in P. Cole and J. L. Morgan (eds), *Syntax and Semantics*, Vol. 3: *Speech acts*, 41–58, New York: Academic Press.
Haeckel, E. (1866), *Generelle Morphologie der Organismen*, Vol. II, Berlin: G. Reimer.
Halliday, M. (2001 [1990]), 'New Ways of Meaning: The Challenge to Applied Linguistics', in A. Fill, and P. Mühlhäusler (eds), *The Ecolinguistics Reader: Language, Ecology and Environment*, 175–202, London, New York: Continuum.
Halliday, M. and C. M. Matthiessen (2004), *An Introduction to Functional Grammar*, 3rd edn, London: Hodder Arnold.
Hartmann, K. (2018), *Die Grüne Lüge. Weltrettung als Profitables Geschäftsmodell*, Munich: Karl Blessing.
Heuberger, R. (2003), 'Anthropocentrism in Monolingual English Dictionaries: An Ecolinguistic Approach to the Lexicographic Treatment of Faunal Terminology', *Arbeiten aus Anglistik und Amerikanistik*, 28 (1): 93–105.
Jakobson, R. (1980), *The Framework of Language*, Ann Arbor: Michigan Slavic Publications.
Kohr, L. (1986), *Das Ende der Großen. Zurück zum Menschlichen Maß*, trans. Edgar Th. Portisch, Vienna: ORAC Verlag.
Mühlhäusler, P. (1999), 'Metaphor and Metonymy in Environmental Advertising', *Arbeiten aus Anglistik und Amerikanistik*, 24 (2): 167–80.
Mühlhäusler, P. (2003), *Language and Environment, Environment of Language: A Course in Ecolinguistics*, London: Battlebridge.
Mühlhäusler, P. (2020), 'Quo Vadis Ecolinguistics?' *Ecolinguistica. Revista de Ecologia e Linguagem*, 6 (1): 5–23.

Orr, D. (1992), *Ecological Literacy: Education and the Transition to a Postmodern World*, New York: SUNY Press.
Pope, A. (1963), *The Poems of Alexander Pope* (a one-volume edition of the Twickenham text, ed. John Butt). Yale University Press ["Essay on Criticism" first published in 1711.]
Precht, R. D. (2016), *Tiere denken. Vom Recht der Tiere und den Grenzen des Menschen*, Munich: Goldmann.
Quirk, R., S. Greenbaum, and G. Leech (1972), *A Grammar of Contemporary English*, London: Longman Group Limited.
Radcliffe-Brown, A. R. (1952), *Structure and Function in Primitive Society. Essays and Addresses*, London: Cohen & Unwin.
Rother, W. (1964), *Die Kunst des Streitens*, Munich: Goldmann tb.
Schumacher, E. F. (1973), *Small Is Beautiful: Economics as if People Mattered*, New York: Harper.
Singer, P. (2009), *Animal Liberation: The Definitive Classic of the Animal Liberation*, New York: HarperCollins Publishers.
Stibbe, A. (2012), *Animals Erased: Discourse, Ecology, and Reconnection with the Natural World*, Middleton: Wesleyan University Press.
Stibbe, A. (2021), *Ecolinguistics: Language and the Stories We Live By*, 2nd edn, London, New York: Routledge.
Trampe, W. (2001), 'Language and the Ecological Crisis. Extracts from a Dictionary of Industrial Agriculture', in A. Fill and P. Mühlhäusler (eds), *The Ecolinguistics Reader: Language, Ecology and Environment*, 232–40, London, New York: Continuum.
Trömel-Plötz, S. (1988), 'Preface', in H. Kotthoff (ed), *Das Gelächter der Geschlechter. Humor und Macht in Gesprächen von Frauen und Männern*, 7–17, Frankfurt/Main: Fischer tb.
Watzlawick, P., J. H. Beavin, and D. Jackson (1982), *Menschliche Kommunikation. Formen, Störungen, Paradoxien*, 6th edn, Stuttgart, Vienna: Hans Huber.
Whorf, B. L. (1956), *Language, Thought and Reality: Selected Writings of B. L. Whorf*, ed. J. B. Carroll, Cambridge: MIT Press.
Wolf, W. (1999), *The Musicalization of Fiction: A Study in the Theory and History of Intermediality*, Amsterdam, Atlanta: Rodopi.

2

A Corpus-Assisted Ecolinguistic Analysis of *Hurricanes* and *Wildfires* and the Potential for Corpus-Assisted Eco-Pedagogy in ELT Classrooms

Robert Poole

Introduction

Since at least 1896 and the research of Svante Arrhenius, the scientific community has understood the deleterious effects that the burning of fossil fuels would one day have on the global climate. Nearly fifty years later, Callendar further advanced the nascent scientific understanding of global climate in his discovery that temperatures and the amount of carbon dioxide in the atmosphere were steadily increasing (1938). As empirical data of climate change grew and our knowledge of climate science expanded, the urgency of climate change slowly became recognized beyond the scientific community as a result of moments such as climate scientist James Hansen's testimony to the US Congress in 1988 and the release of Bill McKibben's *The End of Nature* – often considered the first non-fiction text on climate change for a general audience – in 1989. At that point, global warming – the preferred term at the time – entered public discourse in the United States and widespread public awareness of climate change began to emerge, though not without contention and scepticism. Soon after, the United Nations' Intergovernmental Panel on Climate Change (IPCC) released its first Assessment Report in which it rather cautiously asserted, 'There is concern that human activities may be inadvertently changing the climate of the globe' (IPCC 1990). Such tentativeness was absent by 2021 when in its sixth report on the physical science of climate change, the IPCC concluded, 'It is unequivocal that human influence has warmed the atmosphere, ocean and land' (IPCC 2021). The scientific evidence of the climate crisis – increasing temperatures, warming oceans, retreating glaciers, rising sea levels – has become clearer and more abundant with each passing year.

The analysis of this chapter does not explore climate change through such physical indicators of increasing temperatures, retreating glaciers or rising sea levels. Instead, I investigate whether changes in US English language use display evidence of climate change across the past three decades. To explore this question, I investigate the changing discursive representation of two events – *hurricanes* and *wildfires* – from 1990 to 2019 in the one-billion-word Corpus of Contemporary American English (Davies 2008). Thus, the approach integrates the techniques of corpus linguistics with the framework of ecolinguistics – in other words, the chapter applies and performs corpus-assisted ecolinguistics (Frayne 2019; Poole 2022a).

The following section surveys research in corpus-assisted ecolinguistics with a particular focus on studies in this space which explore diachronic change in language use of ecological relevance. I then present the analysis of *hurricane/s* supported by the implementation of Kendall's Tau correlation coefficient to empirically evaluate the strength of language use trends over time. In the analysis of *wildfire/s*, I produce a more pedagogically accessible path to diachronic analysis, as I aim to demonstrate the possibilities of corpus-assisted activities for the ELT classroom. In closing, I introduce additional activities and assert the potential of corpus-assisted eco-pedagogy for expanding ecoliteracy and cultivating ecocritical language awareness.

2.1 Corpus-assisted ecolinguistics

The discourse analytic strand of ecolinguistics is grounded in Mühlhäusler's assertion that 'perceptions of nature are mediated through language and that in turn such perceptions and lifestyles feed back into the structure of discourse' (2003: 12). In recent years, ecolinguists have more frequently investigated the mediating role of language on 'the life-sustaining interactions of humans, other species and the physical environment' (ecolinguistics-association.org) through the analysis of large, principled collections of authentic language use – that is, corpora. While more qualitatively oriented approaches are well suited for many investigations, particularly the critical analyses of single texts of ecological relevance, the investigation of corpora facilitates the identification of language patterns that operate across prevailing discourses. As Alexander and Stibbe (2014) assert, ecolinguistics should expand its research vision beyond the analysis of ecological discourse – texts and discourses specifically about the environment, that is, 'greenspeak' (Harré, Brockmeier and Mühlhäusler 1999) – to ecological analysis of discourses more broadly in order to explore language use of ecological relevance that similarly, and perhaps even more powerfully, functions to normalize and perpetuate our attitudes, beliefs and actions regarding the more-than-human world. A corpus-assisted approach is well suited for such a task.

The application of corpus-assisted analytic methods has grown increasingly diverse in ecolinguistics in recent years. Perhaps unsurprisingly, the space garnering the most attention has been the analysis of climate change discourse. Much of this work has emanated from communication and media studies with research generally exploring the use of terms such as *global warming*, *climate change* and their equivalents in media of various national contexts (e.g. Aykut, Comby and Guillemot 2012; Dotson et al. 2012; Schmidt, Ivanova and Schäfer 2013). More linguistically oriented analyses have also been conducted (e.g. Grundmann and Krishnamurthy 2010; Grundmann and Scott 2012). In one such study, Grundmann and Krishnamurthy (2010) report a corpus-based investigation of keywords surrounding the issue of climate change in popular media from the United States, the United Kingdom, Germany and France. Their analysis demonstrates an increase in climate change-related media reporting in all four countries. In the United States, the preferred term was *global warming* while in the United Kingdom, climate change was preferred over global warming. However, there was more reporting on the issue in France and Germany. The US discourse mostly concerns scientific frames while the three European nations focus on political framings of the issue. In the United States, there is a noted difference between the use of global warming and climate change; global warming is viewed as 'dramatizing' (Grundmann and Krishnamurthy 2010: 143) and occurs in contexts of threats and fights. In contrast, 'climate change' is framed and discussed with more natural causes.

Representations of non-human animals have also been investigated through the application of corpus techniques (Frayne 2019; Fusari 2018; Goatly 2002; Poole 2022a). In Goatly (2002), representations of nature and non-human animals were investigated in a 2.5-million-word corpus of the BBC World Service. The analysis revealed 'frames of consistency' (2002: 20) as to how nature is represented, observing that the BBC consistently presents nature as acted upon rather than as an actor, and that nature is only extended agency in frames which present it as hostile to human life. Goatly argues that the consistency of the representations may have effects on cognition and how individuals perceive and think about nature. Frayne (2019) and Fusari (2018) are discussed later as each has a diachronic element relevant to this chapter's analysis.

Though the discourse of climate change and the depictions of non-human animals are the most frequent spaces of exploration, corpus linguistic techniques have been implemented to explore representations of the environment in political discourse (Bevitori 2015; Bonnefille 2008), business communication (Lischinsky 2011; Lischinsky 2015; Lischinsky and Sjölander 2014) and religious texts (Castello and Gesuato 2019). Other studies have investigated key ecological terms such as *green* (Bevitori 2011), *wilderness* (Poole 2022a) and *sustainable development* (Mahlberg 2007). This review is not exhaustive, but it does indicate the increasingly diverse collection of contexts and discourses which have been explored in corpus-assisted ecolinguistics.

Though some of the aforementioned studies include a diachronic dimension, I will highlight several examples that more directly inform the analysis of the present chapter. These studies reveal not only how frequencies of use of certain terms and/or constructs of ecological relevance have changed over time but also how these terms/constructs have been variably represented across time periods. Such diachronic research has explored time frames as brief as eight years (Bonnefille 2008), ten years (Grundmann and Scott 2012), twelve years (Grundmann and Krishnamurthy 2010) and fifteen years (Carvalho 2005) to spans as great as fifty (Bevitori 2015; Grant and Walsh 2015), one hundred (Fusari 2018) and even two hundred years (Frayne 2019; Poole 2022a).

Several diachronic studies have focused upon changing representations of the environment within political discourse. In one such study, Bonnefille (2008) explores the eight State of the Union addresses delivered by former US president George W. Bush from 2001 to 2008. In a related yet more comprehensive analysis, Bevitori (2015) broadens the corpus to include acceptance, inaugural and State of the Union speeches but also expands the time frame from the early 1960s to the 2010s. In this diachronic analysis, Bevitori explores these terms through a systemic functional linguistic framework to uncover how the representation of the environment has evolved over fifty years of presidential discourse and demonstrates how depictions of the environment continually evolve, illustrating that the meanings of environment are not 'fixed and stable' but vary according to a complex of factors (2015: 129).

More expansive in scope, Fusari (2018) and Frayne (2019) explore the evolving ways by which non-human animals have been discursively represented. In the former, Fusari (2018) analyses the changing depictions of the single term *animal* in the 50-million-word Strathy Corpus of Canadian English (Davies 2012–) in approximately 100 years of English language use in Canada. The analysis observed that humans were frequently evaluated as rational while non-human animals were contrastingly portrayed as dangerous and irrational. Additionally, there was a tendency to fragment human and non-human animals within language use. Though an emergent practice that reflected a more compassionate understanding of and relationship with non-human animals was noted, Fusari asserted that even within this positive practice, a hierarchical structuring which placed non-human animals as distant and thus less important remained evident across the span of the corpus.

Frayne (2019) explores a broader time period (1800s–2000s) and a more extensive collection of terms (134 species names) in much larger corpora (the 475-million-word Corpus of Historical American English and the massive Google Books Corpus). The study is noteworthy for it investigates the extent to which cultural and technological change is reflected in the frequencies and representations of selected eco-relevant terms over time. Displaying the possibility for corpus-based cultural analysis, Frayne (2019) interrogates whether frequencies of mention of non-human animals have changed in the past two centuries. The study demonstrates that correlation is present between rural population decline and frequency of species references. Frayne asserts that language change reflects 'shifting meanings and values within a society or culture' (2019: 331).

Finally, and likely most informing of the present work, is a study which tracks the frequencies of use of terms such as *unseasonal, cyclone, hurricane, flood* and many others in order to determine whether an emergent social awareness of climate change is reflected in language use through increased use of these terms over time (Grant and Walsh 2015). The study observed that there has indeed been an increase in the use of the terms. As the authors assert, their findings are completely 'unconnected with the traditional physical forms of data' employed to illustrate the reality of the climate crisis, thereby providing supplemental data in support of the physical indicators of a changing climate (2015: 197). The present chapter is informed by this study but diverges in meaningful ways. Namely, the Grant and Walsh study tracks the frequencies of use of the various terms; contrastingly, this chapter aims instead to investigate how certain events have been variably represented in discourse over time. In other words, their study explores whether a certain term is used more frequently, but the present chapter asks whether certain weather events are represented differently in language use across the period. Findings that terms are also represented differently would extend the claims of Grant and Walsh (2015).

These diachronic studies highlight the evolutions in use of ecologically relevant terms over many years of language use. While synchronic studies provide important insights into beliefs and attitudes at a defined point in time, diachronic analysis illustrates the dynamic nature of meaning and representation. Herein lies the potential of diachronic studies within corpus-assisted ecolinguistics, for this research enables researchers to challenge language practices that contribute to ecological degradation and which may be popularly viewed as natural and given. Additionally, such work provides an impetus in the potential cultivation of more ecologically sustainable language use, as we are able to empirically demonstrate that 'our reality is not something ready-made and waiting to be meant – it has to be actively construed' (Halliday 2001: 179). And ecolinguistics can potentially help shape the emergence of more sustainable construals. Further, highlighting the dynamic, emergent qualities of language and discourse presents a pedagogical opportunity to develop ecocritical language awareness (Micalay-Hurtado and Poole 2022) and promote ecoliteracies. In the following sections, I demonstrate two diachronic analyses before elaborating further upon the pedagogical potential of corpus-assisted eco-pedagogy within the ELT classroom.

2.2 Exploring language change

The following analyses of the terms *hurricane/s* and *wildfire/s* aim to answer two questions: (1) What adjective collocates are increasing or decreasing in use with the node terms from 1990 to 2019? (2) Are patterns of use in the adjective collocates reflective of changing environmental conditions due to climate crisis? These questions explore whether social evidence of a worsening climate crisis is present in language patterns attested in a large corpus of contemporary US American language use. If there were indeed such social evidence for climate change, one would anticipate the patterns of use to be increasingly negative and severe in their framing of these events. In essence, it was hypothesized that just as empirical data indicates that global temperatures are increasing and sea levels are rising, so too would the discursive representations of these and related events be increasingly concerning and dire. In other words, one would anticipate that adjectives such as *catastrophic, severe, intense* and others with clearly negative semantic prosodies would be increasing in use while adjectives such as *mild, moderate* or *weak* would be absent or declining.

To explore this hypothesis, the Corpus of Contemporary American English (COCA) (Davies 2008–) was selected for use. This 1-billion-word corpus contains approximately 25 million words for each year from 1990 to 2019 balanced across eight registers of language use (spoken, fiction, magazines, newspapers, academic texts, TV and movies subtitles, blogs and general web pages). One affordance of the COCA for the present analysis is that it is segmented into five-year periods, enabling one to track frequencies of use across six periods of five-year increments. Thus, the collocate searches were completed for each of the six time periods represented in the COCA: 1990–4, 1995–9, 2000–4, 2005–9, 2010–14, 2015–19.

For the analyses of the target words – *hurricane/s* and *wildfire/s* – the adjective collocates in a 4L-4R collocational window for the two terms were collected. In other words, the adjectives occurring four words to the left and four words to the right were captured for the analysis. While it may be viewed as constraining to limit the analysis to adjectives alone, it seemed a reasonable course of action for the present work to focus narrowly on the representations construed by this class of items. It should be noted that collocates for the singular and plural forms of the target terms were captured by using the bracketing function within COCA; conducting the search with the search syntax *[hurricane]* yields data for both the singular *hurricane* and the plural *hurricanes*. This collocation search procedure also captures many adjectives that do not produce representations of the events. For example, adjectives such as *other*, *previous* and *recent* were frequently used with *[hurricane]* but were excluded from the analysis.

Kendall's Tau correlation coefficient was calculated for the adjective collocates to empirically determine the strength by which each collocation was increasing or decreasing. The per million frequencies for each collocational pairing (e.g. *catastrophic* + *hurricane*) were used for the calculation of the Kendall's value. For interpretation, the Kendall's Tau calculation produces a figure between -1.0 and $+1.0$. When the Kendall's Tau produces a figure approaching $+1.0$, the collocation has experienced consistent increases across the time periods. Conversely, as a value approaches -1.0, it is experiencing clear decreases across the time spans. It is important to note that this correlation coefficient does not enable one to identify specific points in time in which meaning or use experienced change; it only indicates whether a feature increased or decreased in use across the time periods under analysis. Such a limitation may be of greater concern if the time period were more expansive and the increments of time more numerous, but as the present study focuses upon use across only six periods, this issue is of minimal concern.

2.3 Representing hurricanes

The analysis begins with the reporting of the trends in use of the most frequent twenty adjective collocates with *[hurricane]* from 1990 to 2019. As this data (see Table 2.1) was primarily marked by strong positive Kendall's values, the discussion starts with those items displaying increases in use across the period.

The adjectives *major* (0.73), *big* (0.73), *powerful* (0.47), *massive* (0.73), *strong* (0.60), *intense* (0.60), *destructive* (0.60), *heavy* (0.70), *catastrophic* (0.55) and *deadly* (0.60) display rather strong positive growth trends. Indeed, *major* and *big* are not only the most frequent adjective collocates with the target word but also record two of the highest Kendall's values; the adjective *massive* is the seventh most frequent but with a Kendall's value matching *major* and *big*. Interestingly, these three adjectives (*major, big, massive*) displaying the strongest increases in use all represent hurricanes in terms of their immense size. These depictions of size are complemented by representations of strength and power: *powerful, strong, intense, destructive, catastrophic* and *deadly*. Additional items recorded positive but rather weak values: *devastating* (0.20), *great* (0.07), *worst* (0.20), *good* (0.07). Only three of the most frequently used adjectives record negative

Table 2.1 Use trends with the top twenty adjective collocates of [hurricane]

Rank	Adjective	Kendall's Tau
1	Major	0.73
2	Big	0.73
3	Devastating	0.20
4	Powerful	0.47
5	Natural	0.47
6	Great	0.07
7	Massive	0.73
8	Strong	0.60
9	Worst	0.20
10	Intense	0.60
11	Destructive	0.60
12	Good	0.07
13	Severe	−0.33
13	Large	0.33
15	Stronger	−0.07
16	Bad	−0.07
17	Different	0.55
18	Heavy	0.70
19	Catastrophic	0.55
20	Deadly	0.60

Kendall's values: *severe* (−0.33), *stronger* (−0.07) and *bad* (−0.07). However, these three adjectives have quite weak Kendall's values; there are twelve items which produce stronger positive correlation scores.

It is not particularly surprising that such representations as *massive, powerful, strong, intense, catastrophic* and so on are commonly ascribed to *hurricanes*, as they are indeed major weather events. However, it is revealing that these items are steadily rising, thereby potentially indicating that hurricanes of recent decades are growing stronger, larger and deadlier. The trends in use of the aforementioned items potentially reflect social evidence of climate change, as frequently deployed representations of these events increasingly point to their immense size and strength. Hurricanes are somewhat common events along the coasts of the Gulf of Mexico and Atlantic Ocean in North America, and recent studies have demonstrated that the number of hurricanes per year has not changed significantly across this period (Gramling 2021). However, though their frequency of occurrence is generally stable, they are increasingly depicted for their great power and size. This indicates that the increased use of these adjectives is not simply a result of the increased frequency of these events but rather an increase in the contextual exigencies that require such a representation. In other words, it appears language users more commonly feel it both necessary and accurate to describe the events in such dire terms.

While the previous analysis focused upon the trajectories of use of the twenty most frequent adjective collocates, this next step explores which adjectives experienced the greatest increases or decreases in use over the thirty-year period. Although these items may not be the highest in frequency, they displayed the strongest changes in use. As hundreds of adjectives occurred with *[hurricane]* over the period, it was necessary to determine which items demonstrated the clearest changes over the period. In this step, a threshold of ±0.75 was established as a cut-off point for inclusion in order to focus upon those items displaying the strongest correlation values.

As Table 2.2 indicates, fifteen adjectives experienced consistent increases in use. As evident in the previous findings, this data suggests that hurricanes are increasing in power and size. The adjective *higher* displays the strongest positive correlation value of all the analysed adjectives. At a value approaching +1.0, its use is consistently and steadily rising in use. A closer inspection of its use in context reveals its presence in patterns discussing higher water temperatures, higher storm surges, higher rainfall, higher winds, higher hurricane activity and higher hurricane costs. Additionally, the items *extreme* and *bigger* also produce rather strong positive correlation scores. In the case of *extreme*, it typically occurs

Table 2.2 Representations of [hurricane] with strongest use trends

Adjective	Kendall's Tau
Higher	0.97
Seasonal	0.90
Coastal	0.87
Similar	0.87
Outer	0.83
Extreme	0.78
Observed	0.78
Bigger	0.78
Busy	0.78
Epic	0.78
Unprecedented	0.78
Multiple	0.75
Best	0.75
Historic	0.75
Financial	0.75
Larger	−0.75
Typical	−0.78
Disastrous	−0.78
Sweeping	−0.78

in contexts where extreme weather events such as hurricanes are discussed generally or in instances where specific extreme events such as Hurricane Irma, Hurricane Sandy or Hurricane Harvey are discussed. Also recording the same correlation value are items *busy, epic* and *unprecedented*.

There are three items displaying strong negative correlations – each of these has Kendall's value of −0.78. In order of appearance on the chart, the first item *typical* seems to support the tentative claims of the previous paragraph, for there is nothing typical about recent hurricanes in the United States. As recent hurricanes seem *different* – an adjective collocate on the rise (see Table 2.1) – they are less frequently modified as *typical*. In fact, hurricanes and their impacts are increasingly *epic, unprecedented* and *historic*. The next item, *sweeping*, seems to indicate great size, but it occurs at a very low frequency with the target term. The final item *disastrous* potentially suggests that the effects of hurricanes have weakened. Perhaps even though hurricanes are increasing in strength, their effects are somehow less disastrous as humans have adapted accordingly.

It was originally hypothesized that the increase in use of adjectives representing intensifying weather events would serve as an indicator of the worsening climate crisis. The data indicates that hurricanes are indeed increasingly depicted in prevailing discourse in dire frames marked by adjectives such as *extreme, bigger, epic, unprecedented* and *historic*. As scientific data for the climate crisis expands and the consequences of rising temperatures are manifested, the linguistic data here suggests that social evidence of worsening conditions is present in prevailing language use.

2.4 Representing wildfires

This illustration simplifies the approach presented in the previous case. While there are affordances of the Kendall's Tau analysis, such a quantitative procedure is likely neither feasible nor accessible for many educational contexts. Although the previous analytic techniques may be useful for comprehensive diachronic analysis of lexical items across a range of periods, a more accessible approach is needed to open space for and facilitate inquiry and discussion in a classroom setting. Thus, the process which produced the data in Table 2.3 was designed to be learner-friendly and more pedagogically achievable.

The items reported in Table 2.3 are the top twenty-five adjectives collocating with *wildfire/s* from the first five-year period of the corpus, 1990–4, along with their frequencies of use from the final time period of the corpus, 2015–19. Most noteworthy are the significant increases in use from the first to the second time period of adjectives indicating increased strength and size of these events. Most frequent of these items is the adjective *deadly* which occurred zero times from 1990 to 1994 but thirty-one times from 2015 to 2019. It seems troublesome that an event not once characterized in such severe terms in the early 1990s is now represented regularly in such a manner. Similar statements may be offered for multiple adjectives: *large, devastating, largest, massive, fast-moving, major, raging, deadliest, destructive, worst* and *growing*. Several of these adjectives occurred zero or one time in the first period, yet experienced rather dramatic growth in the second. For instance, *large* moves from one to eighteen, *devastating* from zero to fourteen, *largest* from one to thirteen, *massive* from zero to twelve, *fast-moving* from zero to ten, *ranging* from zero to ten and *major* from one to nine. It seems reasonable to assert that the linguistic evidence suggests increased frequency, greater strength and larger size of wildfires from one period to the next. Indeed, it is troubling that wildfires are now with much greater frequency being represented in such serious terms. If these adjectives continue along these trajectories of use, it is certainly worrisome to consider the size and ferocity of wildfires yet to occur.

Comparison of diachronic data such as that present in Table 2.3 provides pedagogical value for various learning purposes and contexts. With instructor

Table 2.3 Adjective collocates of [wildfire]

Adjective	1990–4	2015–19	Total
Northern	0	40	40
Deadly	0	31	31
Large	1	18	19
Western	3	14	17
New	1	15	16
Devastating	0	14	14
Largest	1	13	14
Southern	5	8	13
Massive	0	12	12
Recent	2	9	11
Fast-moving	0	10	10
Major	1	9	10
Raging	0	10	10
Other	1	8	9
Vulnerable	0	9	9
Deadliest	1	7	8
Destructive	0	8	8
High	1	7	8
National	2	6	8
Huge	2	5	7
Worst	2	5	7
Growing	0	6	6
Central	0	5	5
Multiple	0	5	5

mediation, such data could serve as a platform for conversations about language, language change and ecological well-being. And while the present analysis did not have space to include sample sentences from the corpus, within the classroom, students could inspect concordance lines as well. The next section outlines the affordances of corpus-assisted pedagogy more fully.

2.5 A case for corpus-assisted eco-pedagogy

The English language classroom has been the site of many social justice-oriented pedagogies. Such approaches to language teaching and learning, namely critical language awareness (CLA) (Fairclough 2001), have centred social justice in the language learning classroom through 'the inclusion of explicit discussions about power issues in the context of literacy and language instruction' (Achugar 2015). Indeed, efforts to produce and empower positive social change for/by language learners are undeniably important. Yet, as the climate crisis grows increasingly severe, it seems evident that oppressed and marginalized peoples whose lives critical pedagogies hoped to better will likely be the most severely impacted. One only has to review data on the rising number of climate refugees to see how climate change is already impacting peoples and communities around the world. In light of present realities, we must now recognize that social justice encompasses environmental justice (Delavan 2020; Stibbe 2014, 2021). It is time the English language classroom expands its critical lens and inspect more deeply the role that its practices and pedagogies serve in the (re)production of attitudes, ideologies, identities and actions which contribute to ecological degradation and climate crisis (Goulah and Katunich 2020; Micalay-Hurtado and Poole 2022). Beyond this reflective ecocritical work, it is necessary to integrate sustainability and ecological well-being into curriculum, pedagogy and practices. The following details how corpus-assisted activities can contribute to these aims.

There is a growing body of research on the affordances of corpus-assisted language teaching and learning with recent meta-analyses demonstrating its efficacy in many contexts and for many purposes (Boulton and Cobb 2017; Chen and Flowerdew 2018). Though it is perhaps most frequently implemented for the learning of vocabulary and grammar, the data-driven approach to teaching and learning has also been implemented successfully to heighten learners' rhetorical awareness (Charles 2007, 2011; Poole 2016; Lee and Swales 2006). In one of my previous studies, I implemented corpus-assisted activities in a first-year composition course for multilingual writers at a university in the United States (Poole 2016). For the course, I created a specialized corpus of blog posts from a community-based environmental advocacy group and another corpus of press releases from a multinational mining corporation. At the time, both groups were engaged in a contentious debate concerning the construction of a massive open-pit copper mine in the mountains visible from our classroom and campus. Corpus data was used as a platform for initiating conversations about language and rhetoric for the novice academic writers, and classroom discussion and assignment prompts directed student attention to the linguistic and rhetorical choices of the opposing groups. While the study assessed student attitudes regarding the corpus activities and their utility for heightening their rhetorical awareness, a plausible development was the heightening of students' CLA regarding how the opposing groups' language use discursively framed an environmental issue.

Corpus-assisted eco-pedagogy, I contend, merits attention for it presents multiple learning affordances. First, corpus-assisted activities in the language learning classroom provide students opportunities to explore authentic language use while testing their own hypotheses about language use. Such activities cultivate learner autonomy and agency as they empower students to ask language-focused questions, analyse authentic language use, forward interpretations based on data and summarize and present their results to peers. In numerous English for Academic Purposes contexts and classrooms, these are the foundational academic skills enumerated on syllabi and reflected in learning outcomes. Thus, at its core, corpus-assisted eco-pedagogy advances the learning of language and the acquisition of key academic skills – the primary goals of learners in such classes. Indeed, developing language proficiency is the central mandate of such educational contexts.

Second, corpus-assisted eco-pedagogy can facilitate the development of ecocritical language awareness as learners analyse, discuss and critique prevailing language practices which contribute to the present climate crisis. Such activities can facilitate discussions aimed at cultivating ecocritical language awareness. In a manner similar to the analysis from earlier in the chapter, students could explore how various climate-related events are depicted in language use, how animals are represented in media, how ecology-relevant words/practices such as 'disposable', 'fast fashion' or 'sustainable' are discussed and much more. Teachers and students would need training on how to exploit existing corpora for such purposes but recent texts such as *A Guide to Using Corpora for English Language Learners* (Poole 2018) and *Corpus Linguistics for English Teachers* (Friginal 2018) provide ready-to-go activities that can be implemented and adapted by teachers. The following provides examples of the sort of corpus-assisted activities that could be productively implemented for engaging learners in conversations about environmental issues.

The first lesson explores the changes in use in the terms *climate change* and *global warming* and is included in the collection *Teaching English with Corpora: A Resource Book* (Viana 2022). In the activity, I engage learners in reflection and discussion regarding their preference of terms, the responses that each potentially elicits and the equivalent phrases in their language (Poole 2022b). As previously asserted, language learners in English for Academic Purposes programmes are frequently asked to analyse and interpret data and subsequently summarize and report findings – such a task is also common on language proficiency tests such as TOEFL and IELTS. The teacher could guide students through the searches within the Corpus of Contemporary American English (Davies 2008–) and ask students to record data as they move through the searches. Additionally, students could be presented with data previously collected by the instructor. Learners could then discuss questions such as those in Table 2.4 in groups and

Table 2.4 Activity no. 1: Climate change or global warming?

1.	What is the general change in use of the term *climate change* since 1990?
2.	What is the general change in use of the term *global warming* since 1990?
3.	Which term is most frequently used at the present date?
4.	Has one term always been the most frequently used? If not, when did the change occur?
5.	In which sections (blog, web, TV/movies, spoken, fiction, magazine, newspaper or academic) are the terms most and least frequently used?
6.	How might you interpret and explain the frequency changes in the use of these two terms?
7.	Is there anything from the data that surprises you? Explain.
8.	What predictions could you make regarding the use of these terms in the coming 5 to 10 years?

present findings in a written report. In the full version of the lesson included in the aforementioned text, additional readings and supporting videos as well as possible adaptations are included. One adaptation that is immediately possible is asking students to compare the use of these terms in English with the equivalents in their language.

Additional activities could similarly explore language change, again providing a space for the sort of interaction and negotiation of meaning central to language learning while also investigating topics of ecological importance. For example, an activity focused upon the adjectives that have been used to evaluate *wilderness* in US language use could demonstrate how US English language users have differently discussed *wilderness* over the past 200 years. Such an activity would not need to implement the Kendall's Tau measure as illustrated previously in this chapter. Instead, students could select various decades in the Corpus of Historical American English (Davies 2010), conduct searches to identify common adjective collocates in each period and then analyse, interpret and report findings. As I reported in my previous research on *wilderness* (Poole 2022a), students would note earlier representations of wilderness as barren, desolate and savage in the early 1800s but a quite divergent representation in recent decades. It would be quite interesting to engage students in a critical discussion of why adjective use with *wilderness* has changed so dramatically and what these changes say about human–nature relationships. Again, it is worth highlighting the possibility for comparisons across languages. As public corpora are now generally available for numerous languages, students could compare how representations of entities such as *wilderness, forests* or *animals* either converge or diverge between English and other languages they use.

While the previous illustrations present activities centred around the exploration of words and phrases of clear ecological relevance, there is no reason such corpus-assisted eco-pedagogy should be constrained to investigations of eco-keywords alone. Learners could investigate and critique keywords that reflect and perpetuate consumerist culture. For example, learners could investigate the common noun collocates of the word *disposable* and reflect upon the variety of nouns increasingly ascribed with such single-use, use-and-discard practices. And though many of these activities have focused upon critiques of language use practices deemed unecological, the activities could be differently designed and implemented to enable students to search for emergent linguistic practices perhaps reflecting greater ecological awareness. For example, learners could investigate the increased use in labels and diets such as *vegetarian* and *vegetarianism* as well as *vegan* and *veganism*.

Additionally possible are activities that move beyond the analysis of lexical items to the exploration of grammatical features. One such feature, nominalizations, has been critiqued within ecolinguistics for they potentially enable language users to obscure and/or diffuse responsibility for an action that causes ecological harm. For example, in perhaps the first ecolinguistics article to explore the functioning of nominalizations in ecological discourse, Martin demonstrated how nominalizations contribute to the 'degree of abstraction' within texts (1986: 240), thereby producing a disconnect between the reality of the event and the grammatical structure which represents it. In the analysis, he noted patterns of nominals such as *the killing of* and *sealing operation* that create distance between the reader and the event through nominals that avoid describing the killing of animals as a verbal process. Reflecting Martin's analysis, students could investigate the nominals *pollution* and *emission*. By reading sample concordance lines, students could note and discuss how frequently the agents responsible for pollution were clearly identified and how responsibility is often shifted and diffused across the general public.

2.6 Conclusion

Corpus-assisted diachronic analysis enables us to challenge present-day language use popularly imagined as inherent, objective and normal regarding the environment, non-human animals and other constructs and issues of ecological relevance. Such research into the evolving discursive depictions of eco-relevant entities provides evidence of the evolving nature of meaning and allows ecolinguists to highlight contemporary discursive practices that transgress or support our broadly shared ecosophies of well-being and sustainability. Additionally, such analysis of social data can illustrate changing relationships with and understandings of the environment. In the present chapter, the analysis reveals traces of social evidence for the worsening consequences of climate change as *hurricane/s* and *wildfire/s* are increasingly represented in terms or great size, severity and strength. While I do not suggest that the limited analysis of a select group of words presented in this chapter is revelatory of climate change, the trajectories by which *hurricane/s* and *wildfire/s* are discursively framed do seem to indicate the accelerating effects of climate change.

Finally, a growing body of research on the use of corpus-assisted activities and corpus-informed materials has demonstrated the efficacy of corpus-assisted language teaching and learning. The activities presented in the chapter could be introduced in language learning classrooms not only to advance language proficiency but also to promote ecocritical language awareness. However, such corpus-assisted eco-pedagogy as presented here may be implemented beyond language learning classrooms as well, as the potential for such activities to develop ecocritical language awareness and cultivate ecoliteracies is not restricted to language learning contexts alone.

References

Achugar, M. (2015), 'Critical Language Awareness Approaches in the Americas: Theoretical Principles, Pedagogical Practices and Distribution of Intellectual Labor', *Linguistics and Education*, 32: 1–4.

Alexander, R. and A. Stibbe (2014), 'From the Analysis of Ecological Discourse to the Ecological Analysis of Discourse', *Language Sciences*, 41: 104–10.

Arrhenius, S. (1896), 'On the Influence of Carbonic Acid in the Air upon the Temperature of the Ground', *The London, Edinburgh, and Dublin Philosophical Magazine and Journal of Science*, 41 (251): 237–76.

Aykut, S. C., J. B. Comby, and H. Guillemot (2012), 'Climate Change Controversies in French Mass Media 1990–2010', *Journalism Studies*, 13 (2): 157–74.

Bevitori, C. (2011), '"Jumping on the Green Bandwagon": The Discursive Construction of GREEN Across "Old" and "New" Media Genres at the Intersection Between Corpora and Discourse', *Proceedings of the Corpus Linguistics Conference 2011– Discourse and Corpus*, 1–19.

Bevitori, C. (2015), 'Discursive Constructions of the Environment in American Presidential Speeches 1960–2013', in P. Baker and T. McEnery (eds), *Corpora and Discourse Studies: Integrating Discourse and Corpora*, 110–33, London: Palgrave Macmillan.

Bonnefille, S. (2008), 'When Green Rhetoric and Cognitive Linguistics Meet: President GW Bush's Environmental Discourse in His State of the Union Addresses (2001–2008)', *Metaphorik.de*, 15: 27–61.

Boulton, A. and T. Cobb (2017), 'Corpus Use in Language Learning: A Meta-Analysis', *Language Learning*, 67 (2): 348–93.

Callendar, G. S. (1938), 'The Artificial Production of Carbon Dioxide and its Influence on Temperature', *Quarterly Journal of the Royal Meteorological Society*, 64: 223–40.

Carvalho, A. (2005), 'Representing the Politics of the Greenhouse Effect: Discursive Strategies in the British Media', *Critical Discourse Studies*, 2 (1): 1–29.

Castello, E. and S. Gesuato (2019), 'Pope Francis's Laudato Si: A Corpus Study of Environmental and Religious Discourse', *Lingue e Linguaggi*, 29: 121–45.

Charles, M. (2007), 'Reconciling Top-down and Bottom-up Approaches to Graduate Writing: Using a Corpus to Teach Rhetorical Functions', *Journal of English for Academic Purposes*, 6 (4): 289–302.

Charles, M. (2011), 'Using Hands-on Concordancing to Teach Rhetorical Functions: Evaluation and Implications for EAP Writing Classes', in A. Frankenberg-Garcia, L. Flowerdew, and G. Aston (eds), *New Trends in Corpora and Language Learning*, 26–43. London: Continuum.

Chen, M. and J. Flowerdew (2018), 'A Critical Review of Research and Practice in Data-Driven Learning (DDL) in the Academic Writing Classroom', *International Journal of Corpus Linguistics*, 23 (3): 335–69.

Davies, M. (2008–), 'The Corpus of Contemporary American English'. https://www.english-corpora.org/coca/ (accessed January 2022).

Davies, M. (2010), 'The Corpus of Historical American English'. https://www.english-corpora.org/coha/ (accessed January 2022).

Davies, M. (2012–), 'The Strathy Corpus of Canadian English (from the Strathy Language Unit, Queen's University)'. Available online: https://www.english-corpora.org/can/.

Delavan, M. G. (2020), 'Earth Democracy as Empowerment for TESOL Students and Educators: Though the Crisis Speaks English, Englishes Can Become a Commons Language of Sustainability', in J. Goulah and J. Katunich (eds), *TESOL and Sustainability: English Language Teaching in the Anthropocene Era*, 19–40, London: Bloomsbury.

Dotson, D. M., S. K. Jacobson, L. L. Kaid, and J. S. Carlton (2012), 'Media Coverage of Climate Change in Chile: A Content Analysis of Conservative and Liberal Newspapers', *Environmental Communication: A Journal of Nature and Culture*, 6 (1): 64–81.

Fairclough, N. (2001), *Language and Power*, 2nd edn, New York City: Longman.

Frayne, C. (2019), 'An Historical Analysis of Species References in American English', *Corpora*, 14 (3): 327–49.

Friginal, E. (2018), *Corpus Linguistics for English Teachers*, London: Routledge.

Fusari, S. (2018), 'Changing Representations of Animals in Canadian English (1920s–2010s)', *Language and Ecology*, 1–32.

Goatly, A. (2002), 'The Representation of Nature on the BBC World Service', *Text*, 22 (1): 1–27.

Goulah, J. and J. Katunich, eds (2020), *TESOL and Sustainability: English Language Teaching in the Anthropocene Era*, London: Bloomsbury.

Gramling, C. (2021), 'Hurricanes May not Be Becoming More Frequent, but They're Still More Dangerous', *Science News*. Available online: https://www.sciencenews.org/article/hurricanes-frequency-danger-climate-change-atlantic (accessed 1 March 2022).

Grant, W. J. and E. Walsh (2015), 'Social Evidence of a Changing Climate: Google Ngram Data Points to Early Climate Change Impact on Human Society', *Weather*, 70 (7): 195–7.

Grundmann, R. and R. Krishnamurthy (2010), 'The Discourse of Climate Change: A Corpus-Based Approach', *Critical Approaches to Discourse Analysis across Disciplines*, 4 (2): 125–46.

Grundmann, R. and M. Scott (2012), 'Disputed Climate Science in the Media: Do Countries Matter?', *Public Understanding of Science*, 23 (2): 220–35.

Halliday, M. (2001), 'New Ways of Meaning: The Challenge to Applied Linguistics', in A. Fill and P. Mühlhäusler (eds), *The Ecolinguistics Reader: Language, Ecology, and Environment*, 175–202, London: Continuum.

Harré, R., J. Brockmeier, and P. Mühlhäusler (1999), *Greenspeak: A Study of Environmental Discourse*, London: Sage.

Intergovernmental Panel on Climate Change (IPCC) (1990), 'First Assessment Report'. Available online: https://www.ipcc.ch/assessment-report/ar1/ (accessed 15 February 2022).

Intergovernmental Panel on Climate Change (IPCC), 'Climate Change 2021: The Physical Science Basis'. Available online: https://www.ipcc.ch/report/sixth-assessment-report-working-group-i/ (accessed 15 February 2022).

Lee, D. and J. Swales (2006), 'A Corpus-Based EAP Course for NNS Doctoral Students: Moving from Available Specialized Corpora to Self-Compiled Corpora', *English for Specific Purposes*, 25 (1): 56–75.

Lischinsky, A. (2011), 'The Discursive Construction of a Responsible Corporate Self', in A. E. Sjölander and J. Gunnarsson Payne (eds), *Tracking Discourses: Politics, Identity and Social Change*, 257–85, Lund: Nordic Academic Press.

Lischinsky, A. (2015), 'What Is the Environment Doing in My Report?: Analyzing the Environment-as-Stakeholder Thesis through Corpus Linguistics', *Environmental Communication*, 9 (4): 539–59.

Lischinsky, A. and A. E. Sjölander (2014), 'Talking Green in the Public Sphere: Press Releases, Corporate Voices and the Environment', *Nordicom Review*, 35: 125–39.

Mahlberg, M. (2007), 'Lexical Items in Discourse. Identifying Local Textual Functions of Sustainable Development', in M. Hoey, M. Mahlberg, M. Stubbs, and W. Teubert (eds), *Text, Discourse and Corpora: Theory and Analysis*, 191–218, London: A&C Black.

Martin, J. R. (1986), 'Grammaticalizing Ecology. The Politics of Baby Seals and Kangaroos', in T. Threadgold, E. Grosz, G. Kress, and M. Halliday (eds), *Semiotics, Ideology, Language*, 225–67, Sydney: Sydney Association for Studies in Society and Culture.

McKibben, B. (1989), *The End of Nature*, New York City: Random House.

Micalay-Hurtado, M. and R. Poole (2022), 'Eco-Critical Language Awareness for English Language Teaching (ELT): Promoting Justice, Wellbeing, and Sustainability in the Classroom', *Journal of World Languages*, 8 (2): 371–90.

Mühlhäusler, P. (2003), *Language of Environment, Environment of Language: A Course in Ecolinguistics*, London: Battlebridge.

Poole, R. (2016), 'A Corpus-Aided Approach for the Teaching and Learning of Rhetoric in an Undergraduate Composition Course for L2 Writers', *Journal of English for Academic Purposes*, 21: 99–109.

Poole, R. (2018), *A Guide to Using Corpora for English Language Learners*, Edinburgh: Edinburgh University Press.

Poole, R. (2022a), *Corpus-Assisted Ecolinguistics*, London: Bloomsbury.

Poole, R. (2022b), 'Global Warming or Climate Change? Analyzing, Interpreting, and Reporting Findings', in V. Viana (ed), *Teaching English with Corpora: A Resource Book*, 295–99, London: Routledge.

Schmidt, A., A. Ivanova, and M. S. Schäfer (2013), 'Media Attention for Climate Change around the World: A Comparative Analysis of Newspaper Coverage in 27 Countries', *Global Environmental Change*, 23 (5): 1233–48.

Stibbe, A. (2014), 'An Ecolinguistic Approach to Critical Discourse Studies', *Critical Discourse Studies*, 11 (1): 117–28.

Stibbe, A. (2021), *Ecolinguistics: Language, Ecology and the Stories We Live By*, 2nd edn, Oxfordshire: Routledge.

Viana, V., ed (2022), *Teaching English with Corpora: A Resource Book*, London: Routledge.

Part II

Multimodal Discourses for Ecological Action

3

Discourses of Cycling Advocacy and Power amidst Wars, Petro-Masculinity and Climate Inaction

M. Cristina Caimotto

Introduction

This chapter was written after two years of ongoing Covid-19 pandemic and weeks into a war conflict, as Russia invaded Ukraine. With a chilling sense of déjà vu, in 2022, the second anniversary of the beginning of the pandemic was remindful of the discourses circulating in March 2020, the acknowledgement that an apparently unexpected situation, unimaginable until it was a tangible fact, was actually expected by some experts. Worse, the situation had been at least partially preventable, if only some other choices had been made, if more attention had been paid to the dangers, to the warning signs. It is clearly beyond the scope of this chapter to attempt an even superficial analysis of the actual ways in which most countries were not ready to face the Covid-19 pandemic or how most European citizens were not even thinking of the brutal war in Ukraine as something possible in Europe in 2022. The point here is that the reaction and the lack of anticipation of ordinary people to the pandemic and the war resemble too closely the dominant attitude towards the climate crisis.

The existence of pandemic plans was unknown to most citizens, until they faced the fact that many governments did not appear prepared to face a pandemic. The amount of money European countries were paying Russia for gas and oil and how that money would be employed to attack Ukraine was not acknowledged by most European citizens until they learnt their governments were even considering the hypothesis of reviving coal power plants in order to be able to face a reduction or lack of Russian gas, oblivious to their recent pledges towards the reduction of coal energy. It is not difficult to imagine how each of these choices – not updating the pandemic plans, cutting spending for the national health system, building a new gas pipeline instead of focusing on renewables or on the reduction of energy consumption and in general not taking proper action to reduce the effects of the climate crisis – was driven by governments focusing mainly on short-term goals.

This may appear as a populist argument, but the point this chapter wants to make is more subtle. We humans are underestimating – more or less consciously – the most dangerous threat for our planet and for life as we know it, the climate crisis. Many people would not label the economic crisis in 2008, the Covid-19 pandemic and the various wars that have been fought in recent years as 'environment related'. The only news items that a vast number of people will recognize as 'environmental' are the news stories concerning extreme weather events such as huge fires in California and Australia or floods in Germany. Why are we being overwhelmingly oblivious to the fact that most, if not all, crises we have faced in recent years derive from the ways in which we are not dealing properly with the climate crisis?

This difficult question, which can be approached from a variety of disciplines, is observed here from a discursive perspective. Starting from discourses concerning the war in Ukraine and the climate crisis, the chapter zooms on discourses promoting active mobility in urban environments. The aim of this analysis is to observe some of the deep assumptions that influence our perception of reality and how these assumptions are reinforced through discourse. What holds together the goal of increasing the number of people cycling in urban environments and the war against Ukraine may not seem obvious. The aim of this analysis is to bring to the surface the deep connection linking them through an approach that brings together ecolinguistics (Stibbe 2021), mobility justice (Sheller 2018) and the notion of petro-masculinity (Daggett 2018) by observing texts from institutional sources comparing them to grassroots discourse in order to show how grassroots sometimes proves to be more effective and closer to reality, as it is naturally better detached from the dominant fossil fuel mentality. The words pronounced by M. A. K. Halliday back in 1990 appear more topical than ever: 'the hegemony arrogated by the human species is inseparable from the hegemony usurped by one human group over another, and that neither will come to an end as long as the other still prevails' (2001: 198–9).

Section 3.1 introduces the notions of ecolinguistics and mobility justice, showing their connections with Critical Discourse Studies (CDS) and explaining how they are related to fossil fuel lifestyles. Section 3.2 observes some of the discourses that circulated when Russia invaded Ukraine and the role attributed to fossil fuels, underlining how our environmental hypocognition shapes our understanding of the events. In contrast to this, Section 3.3 shows the clarity with which grassroots movements can sometimes convey effective messages that require a much longer time to become common knowledge for the general population. Section 3.3 also brings in the local issue of cycling promotion, showing its ties with global, fossil-related tragedies. But given the vast amount of evidence to show how beneficial an increase in everyday cycling would be, why is cycling not promoted enough in our cities? Section 3.4 tries to answer this question. Sections 3.5 and 3.6 analyse some case studies, observing discourses about the promotion of active mobility and highlighting the differences between those that recognize the need for changes in the system – how roads are built – and those that limit their focus on convincing people to change their behaviour, a strategy unlikely to work as it is assumed that our mobility choices are mainly or exclusively rational.

3.1 Ecolinguistics, mobility justice and petro-masculinity

Before analysing some of the texts that shape or reshape the discourses of automentality, and our dependence on fossil fuel, we shall introduce the approaches that are employed here in addition to CDS, that is, ecolinguistics, mobility justice and petro-masculinity. Discourse consists in a particular representation of the world, verbal and non-verbal, and as a form of social practice: there is a dialectical relationship between a discursive event and the situation(s), institution(s) and social structures that frame it and are shaped by it at the same time. Discursive practices give rise to important power-related issues, as they contribute to the production and reproduction of unequal power relations through the ways in which they position people and represent things (Fairclough and Wodak 1997: 258).

Ecolinguistics is an approach that brings together language and ecology, by critiquing forms of language that contribute to ecological destruction and contributing to the search for new discourses and forms of language that can inspire people to protect the natural world (Stibbe 2021: 1). The aim of ecolinguistics, Stibbe explains, is to observe how 'there are certain key stories about economic growth, about technological progress, about nature as an object to be used or conquered, about profit and success, that have profound implications for how we treat the systems that life depends on' (2021: 1).

A CDS approach is mainly concerned with the power-related aspects of discourse, and an approach based on ecolinguistics focuses mainly on the role language and discourse play in shaping our relation with environment-related issues. The influence played by language on how we conceive, understand and talk about mobility and power has seldom been investigated and when it has happened, the research field was different from linguistics most of the time. Ralph et al. (2019), Goddard et al. (2019) and Fevyer and Aldred (2022) belong to different disciplines but they have analysed how the wording employed in newspapers to report collisions is likely to influence the way in which readers understand events and attribute agency and blame. It is thus useful to observe how scholars belonging to other disciplines focus on discourse-related issues even if they do not present their research as focused on language (see Caimotto 2020: 31–49 for more details).

The disciplines employed for the theoretical framework for this chapter are sociology (Sheller 2018), political science (Daggett 2018) and geography (Henderson and Gulsrud 2019). Sheller's book *Mobility Justice* brings together the three main crises that humanity is dealing with, climate, urbanization and migration, and shows how they all have the common denominator of mobility, as 'together they bring into focus the unjust power relations of uneven mobility' (2018: 1). In her chapter 'Beyond Automobility and Transport Justice' she summarizes the article (Sheller and Urry 2000) that she co-authored with John Urry back in 2000:

> we described automobility as the 'quintessential *manufactured object*' of Western capitalism, the 'major item of *individual consumption* after housing', an 'extraordinarily powerful *machinic complex* constituted through the car's technical and social interlinkages with other industries', the 'predominant global form of "quasi-private" *mobility* that subordinates other "public" mobilities of walking, cycling, traveling by rail and so on'. It is the 'dominant *culture* that sustains major discourses of what constitutes the good life, what is necessary for an appropriate citizenship of mobility and which provides potent literary and artistic images and symbols.' And finally, it is the 'single most important' cause of *environmental resource-use*'. (Sheller 2018: 68)

Her analysis highlights what links automobility to capitalism, and she underlines how modern infrastructures of urban mobility have been shaped by 'historically dominant forms of *white, male, elite* automobility' (Sheller 2018: 74) thus limiting the access of others to its privileges. This discrimination is mirrored by the data concerning the victims of collisions: as reported by Baker (2019),

> within the US, pedestrian death occurs disproportionately in neighbourhoods populated by people with low-incomes and people of colour. Is distraction

really more endemic in those neighbourhoods, or among people driving through them, than it is in wealthier, whiter areas? Or is it more likely that these neighbourhoods are more likely to be criss-crossed by high-speed roads, and less likely to receive investment in transit interventions that protect pedestrians?

The elitism of owning cars is further confirmed by the fact that, as demonstrated by Gössling, Kees and Litman (2022), both car owners and policymakers underestimate the real costs of driving a car, which represents a cost equal to housing, as the total lifetime cost of car ownership (fifty years) ranges between €599,082 and €956,798. However, conservatives often paint anti-car activists and environmentalists as elitist and this, as Furness (2010: 134–5) points out, is the way 'by which one of the cheapest forms of transportation [cycling] on the planet in construed as elitist, whereas one of the most expensive and resource-intensive technologies [cars] is considered populist'. Defining elitism, he explains, as a moral or behavioural disposition rather than as the result of a privileged role in society allows for the backgrounding of the actual privilege that car owners benefit from.

Daggett's research adds a significant layer to this complex web: petro-masculinity, a concept that emphasizes the relationship between fossil fuels and white patriarchal orders (2018: 28). This approach allows her to bring together misogyny and climate denial. They are treated as separate most of the time but, through the prism of petro-masculinity, it is possible to see more clearly how the patriarchal order explains the lack of political responses to the climate crisis. According to Daggett's analysis, the Anthropocene has aroused authoritarian desires and anxieties and we are witnessing what she describes as 'catastrophic convergence': the climate crisis, the threat to the fossil fuel system and an increasing fragile Western hypermasculinity (29). She draws thought-provoking parallels between masculinity, sexuality, misogyny and the active refusal of climate change. Daggett observes, 'when petro-masculinity is at stake, climate denial is thus best understood through desire, rather than as a failure of scientific communication or reason. In other words, an attachment to the righteousness of fossil fuel lifestyles, and to all the hierarchies that depend upon fossil fuel, produces a desire to not just deny, but to refuse climate change' (41).

Her work focuses on petro-masculinity in the United States. She explains that '[c]ars, suburbs, and the nuclear family, oriented around white male workers, formed a triumvirate that yoked the desires of Americans not only to wage labour, but to the continued supply of cheap energy that made the dream possible' (Daggett 2018: 32). We start seeing here the thread that links fossil fuel burning and everyday mobility. The author talks about 'fossil fuel lifestyle', a useful expression that describes the kind of deep link between car dependency and identities. This notion of fossil fuel lifestyle appears close to Walks's notion of 'automentality' (2015: 12), that is, the assumption that the automobile and all the infrastructure supporting automobility are the result of the desire of the majority of people, autonomous individuals exercising their free choice in an open and free market. Walks explains that, within this logic, restrictions to car use of any kind are perceived as a limitation of people's personal rights. As we shall observe, issues of mobility justice, elitism and petro-masculinity all affect the ways in which cycling is promoted and resisted. But before discussing the promotion of cycling, we shall observe discourses around the Russian war in Ukraine through the lenses of Western fossil fuel lifestyle.

3.2 Fossil wars, power and hypocognition

The speech delivered by Svitlana Krakovska on 28 February 2022 during a Zoom meeting of the International Governmental Panel on Climate Change (IPCC), in view of the release of the IPCC report about Adaptation and Vulnerability, points to how the crises are connected. Krakovska – a senior scientist at the Ukrainian Hydrometeorological Institute – spoke from her home in Kyiv as her house was being threatened by Russian missiles:

> Someone could question us that IPCC is not a political body, and should only assess science related to climate change. Let me assure you that this human-induced climate change and war against Ukraine have direct connections and the same roots. They are fossil fuels and humanity's dependence on them. While emissions of greenhouse gas have changed the energy balance of the planet, the ease of receiving energy from burning coal, oil and gas has changed the balance of power in the human world. We cannot change laws of the physical world but it is our responsibility to change laws of human civilization towards a climate resilient future. (Rathi 2022)

Twelve years earlier, Lakoff (2010: 76) already pointed out that

> we are suffering from massive hypocognition in the case of the environment. The reason is that the environment is not just about the environment. It is intimately tied up with other issue areas: economics, energy, food, health, trade, and security. In these overlap areas, our citizens as well as our leaders, policymakers, and journalists simply lack frames that capture the reality of the situation.

Lakoff then explained how we tend to consider the environment as something surrounding us rather than something we are part of, how we accept the idea that the natural world can be exploited for short-term private enrichment and, in general, how we tend to consider the economy and the environment as separate issues, somehow in contrast in a narrative that envisages environmentally friendly choices as 'bad for the economy'. Several scholars (Jackson 2017; Raworth 2017) have demonstrated that a new approach to the economy can actually provide useful responses to both crises but, for a number of complex reasons that cannot be discussed here, our systems still tend to focus on the short-term.

In her speech, Krakovska referred to the change in the balance of power as related to the burning of fossil fuels. The same message is visible in the EU's 'REPowerEU plan' (European Commission 2022), with a name that clearly plays on the multiple meaning of the word 'power', highlighting the connection between controlling sources of energy and being in control. The growing pressure on politicians created by the evidence emerging from Bucha of murders, tortures, rapes and abuses by Russian soldiers against civilians increasingly brought the connection between fossil fuel and the war under the spotlight. On 7 April 2022 the European parliament passed a non-binding resolution calling for 'an immediate full embargo on Russian imports of oil, coal, nuclear fuel and gas' (Europarl 2022). The previous day Josep Borrell, the EU's foreign policy chief, stated:

> We have given Ukraine 1 billion Euros. It might seem a lot, but 1 billion Euros is what we give Putin every day for the energy he provides us. Since the beginning of the war we have given him 35 billion euros, compare that to the one billion we have given to the Ukraine in arms and weapons. This gigantic difference has to highlight the importance and need of implementing what the European Council has ordered us: we have to reduce our energy dependence. There is no doubt about the fact that the Commission will exercise its leadership, putting forward the necessary measures to achieve this.
>
> Today we put an end to coal, but this is only a small part of the bill. Our independence, our energy autonomy hinges on developing renewable energies and, for once, geopolitics and climate change go hand in hand.[1] (EEAS 2022)

While the content of this speech is significant in itself, from a discursive perspective it is worth observing the use of 'for once', implying that geopolitics and climate change usually do not go hand in hand. The English translation provided by the simultaneous interpreter was 'climate change and geopolitics actually go hand in hand for the first time' (Audiovisual Service 2022) further reinforcing the implication in the speech delivered in Spanish. Both Borrell and the interpreter, through this phrasing, reveal the kind of framing and hypocognition described by Lakoff (2010) which tend to see geopolitics and economic interests in contrast with the protection of the environment (see also Caimotto and Raus 2023, about ideology in translation).

3.3 Grassroots and the promotion of active mobility

It took several weeks and a large amount of horrific pictures from Ukraine to start a mainstream debate around the way in which European countries are providing money for the Russian war through their dependence on Russian fossil fuels. However, if we look at grassroots movements, it took only one day for environmental activists to bring attention to this aspect, with Twitter users sharing images that point out the connection between a war initiated by a country whose power rests on fossil fuels and our dependence on automobility. Two images inviting people to change their mobility habits in order to curb their energy consumption immediately became viral on Twitter and travelled across countries within a few days after the Russian invasion (Figure 3.1):

Figure 3.2 was based on a 1943 poster, reciting 'When you ride ALONE you ride with Hitler! Join a Car-Sharing club today.' Campaigners also focused quickly on the uncomfortable position of European countries, for example, the Europe Beyond Coal campaign created a tracker to show how much money EU nations paid for Russian fossil fuels since the day of the invasion of Ukraine (Beyond Coal 2022a). In their statement on the invasion of Ukraine, they make an explicit reference to cycling as one of the measures that should be promoted:

> Every heat pump, every lowered highway speed limit, every new LED street lamp and insulated house, every solar panel and wind turbine, every bicycle ride replacing a trip with a car, every reduced train fare protects citizens from high energy costs and gas shocks in the near term, while promoting peace for Europe and globally. (Beyond Coal 2022b)

Other observers have underlined the link between importing oil and car dependency. For example, on 31 March the NGO Transport and Environment published an article explaining why the introduction of subsidies on transport fuel exacerbates the very problem that governments are trying to solve by introducing them. The article closes with the words: 'Putin is probably convinced that Europeans are so obsessed with their cars that they will not quit using them

Figure 3.1 Tweet 'Fight Putin, ride a bike' by @HarryHamishGray.

even temporarily, no matter what he does in Ukraine. Let's prove that he is wrong' (Lukács 2022).

In her work about mobility justice, Sheller observes that grassroots community organizations had already highlighted the links between crises that most people would perceive as separate, connecting 'contemporary racial inequalities in mobility and urban access to long histories of colonialism, capitalist exploitation, and appropriation of land, processes that have displaced people, disrupted their forms of moving and settling, and made alternative forms of life untenable' (Sheller 2018: 2).

It goes without saying that promoting a reduction in the consumption of fossil energy is not new and not exclusively related to the invasion of Ukraine. In 2018, the International Environmental Agency (IEA) published an updated version of its 2005 report 'Saving Oil in a Hurry'. Its aim is to provide an 'updated set of actionable recommendations for governments on how to effectively reduce oil demand in a sudden restriction in oil supplies', and the new version focuses more on the role of modal shifts compared to the previous version. The report observes how countries that already have a solid biking/walking infrastructure

Figure 3.2 Tweet 'When you drive a car, you drive with Putin' by @no_face.

would be well positioned during an oil supply disruption, as citizens would be able to carry out many everyday activities on bikes (IEA 2018: 14).

3.4 Why is cycling not promoted enough?

Up to now, we have highlighted the tragic consequences of the huge amounts of money paid to Russia and the role of that money in making the war in Ukraine economically possible. In addition, we have discussed the positive effects that a rise in the number of people cycling would have in terms of freedom from uncomfortable international ties and of pollution – even if, of course, the benefits of cycling are wider than this. Why then, a reader might ask, is cycling not much more common in our cities? In this section, we shall provide some tentative answers by observing discursive practices. The aim of this analysis is to show more clearly the ties connecting capitalism, patriarchy, individualism and automentality. The connection between patriarchy and automentality is useful not only because, as explained by Daggett (2018), misogyny and fossil fuel lifestyles are closely interconnected but also because both consist in a dominant mental framework which pervades all discourses. When we want to reflect on the position of women in society, we need to envisage rape and femicide as extreme manifestations of a continuum that degrades into forms of discrimination that are less tragic but belong to the same kind of patriarchal mentality and discourse. Rather than the dominant approach of discussing rape and femicide as perpetrated by 'monsters' and detached from the other subtler forms of injustice, this vision based on a continuum helps us to identify and address the roots of a mentality that is reinforced by everyday sexist discourse (Clark 1992).

In similar ways, automentality is a dominant mental frame that manifests itself in the extreme hate crimes of drivers deliberately attacking and killing cyclists (Sparks 2011; Spagnolo 2016) and is part of a continuum which includes verbal attacks and intimidations on the road, such as close passes (Aldred 2016), rollin' coal (Sheller 2018: 83), down to the everyday discrimination that prioritizes automobility over other forms of transport, oblivious to all the negative effects this prioritization has on public health, public spending and the natural environment. This prioritization is most obviously present in our cities if we calculate the amount of public space dedicated to car traffic and car parking. While this is obvious and very visible, it is at the same time overlooked exactly because it is so dominant and taken for granted. Discursively, this is reinforced by expressions such as 'road tax' and 'jaywalking'. The actual name of the tax is vehicle excise duty, and as it is based on the size of engine and emissions, it actually consists in a tax on pollution (Harrabin 2013). Road maintenance is paid for via general and local taxation so that all citizens, whether they move around by car or not, contribute to its costs. As for jaywalking, Norton (2007) describes from a historical perspective the strategic effects the word and the notion had when the car industry was struggling to make sure cars would not be banned from urban environments but rather prioritized over people walking and cycling.

Both the discourses of patriarchy and automentality also have in common the role played by hyper and toxic masculinity. From a discursive perspective, various studies observe how dangerous driving is associated to performances of masculinity and, more in general, car travel and car-associated stereotypes of freedom and movement are associated to masculine identity (Balkmar 2012; Mellström 2004; Redshaw 2008). At the same time, we observe an ambivalent attitude towards people who cycle, as the stereotypical negative images of cyclists are constructed as aggressive MAMILS (middle-aged man in lycra), urban male cyclists behaving particularly carelessly and ruthlessly. This is ambivalent because cycling gear is sometimes ridiculed as feminized[2] and, as observed by Balkmar (2018: 726), the position of a cyclist in urban traffic is associated to weakness and being vulnerable, characteristics stereotypically attributed to femininity. According to Fevyer and Aldred (2022: 4), 'bicycle mobility is subject to a discourse of othering predicated on the perceived transgression or disruption of a normative automobility' and the weakness attributed to (white male) cyclists is framed as particularly problematic within derogatory discourse as the individual chooses to cycle, voluntarily identifying with the weak identity when he could decide to choose the strong, dominant identity of the driver promoted by a form of toxic masculinity. The stereotypical power associated to automobility may inform fictional characters or may emerge in car advertising or collision reporting in subtler ways. It plays an important role in the way in which most urban inhabitants do not question the disproportionate amount of space and resources allocated to cars.

3.5 Discourses on active mobility

The contribution that ecolinguistics can offer to the promotion of active mobility focuses on the 'stories we live by', the stories (discourses, narratives) that are employed by policymakers and how these shape the dominant perception of how we should organize and share public urban space. One of the aims of ecolinguistics is to observe and classify discourses as destructive, beneficial and ambivalent (Stibbe 2021: 19–38) in order to find ways to reinforce the discourses deemed beneficial according to the ecosophy of the analyst. In order to carry out this analysis in our case study, we shall employ the tripartite framework provided by Henderson and Gulsrud (2019), which in many ways parallels Stibbe's. Their work analyses the urban transport policy in Copenhagen, a city often employed as an iconic model around the world by cities trying to improve their cycling system and reduce car dependency even if, the authors point out, the political issues and controversies concerning cars and cycling are remarkably similar to those happening in almost all cities around the world (Henderson and Gulsrud 2019: 3).

Henderson and Gulsrud identify three mobility politics: Left/Progressive, Neoliberal, and Right/Conservative. In their detailed history of cycling in Copenhagen, they point out how the bicycle, when it was invented, was very far from being an inherently social democratic form of transport. Its relatively high cost made it a status symbol of upper-class leisure and 'the bicycle industry was built on speculation, the rise of mass production, and monopolistic pursuits' (2019: 48). In the course of the twentieth century, cycling rates in Copenhagen climbed together with social democracy and while the bicycle itself is not necessarily social democratic, social democracy is well suited to cycling. They observe how 'working-class identity, women's emancipation, and social levelling undergirded and subsequently sustained cycling' (2019: 48). Let us then describe more in detail the characteristics of the three-way politics of mobility.

By 'Left/Progressive', Henderson and Gulsrud describe a politics that challenges the system of capitalism and strongly believes in the ability of the public sector and the government to work meaningfully for the people. They underline that their choice to use 'Left' wants to clarify the distinction between left-leaning and neoliberal politics, which, especially in the United States, are often bundled together under the label 'Progressive' thus obfuscating the differences between the two. While both political currents may promote a progressive mobility agenda, the neoliberal approach will support a much greater role of private sector involvement and will not favour car restraint. In fact, the neoliberal politics does not support the leftist critique of capitalism or of the car, nor the Left/Progressive discourse of 'right to the city'. A neoliberal approach rather favours a market-oriented housing and mobility, supports green growth and considers the car part of the economic growth, which is obviously considered good in their vision. This contrast between the two approaches, which the authors describe as clearly recognizable in Copenhagen and associate to specific local political parties, is much less clearly visible elsewhere. While the two discourses certainly exist, they often tend to be supported by different people who belong to the same party and the contrast separating them is toned down, also thanks to the use of neoliberal buzzwords (e.g. 'stakeholders') that tend to hide the conflict.

The Right/Conservative discourse identified by Henderson and Gulsrud mainly focuses on the need for cars. Cars are narrated as necessary for families, framing parents who drive their children to school as good parents and those who let their children cycle to school as bad parents (2019: 100). The whole notion of restraining cars is rejected as leftist and ideological, and on the contrary, car taxes are opposed, as families with children should be allowed to afford larger cars and 'safer' sport utility vehicles (SUVs), something that they are not able to do because of the car tax, according to the Right/Conservative narrative. Henderson and Gulsrud conclude their analysis of political conflicts in Copenhagen, observing that

> For green mobility advocates worldwide, it is important to incorporate right to the city thinking, but it is equally important that the right to the city movement prioritize cycling. Globally, urban-based left-wing movements frequently ignore mobility, or fail to connect the deep inequities of the car system, and thus undermine green mobility. (2019: 192)

Sheller (2018: 20–44) approaches the different kinds of politics employed when discussing mobility from a more philosophical perspective and identifies the utilitarian view, the libertarian view, the accessibility approach and then proposes an approach based on equity. The utilitarian view is very common in transport planning, it takes the form of cost-benefit analysis (CBA) and it is often used to determine transportation investments. This approach assumes that transport is about getting from A to B as efficiently as possible. Therefore, higher earners tend to have higher priority and investments tend to be employed to build automobile infrastructure and motorways. The problem with this kind of approach, Sheller observes, is that decisions over transport cannot be left to the market because this will prevent subordinate groups from giving free consent as those with power will dominate choices: congestion, air pollution and collisions will only get worse.

The accessibility approach moves away from the idea of increasing mobility for all – which is obviously impossible with limited resources and will only worsen pollution and congestion – and rather focuses on the ease with which different citizens can reach places. While better than the utilitarian and libertarian approaches, this approach still views the journey as something between A and B, and space as an empty background, Sheller observes (2018: 26–7). This reminds us of Lakoff's observation concerning how we conceive of the environment as external, as surrounding us, rather than something of which we are part. Introducing equity in the equation, Sheller explains:

> Transport justice, like other distributive theories of justice, presumes that there is a pre-existing space in which goods are distributed, or in which procedural justice occurs or entitlements are enforced, rather than presuming that space itself is up for grabs. Mobility justice, in contrast, built on a mobile ontology, suggests that political claims to access and goods (such as vehicles, transport and accessibility) re-make spaces and subjects; it brings into play historical bodily relations, ecological relations, and wider global relations in the political arena. (2018: 28)

With these frameworks in mind, let us now observe how discourse is deployed in some official documents.

3.6 IPCC AR6 WGIII and London in 2030

Analysing the fifth IPCC report, Sheller (2018: 84–6) underlines that the emphasis on personal choices as key drivers of transport decisions – travel-time budgets, costs and prices – relies on older ways of thinking based on rational choice economic thinking, assuming that the management of travel demand is mainly a matter of individual choice that can be adjusted through pricing mechanisms. But, Sheller observes, this hopeful scenario ignores class, race, gender and ability. It tends to ignore suburban and extra-urban transport issues, focusing almost exclusively on the 'young, healthy, middle-class, implied white consumer' who can afford to give up driving. Nevertheless, pricing mechanism is likely to end up worsening the economic situation of the lower-middle-class, thus fuelling resentment and backlash against environmentalists.

If we look at the latest report, at the time of writing, IPCC AR6 WGIII[3] (2022), we notice that the systemic changes have gained a more prominent role, not expecting consumers to simply change their behaviour because they are advised to do so but rather changing the urban space, making it less car dependent to encourage behaviour change.

> Changes in urban form (e.g., density, land use mix, connectivity, and accessibility) in combination with programmes that encourage changes in consumer behaviour (e.g., transport pricing) could reduce transport related greenhouse gas emissions in developed countries and slow growth in emissions in developing countries (*high confidence*). Investments in public inter- and intra-city transport and active transport infrastructure (e.g., bike and pedestrian pathways) can further support the shift to less GHG-intensive transport modes (*high confidence*). (C.8.2)

> Cities can reduce their transport-related fuel consumption by around 25% through combinations of more compact land use and the provision of less car-dependent transport infrastructure. Appropriate infrastructure, including protected pedestrian and bike pathways, can also support much greater localised active travel. (TS 5.3 Transport) (IPCC 2022)

Nevertheless, if we observe the *Analysis of a Net Zero 2030 Target for Greater London* report (ElementEnergy 2022) commissioned by the Greater London

Authority, the behavioural lens is still very prominent. The first subtitle of the 'Transport' chapter is titled 'Behaviour change' and opens by stating:

> Due to limited supply chains, slow turnover of vehicle stock, and reliance on grid decarbonisation, reaching net zero early cannot be achieved by technology alone. The earlier the net zero target date, the greater the importance of behaviour change to reduce demand for travel in high carbon modes (primarily private vehicles). (ElementEnergy 2022)

The focus, once again, is on the individual, requiring behaviour change rather than focusing on changes in the road infrastructure to make active mobility more attractive. But marginalized communities are likely to feel alienated by the fact they are made responsible for something they consider out of their control. Precarious financial circumstances also make it difficult to take action. The effective response to this is to co-design the solution, empowering rather than simply engaging with communities and reaching consensus from a group, overcoming individual views (Future of London 2021).

We shall now compare the discourses observed earlier to a report published by the London Cycling Campaign (LCC) in 2020, a cycling advocacy association based in London. Under a section titled 'fairer mobility', they observe:

> Transport is a social justice issue. The vast majority of Londoners don't have access to a car for most journeys. Moreover, studies have shown that those who suffer from the effects of private motor travel – delays, ill health, injury or death in collisions – are disproportionately those who are less well-off. All Londoners, irrespective of background of wealth, have the right to travel safely, healthily and efficiently. Those on low incomes who have no or very limited access to car travel for most trips deserve better alternatives than they currently have. Improving conditions for walking and cycling and providing better and cheaper public transport services are at the heart of making streets Climate Safe. (LCC 2020: 35)

From a discursive perspective, apart from the already mentioned focus on the community rather than the individual, we notice here a few strategies. The use of the stative verb to be in the opening sentence, which frames the statement as an irrefutable fact. The use of 'Londoners' to refer to the people concerned, which reinforces the sense of community and backgrounds the differences between the various Londoners concerned. Even if the topic discussed in this passage is class related and highlights that people who earn less are disadvantaged also in terms of safety and health, the passage manages to convey a sense of community and common goals rather than conflict between different interests. Differently from the kind of obfuscating effect created with the word 'stakeholder' we discussed earlier, this document clearly states that citizens who can afford car travel should be restrained by authorities, with policies hindering their ability to drive. Groups exist here, and their needs should not be given the same attention; rather, the priority should be the improvement of the situation for all and the attention to the climate crisis, even if this means reducing the comfort of the citizens who are better off. Another strategy worth analysis is that of lexical choices: 'have the right', 'deserve better' and 'improving conditions' contribute to the positive perception of the solutions proposed.

3.7 Concluding remarks

This chapter touches upon many aspects concerning our fossil fuel lifestyles and how they affect life from a very local to a global scale. When Russia invaded Ukraine in February 2022, it took months before the public debate started focusing on how Western countries were actually financing the war they were trying to oppose, by buying fossil fuels from Russia. In Western countries, we are not ready to question or give up our fossil fuel lifestyles, even when we know how tragically the money of those revenues will be employed. On the other side of the spectrum, on a local scale, we observe how the promotion of active mobility tends to appeal to rational choices rather than implementing systemic change and focus on individuals rather than communities. We have shown how the kind of discourse promoted by advocacy groups and environmentalists is more apt to convey a sense of community, which tends to be absent or very weak in discourses that are institutional and tend to concentrate more on the individual and on behavioural change. The discourse categories identified by Henderson and Gulsrud (2019) and those described by Sheller (2018), even if coming from different disciplinary perspectives, similarly point to the need of a better focus on communities rather than individuals and both point to the need to move away from a capitalistic mental framework when promoting changes concerning people's everyday mobility. The hypocognition revealed by the subtle phrasing in Borrell's statement (see Section 3.2), reinforced in the English translation, shows how the problems highlighted by Lakoff (2010) are still present in our approaches to the climate crisis. The conclusion we can draw from all the texts observed in this chapter is that politicians and policymakers who actually want to bring about change, reduce pollution and improve mobility systems should draw inspiration from discourses coming from advocacy and grassroots groups, rather than trying to pass left-wing, anti-capitalist policies by obfuscating them inside a 'progressive' 'behaviour-changing' 'lifestyle-oriented' language, as the choice of using obfuscating language will end up weakening their own message, making it hard to distinguish between actual pro-communities, pro-environment policies from individualistic and market-centred mobility strategies. We need reframing the stories we live by from efficiency to liveability, from competition to well-being, from space to place, from individual to community, from stakeholders to citizens, from wealth to prosperity, from patriarchy to justice.

Notes

1   My translation is from the Spanish source text 'Hemos dado a Ucrania pronto 1.000 millones de euros. Que puede parecer mucho, pero 1.000 millones de euros es lo que pagamos a Putin cada día por la energía que nos suministra. Desde que empezó la guerra le hemos dado 35.000 millones de euros, compárenlo con los 1.000 millones que les hemos dado para armarles a los ucranianos. Esta gigantesca diferencia debe señalar también la necesidad de llevar a la práctica lo que el Consejo Europeo nos ha ordenado: disminuir la dependencia energética. Y, en eso, la Comisión ejercerá sin duda su liderazgo, proponiendo las acciones necesarias para ello.

Hoy, acabamos con el carbón, pero es una parte muy pequeña de la factura. Nuestra independencia, nuestra autonomía energética pasa por el desarrollo de las energías renovables y, por una vez, la geopolítica y el cambio climático se dan la mano en un objetivo común.'
2   Which is but another instance of sexism and the notion that 'feminine' is somehow a synonym of 'diminishing' when referred to men.
3   AR6 refers to 'Sixth Assessment Report' and WGIII stands for 'Working Group III'.

References

Aldred, R. (2016), 'Cycling Near Misses: Their Frequency, Impact, and Prevention', *Transportation Research Part A: Policy and Practice*, 90: 69–83. http://doi.org/10.1016/j.tra.2016.04.016.

Audiovisual Service (2022), 'Opening Statement by Charles Michel, Ursula von der Leyen, and Josep Borrell Fontelles on the Conclusions of the European Council (24-25/03/2022), Including the Latest Developments of the War Against Ukraine and the EU Sanctions Against Russia and their Implementation', 6 April. Available online: https://audiovisual.ec.europa.eu/en/video/I-223089?lg=EN (accessed 30 April 2022).

Baker, P. C. (2019), 'Collision Course: Why are Cars Killing More and More Pedestrians?', *The Guardian*, 3 October. Available online: https://www.theguardian

.com/technology/2019/oct/03/collision-course-pedestrian-deaths-rising-driverless-cars (accessed 30 April 2022).

Balkmar, D. (2012), 'On Men and Cars: An Ethnographic Study of Gendered, Risky and Dangerous Relations', PhD diss., Linköping University.

Balkmar, D. (2018), 'Violent Mobilities: Men, Masculinities and Road Conflicts in Sweden', *Mobilities*, 13 (5): 717–32.

Beyond Coal (2022a), 'Eu Member State Spending on Russian Fossil Fuels'. Available online: https://beyond-coal.eu/russian-fossil-fuel-tracker/ (accessed 30 April 2022).

Beyond Coal (2022b), 'Statement on the Invasion of Ukraine'. Available online: https://beyond-coal.eu/2022/03/04/statement-on-the-invasion-of-ukraine/ (accessed 30 April 2022).

Caimotto, M. C. (2020), *Discourses of Cycling, Road Users and Sustainability. An Ecolinguistic Investigation*, Cham: Palgrave Macmillan.

Caimotto, M. C. and R. Raus (2023), *Lifestyle Politics in Translation: The Shaping and Re-Shaping of Ideological Discourse*, Oxon, New York: Routledge.

Clark, K. (1992), 'The Linguistics of Blame: Representations of Women in *The Sun*'s Reporting of Crimes of Sexual Violence', in M. Toolan (ed), *Language, Text and Context*, 208–24. London: Routledge.

Daggett, C. (2018), 'Petro-masculinity: Fossil Fuels and Authoritarian Desire', *Millennium*, 47 (1): 25–44. https://doi.org/10.1177/0305829818775817.

EEAS (2022), 'Russia/Ukraine: Speech by High Representative/Vice-President Josep Borrell at the EP Plenary', 6 April. Available online: https://www.eeas.europa.eu/eeas/russiaukraine-speech-high-representativevice-president-josep-borrell-ep-plenary_en (accessed 30 April 2022).

ElementEnergy (2022), 'Analysis of a Net Zero 2030 Target for Greater London – Final Report'. Available online: https://www.london.gov.uk/sites/default/files/nz2030_element_energy.pdf (accessed 30 April 2022).

Europarl (2022), 'MEPs Demand Full Embargo on Russian Imports of Oil, Coal, Nuclear Fuel and Gas', *Press Release*, 7 April. Available online: https://www.europarl.europa.eu/news/en/press-room/20220401IPR26524/meps-demand-full-embargo-on-russian-imports-of-oil-coal-nuclear-fuel-and-gas (accessed 30 April 2022).

European Commission (2022), 'REPowerEU: Joint European Action for More Affordable, Secure and Sustainable Energy', COM(2022)108.

Fairclough, N. and R. Wodak (1997), 'Critical Discourse Analysis', in T. A. Van Dijk (ed), *Discourse as Social Interaction*, 258–84, London: Sage.

Fevyer, D. and R. Aldred (2022), 'Rogue Drivers, Typical Cyclists, and Tragic Pedestrians: A Critical Discourse Analysis of Media Reporting of Fatal Road Traffic Collision', *Mobilities*, 17 (6): 759–79 http://doi.org/10.1080/17450101.2021.1981117.

Furness, Z. (2010), *One Less Car: Bicycling and the Politics of Automobility*, Philadelphia: Temple University Press.

Future of London (2021), 'Achieving Net Zero Report'. Available online: https://www.futureoflondon.org.uk/wp-content/uploads/delightful-downloads/2021/03/Achieving-net-zero-report-1.pdf (accessed 30 April 2022).

Goddard, T., K. Ralph, C. G. Thigpen, and E. Iacobucci (2019), 'Does News Coverage of Traffic Crashes Affect Perceived Blame and Preferred Solutions? Evidence from an Experiment', *Transportation Research Interdisciplinary Perspectives*, vol. 3.

Gössling, S., J. Kees, and T. Litman (2022), 'The Lifetime Cost of Driving a Car', *Ecological Economics*, 194: 107335. http://doi.org/10.1016/j.ecolecon.2021.107335.

Halliday, Michael A. K. (2001), 'New Ways of Meaning: The Challenge to Applied Linguistics', in F. Alwin and P. Mühlhäusler (eds), *The Ecolinguistics Reader: Language, Ecology and Environment*, 175–202. London, New York: Continuum.

Harrabin, R. (2013), 'Is There Any Such Thing as "Road Tax"?' *BBC News Website*, 15 August. Available online: https://www.bbc.com/news/magazine-23694438 (accessed 30 April 2022).

Henderson, J. and N. M. Gulsrud (2019), *Street Fights in Copenhagen: Bicycle and Car Politics in a Green Mobility City*, Oxon, New York: Routledge.

IEA (2018), *Saving Oil in a Hurry*, Paris: IEA. Available online: https://www.iea.org/reports/saving-oil-in-a-hurry (accessed 30 April 2022).

IPCC (2022), 'Climate Change 2022: Mitigation of Climate Change', in P. R. Shukla, J. Skea, R. Slade, A. Al Khourdajie, R. van Diemen, D. McCollum, M. Pathak, S. Some, P. Vyas, R. Fradera, M. Belkacemi, A. Hasija, G. Lisboa, S. Luz, and J. Malley (eds), *Contribution of Working Group III to the Sixth Assessment Report of the Intergovernmental Panel on Climate Change*, Cambridge, New York: Cambridge University Press. http://doi.org/10.1017/9781009157926.

Jackson, T. (2017), *Prosperity Without Growth: Foundations for the Economy of Tomorrow*, 2nd edn, London, New York: Routledge.

Lakoff, G. (2010), 'Why It Matters How We Frame the Environment', *Environmental Communication*, 4 (1): 70–81.

LCC (2020), 'Climate Safe Streets Report'. Available online: https://s3.amazonaws.com/lcc_production_bucket/files/13596/original.pdf?1584617987 (accessed 30 April 2022).

Lukács, A. (2022), 'Let's Prove That Putin Is Wrong!' 31 March. Available online: https://www.transportenvironment.org/discover/lets-prove-that-putin-is-wrong/ (accessed 30 April 2022).

Mellström, U. (2004), 'Machines and Masculine Subjectivity: Technology as an Integral Part of Men's Life Experiences', *Men and Masculinities*, 6 (4): 368–82. http://doi.org/10.1177/1097184X03260960.

Norton, P. D. (2007), 'Street Rivals: Jaywalking and the Invention of the Motor Age Street', *Technology and Culture*, 48 (2): 331–59.

Ralph, K., E. Iacobucci, C. G. Thigpen, and T. Goddard (2019), 'Editorial Patterns in Bicyclist and Pedestrian Crash Reporting', *Transportation Research Record*, 2673 (2): 663–71.

Rathi, A. (2022), 'Ukraine Climate Scientist Fears for Russian Peer Who Apologized for War', Bloomberg, 28 February. Available online: https://www.bloomberg.com/news/articles/2022-02-28/ukraine-climate-scientist-fears-for-russian-peer-who-apologized-for-war (accessed 30 April 2022).

Raworth, K. (2017), *Doughnut Economics: Seven Ways to Think Like a 21st-Century Economist*, White River Junction: Chelsea Green Publishing.

Redshaw, S. (2008), *In the Company of Cars: Driving as a Social and Cultural Practice*, Aldershot: Ashgate.

Sheller, M. and J. Urry (2000), 'The City and the Car', *International Journal of Urban and Regional Research*, 24 (4): 737–57.

Sheller, M. (2018), *Mobility Justice: The Politics of Movement in an Age of Extremes*, London, New York: Verso.

Spagnolo, C. (2016), 'Lecce, Piomba con l'Auto sui Ciclisti e Fugge: Uno è Morto, un Altro è Grave. Forse una Lite, un Fermato', *La Repubblica*, 22 January. Available online: https://bari.repubblica.it/cronaca/2016/01/22/news/auto_pirata-131829166/ (accessed 30 April 2022).

Sparks, M. (2011), 'Driver Ploughs into Critical Mass Ride in Brazil', *The Guardian*, 1 March Available online: https://www.theguardian.com/environment/bike-blog/2011/mar/01/diver-brazilian-critical-mass-ride (accessed 30 April 2022).

Stibbe, A. (2021), *Ecolinguistics: Language, Ecology and the Stories We Live By*, Oxon, New York: Routledge.

Walks, A., ed (2015), *The Urban Political Economy and Ecology of Automobility: Driving Cities, Driving Inequality, Driving Politics*, London, New York: Routledge.

'When You Ride ALONE You Ride with Hitler!' Government Printing Office for the Office of Price Administration, NARA Still Picture Branch (NWDNS-188-PP-42). Library Item date: 1943.

4

Communicating the Urgency of the Climate Emergency through Verbal and Non-Verbal Metaphors

Elisabetta Zurru

Introduction, aims and scope

The word 'Anthropocene' gained popularity in the year 2000 when Crutzen and Stoermer published their article about it in no. 41 of the *IGBP Newsletter* (Crutzen and Stoermer 2000: 17–18). Even though the term had been used for at least two decades by then, it was this publication that gave structure to a notion that was becoming clearer and clearer at the time, and that is even more evident now, some twenty years later: the increasingly impactful presence of *Homo sapiens* on planet Earth has changed its natural rhythms so profoundly that the time we are living in can be identified as a new geological period, in which human activity is responsible for staggering changes in the balance of most ecosystems. In other words, previous periods in the geological history of the planet followed its physiological patterns, to which humans have had to adapt to since they first appeared; the current one, however, is influenced by human lifestyles to such an extent that the earth is being forced to find ways to try and adapt to them instead. The result is an unprecedented ecological crisis which is entirely human-made and has its roots in the Western world starting to influence the climate since the first industrial revolution. The scientific literature nowadays shows a 99 per cent consensus about extreme weather events being related to anthropocenic-caused climate change (Lynas, Houlton and Perry 2021).

The scientific and visual representation of the alarming increase in the earth's temperature typical of the Anthropocene is known through one of the most famous visual metaphors (Yus 2009) in climate change discourse: the hockey stick. This term was first used by climatologist Jerry Mahlman in reference to the graph by Mann, Bradley and Hughes in their 1999 publication reconstructing the planet's temperature trend since 1000 CE (Biello 2012: 74), which follows a fairly linear pattern until the end of the twentieth century, when it spikes vertically, thus resembling a reversed ice hockey stick with the handle horizontal and the blade turning upward and giving rise to the visual metaphor TEMPERATURE GRAPH IS HOCKEY STICK.[1] This research was included in the 2001 United Nations Intergovernmental Panel on Climate Change (IPCC) report, and other studies drew similar conclusions in the following years (Biello 2012: 74; Mann 2012: 11). However, it was this specific research that became the focus of attention of climate change deniers, in an attempt to discredit it and its authors and, in so doing, cast doubt on the science behind climate change as a whole (Mann 2012: 11). According to one of its authors (Mann 2012: 12), it was possibly the visual nature of the graph that stirred so much interest in the anthropogenic climate change-denying circles, because of its ability to represent in a clear and immediate way 'the critical question of whether there was truly anything unusual about modern global warming' and its potential to transcend the bounds of specialized communication and easily reach the general public. This episode is symbolic both of the importance visual communication has acquired in environmental discourse in the past decades – as we shall discuss in detail later – and of what has been labelled as 'the denial machine' (Piltz 2008), namely the political (and corporate) interference with climate change research between the end of the twentieth and the beginning of the twenty-first century.

The need to raise awareness and counteract anti-ecological and/or climate change-denying narratives is as strong today as it was at the turn of the millennium. Indeed, attempts to sway public opinion by pushing narratives of 'growthism' (Halliday [1990] 2001: 196) – namely the ideal that human progress equates with continuous growth and accumulation of wealth and material possessions – and/or issuing warnings against environmental alarmism are still made. Elon Musk, one of the richest men in the world, who has recently acquired one of the largest social platforms, which he renamed X, tweeted that 'Population collapse due to low birth rates is a much bigger risk to civilization than global warming'[2] not so long ago. To date, this tweet has almost 40,000 retweets and 345,000 likes even though it (1) belittles the dangers connected to global warming, (2) pushes for human population growth on a planet which is already struggling to sustain its 8 billion human inhabitants (a milestone that was reached in October 2022, only twelve years after the 7 billion milestone had been reached; Welch 2022), and (3) is grounded in a Western-centric mentality which equals low birth rates in the Western world to worldwide population and civilization collapse. By the same token, Matt Walsh, a writer with a large platform and self-professed 'theocratic fascist', has recently tweeted 'Remember when they spent years telling us to panic over the hole in the ozone layer and then suddenly just stopped talking about it and nobody ever mentioned the ozone layer again?'[3] Once again, this tweet has over 6,000 retweets and almost 40,000 likes, even though it ridicules and tries to undermine the most successful collective ecological action to date, which led to the Montreal Protocol in 1987 and the stabilization of the ozone layer:[4] the lack of a consistent public conversation about this topic is provided as an example of environmental alarmism ('they spent years telling us to panic') rather than as a sign of its success and consequent lack of a need to keep discussing it.

It is unsurprising then that more and more disciplines in the humanities (see e.g. Stibbe [2015] 2021: 9; Zurru 2017: 191–2) have started taking an interest in how the relation between humans and the ecosystem(s) is presented in such areas as philosophy, history, sociology, literature, the media, political arenas and so on and through which textual, discursive and linguistic patterns. These disciplines are conscious that these patterns are a key factor in both supporting *and* challenging the narrative that puts humans higher in the hierarchy of life on the planet, and that a change in anti-ecological linguistic, textual and discursive practices can help foster a change in mentality and actions both at the individual and the social level. As data shows,[5] ever since calls for climate action became more insistent over the 1980s and led to the so-called Earth summit in 1992, some progress has been made, and nowadays a considerably larger number of people are conscious of the dangers connected to the ecological crisis. However, targets are not being met within the agreed-upon deadlines by countries around the world.[6] This has prompted an increase in calls for urgent environmental action in both institutional and non-institutional settings directly proportionate to the worsening of the ecological crisis, in order to put as much pressure as possible on governments and corporations. Some of these initiatives are extreme or even hiding behind environmental discourse to disguise other goals, such as eco-fascism (Del Valle 2022); others have a sensationalist approach, such as the recent protest by a group of young activists gluing themselves to one of Botticelli's painting (Gayle 2022); others try to inspire ecological action through art, with an approach referred to as 'artivism' – or activism through art – epitomized by the United Nations tweeting a picture of a sculpture by artivist Von Wong;[7] this sculpture shows an array of plastic products pouring out of a sink, which creates the visual metaphor PLASTIC IS WATER to raise awareness about plastic pollution in the oceans, whose decrease is a sustainable development goal.[8]

As this last example suggests, a communicative strategy that has proven to be pervasive in environmental communication is metaphor, in both its verbal and non-verbal forms (see e.g. Deignan 2017; Goatly 2000, [1996] 2001, 2007, 2017; Li and Ye 2017; Meijers, Remmelswaal and Wonneberger 2019; Nerlich and Jaspal 2012; Penz 2018; Thibodeau, McPherson Frantz and Berretta 2017; Virdis 2022). Notably, the metaphor of the TICKING CLOCK, which used to be very commonly associated with chronobiology (cf. Aviram and Manella 2020; Barrera-Mera and Barrera-Calva 1998; Moss and Maner 2014), has been more and more consistently used in the past few years to communicate the urgency of the climate emergency and foreground how very limited the time left to take action is, before the consequences of the ecological calamity we are facing become irreversible. The aim of this chapter is to investigate how verbal and non-verbal instantiations of the TICKING CLOCK metaphor are exploited in a number of case studies retrieved from both mainstream and more recently developed communication channels, such as artivism, news reports and social media, and for which communicative purposes. Given the aims and scope of the chapter, the theoretical and methodological scaffolding of the study is interdisciplinary. Ecolinguistics (Fill and Mühlhäusler 2001; Fill and Penz 2018a; Stibbe [2015] 2021) and verbal and non-verbal metaphor studies (Forceville and Urios-Aparisi 2009; Kövecses [2002] 2010, 2020a, 2020b, 2021; Lakoff and Johnson [1980] 2003; Pérez Sobrino 2013, 2017; Steen 2019; Steen et al. 2010) will be integrated to investigate the case studies selected and reflect on the communicative effectiveness of the use of the TICKING CLOCK metaphor within the current debate on the climate emergency.

After some theoretical notes in Section 4.1, the analysis presented in Section 4.2 will show that the overarching communicative function of the TICKING CLOCK metaphor in the examples scrutinized is urging for immediate climate action while frequently showcasing an apocalyptic narrative at the same time. Concluding remarks in Section 4.3 will bring the chapter to a close.

4.1 Theoretical notes

As discussed in the Introduction, now more than ever social, cultural, religious, economic, technological, political agendas are intersectional with the environmental crisis, and how this crisis is presented to the general public *can* make a difference (see Lakoff 2010; Penz 2018). Decades of research in applied linguistics have demonstrated how language and textual strategies can be manipulated to share facts and figures in order to lead audiences towards certain interpretations rather than others (see e.g. Carter and Simpson [1989] 2005; Fairclough 1992, [1989] 2013; Fairclough and Wodak 1997; Flowerdew and Richardson 2018; Fowler 1986; Fowler et al. [1979] 2019; Jeffries 2010; Simpson [1993] 2005; van Dijk 2008). As the examples briefly discussed earlier show, the discourse about the environmental crisis is a battleground between competing narratives where communication plays a key role. Other interests, especially the economic one, are obviously at stake. A clear-cut example was provided by Mann (2021) and Solnit (2021), when they reminded readers that the concept of personal carbon footprint – incidentally, a very effective and rapidly popularized metaphor – was suggested by a professional public relations agency hired by one of the largest oil companies on the planet, British Petroleum (BP), in order to shift the attention from the responsibility of the fossil fuel industry to that of the individual. The carbon footprint calculator that was released by BP in 2004 (Solnit 2021) is precisely intended to show each person how their individual choices are contributing to global warming. This is a tool which is still consistently and massively used, for example, by some banking corporations (e.g. the Italian *Intesa Sanpaolo*), which automatically calculate their clients' carbon footprint based on their account transactions. As useful as that might be to help each of us keep track of our own impact on the earth's resources, it is highly improbable that a single person might have a bigger carbon footprint than an oil giant like BP. Yet, this strategy has proven very fruitful in framing the environmental crisis as a predicament that can and, in fact, *should* be tackled through individual sacrifice first and foremost. However, as the above-mentioned success following the Montreal Protocol demonstrates, positive change takes place through *collective* action, when all the key parties are truly invested. And if it is true that each single person can – and should – start making more environmentally conscious choices, it is just as true that individuals must be put in the condition of being able to make those choices, for example, by cities giving them a chance to opt for efficient public transportation or riding a bike (see Caimotto 2020), rather than using a car.

It is not surprising, then, that countless institutional and non-institutional initiatives are now taking place to bring the focus back where it should be, by pressing governments and corporations to opt for swift ecological action. Any of these initiatives represents an incredibly stimulating area of investigation for humanities, first and foremost for eco-disciplines with a critical and applied approach such as ecolinguistics. They offer the opportunity to both explore *and* contribute to change in the making about issues that can guarantee the survival of human and non-human life on earth, or its extinction.

Understandably, the calls for attention to the debilitating climate conditions have increased after 2010, given that the last decade was characterized by extreme events connected to climate change like never before (Freedman et al. 2020). Examples of such calls are countless by now and an exhaustive list would be impossible to make and go beyond the scope of this contribution. However, it is worth mentioning that an institution like the World Health Organization chose the theme 'Our Planet, Our Health' for the 2022 World Health Day[9] and produced a short animated film to explain the dangers to human health if the environmental crisis is not faced, even though the Covid-19 pandemic was still ongoing and might have been selected as the 2022 theme instead. It is also notable that the number of freely accessible platforms monitoring the ecological crisis has increased, both at the institutional level, for example, EU's *Copernicus: Europe's Eyes on Earth*,[10] and at the independent level, for example, *The Climate Action Tracker*.[11] Individuals also take to the web, especially social media, to share their concern about the ecological crisis. A tweet by @ClimateDad77 stating that 'We need to stop thinking like consumers living in an economy. And start thinking like organisms living in an ecosystem'[12] recently went viral. Even more engagement characterized the tweet by @ashtpmny with the message 'the world is ending y'all'[13] accompanied by the video of a visibly rattled NASA scientist working on climate projections who joined the organization 'Scientist rebellion' (which stages protests for environmental protection worldwide) and chained himself to a bank branch of the banking corporation Chase, which invests in fossil fuels more than any other bank, to call attention to the lack of effective climate policies the world over. These are but a few examples of the many institutional and non-institutional, individual and/or collective attempts to engage the general public in the conversation about the urgency of the environmental emergency and to put pressure on key actors, such as governments and corporations. It is important to underline how many of these attempts try to appeal to people's emotions and sensitivity rather than to their understanding of data. This is a fundamental aspect of environmental communication nowadays. Already in 2010 Lakoff (2010: 76) envisaged a case of 'hypocognition' related to the environment, namely a lack of the necessary cognitive frames to fully understand the issue of the environmental crisis, mainly due to its intersectionality with so many other aspects of human life, that is, food, trade, energy, economics and so on. In the author's words:

> The Environment Frame sees the environment as separate from, and around, us. Yet, we are not separate from Nature. We are an inseparable part of Nature. Yet we separate self from other, and conceptualize Nature as other. This separation is so deep in our conceptual system that we cannot simply wipe it from our brains. It is a terribly false frame that will not go away. (Lakoff 2010: 76–7)

As mentioned in the Introduction to the volume, this frame is pervasive in Western ideology, as also addressed by the tweet by @ClimateDad77 mentioned earlier. According to Lakoff (2010: 74), frames of this kind need to be 're-framed' before a considerable number of people will be ready to fully grasp and accept the reality of the situation, and such a reframing takes time and can only take place thanks to a constant, massive and coordinated effort to create the correct background frames while, at the same time, inhibiting false ones. These efforts can be of different nature. We mentioned some of them earlier. The ever-increasing academic work within eco-disciplines is another example, including attempts to reshape vocabulary itself, such as the creation of the word 'convironment', from German 'Mitwelt', by Fill (2001 [1998]: 50, 2020: 2039),[14] to underline 'the togetherness of humans and Nature'. As mentioned earlier, Lakoff further underlines that these efforts should also be characterized by a change in the usual communicative practices adopted by environmental communication: these should stop relying on the 'the old, false view of reason and language' based on the tenet that 'if you just tell people the facts, they will reason to the right conclusion' (Lakoff 2010: 77). On the contrary, he suggests that environmental communication should revolve around different strategies, namely linking frames with moral values, using narratives that illustrate those values and stir emotions and paying attention to the context by addressing everyday concerns, avoiding terminology, using words easy to understand and bearing in mind that 'the messenger matters. Visuals matter. Body language matters' (Lakoff 2010: 79–80).

Remarks such as these, as well as those by Mann (2012) discussed earlier, are in line with the increasing importance of visuality and multimodality within communication as a whole, and environmental communication in particular, which have been greatly influenced by the multiplying of communicative channels, texts and genres following the invention of the internet first and social media later. This is also the reason why the research question of the present study revolves around non-verbal metaphors in environmental communication as well as verbal ones. Indeed, metaphor is a very effective framing device (see Lakoff and Johnson [1980] 2003; Thibodeau, Hendricks and Boroditsky 2017), in that it helps humans perceive, categorize and communicate abstract notions in more concrete terms (e.g. 'the hockey stick' metaphor discussed on pages 88 and 89) and can thus be used just as effectively to 're-frame' pre-existing notions. For example, Hendricks et al. (2018) discussed the change in attitude in oncological patients when their illness is framed as a 'journey' rather than as a 'battle'. By the same token, the #ReframeCovid initiative[15] was launched to propose the use of metaphors and other instances of figurative language alternative to war-related expressions, in order to shift the framing of the pandemic away from a war against the virus and its negative and potentially paralysing undertones. In addition, metaphor is also a very economical strategy able to encapsulate multiple layers of meaning by allowing us to map the characteristics of a concept into another even though the two concepts are not otherwise objectively related (e.g. 'CANCER IS A JOURNEY'). This, in turn, proves strategic when space is a serious constraint, as in the case of protest posters or tweets, or the topic to discuss has many facets and ramifications, such as climate change (see Zurru 2022). In addition, metaphor is capable of appealing to people's emotional intelligence and can thus be exploited to inspire their emotional responses (see e.g. Citron and Goldberg 2014; Hendricks et al. 2018; see also Meijers, Remmelswaal and Wonneberger 2019; Pérez-Sobrino 2016). By applying an ecolinguistic approach to the study of metaphorical communication within environmental discourse, this chapter aims at contributing to the study of visuality and multimodality within both metaphor studies and environmental discourse studies. Indeed, if the number of contributions exploring verbal aspects is extremely large in both these areas of research, studies focusing on visual and multimodal aspects are decidedly fewer (see Fill and Penz 2018b: 441–2; Zurru 2022), and the need to explore the non-verbal aspects of environmental discourse more extensively has been underlined in neighbouring eco-disciplines, such as visual environmental communication (Hansen 2011, 2018; Hansen and Machin 2013). In order to do so, the following section will present the case studies selected, their analysis and discussion of results.

4.2 Analysis and discussion

The case studies selected vary in both text type and communicative context. As anticipated in the Introduction, this choice was made to test the hypothesis that the TICKING CLOCK metaphor might be found in different contexts of use within climate change and environmental discourse, in both mainstream communicative channels, such as visual arts and news reports, and more recently developed media, such as social media platforms, and to establish whether its use has similar communicative purposes and effects in different contexts or not. This implies that the texts analysed vary in terms of mode(s) (e.g. only visual VS visual + verbal), in terms of formality or informality and in terms of communicative skills of the addressor(s) (e.g. a journalist VS a young #FridaysForFuture striker), among other things. This also entails that an integrated approach to the analysis of these texts was necessary, combining methodologies focused on verbal as well as non-verbal communication and metaphor usage, as discussed in the previous two sections. News articles from established publications such as the *New York Times*, art installations and social media texts retrieved from X, formerly known as Twitter, constituted the sources from which the case studies analysed in this chapter were retrieved. Three subsections will follow, which present analyses of the TICKING CLOCK metaphor in visual arts (4.3.1), in news reports (4.3.2) and in social media (4.3.3). Because of space constraints, two case studies will be analysed in each subsection.

4.2.1 The ticking clock in visual arts

The present subsection will focus on the first two case studies: the Ice Watch and the Climate Clock.

The Ice Watch is an art installation by Olafur Eliasson that was launched in December 2015 on the occasion of the 21st United Nations Conference on Climate Change (COP 21) (Zarin 2015). The dedicated website[16] describes the installation as follows:

> Twelve immense blocks of ice, harvested as free-floating icebergs from a fjord outside Nuuk, Greenland, were arranged in clock formation at the Place du Panthéon, where they melted away from 3 to 12 December 2015, during COP21.

This description is followed by a slide show of videos and pictures taken during the event, which show how the twelve ice blocks are placed in a circle, so that people can both see and hear their melting process from within and without the circle itself. The TICKING CLOCK metaphor is, in this case, activated through a pattern of interaction that Pérez Sobrino (2017) defines as multimodal metaphtonymy, since the mapping between the domains MELTING ICE CUBES and TICKING CLOCK is cued both through visual and auditory modes and hinges on an essential metonymy-metaphor relation. Indeed, if the relation between metaphor and metonymy has been established in the context of verbal and cognitive metaphors (e.g. Kövecses 2013; Polzenhagen et al. 2014), it has proved essential for both the creation and decoding of non-verbal ones (Forceville and Urious-Aparisi 2009: 12; Pérez Sobrino 2013, 2017). In this instance, the metaphoric A IS B relation and the metonymic A FOR B relation give rise to the metaphtonymy (ICE FOR) CLOCK (HANDS) IS (MELTING FOR) CLICKING. In terms of communicative effect, this installation is both informative and persuasive, as it is meant to raise awareness on the alarming rate with which the Arctic cap is melting while at the same time provoking a strong emotional response, which is one of the communicative practices suggested by Lakoff in his 2010 article. This is also confirmed by the artist on the website of the project:[17]

> As an artist I hope my works touch people, which in turn can make something that may have previously seemed quite abstract into reality. Art has the ability to change our perceptions and perspectives on the world and Ice Watch makes the climate challenges we are facing tangible. I hope it will inspire shared commitment to taking climate action.

The fact that the metaphorical clock disappears altogether once the melting process is concluded, however, implicitly conveys an apocalyptic message which hints at the complete dissolution of the permafrost rather than its safeguard and continued existence and might, therefore, be counterproductive.

The second case study follows a similar path. The 'Climate Clock' is an art installation by Gan Golan and Andrew Boyd and was launched in September 2020, when the famous Metronome's digital clock in Manhattan, one of the most famous public art projects in New York City, was reprogramed to become the 'Climate Clock' (Moynihan 2020). This reprogramming brought about a cognitive reframing. Indeed, while the Metronome's digital clock acted as an actual clock counting the twenty-four hours of each day, while also providing a countdown of the remaining hours of the day, the Climate Clock is primarily a countdown of the time left to limit global warming to 1.5 °C which is based on the awareness that 'Earth has a deadline'.[18] Therefore, the installation itself seems to be based more on the TIME IS RUNNING OUT metaphor than on the TICKING CLOCK one. As pointed out by Mühlhäusler (2022: 5), the TIME IS RUNNING OUT metaphor originates in the measuring of time by the hourglass,[19] in which time (measured by the sand) would run out of the top bulb and into the bottom one. Moreover, it is connected to 'a linear perception of time [which] underlies the view of accelerated decline and the associated perception [. . .] that there is a "downhill" arrow that leads from a golden past to eventual catastrophe and the end of the world [which] is deeply embedded in Western thought' (Mühlhäusler 2022: 5). Since this metaphor, like other time-related metaphors (e.g. 'save time'), hinges on the conceptual metaphor TIME IS A RESOURCE, its framing of time in terms of loss (time, like sand, slips away) is potentially discouraging, as it depicts time as an alarmingly decreasing resource. The paratextual resources developed to publicize this work of art and keep it alive, namely a publicly available video on YouTube[20] and a dedicated website,[21] however, both make use of the TICKING CLOCK metaphor. The video is 1 minute and 24 seconds long and shows a clock with ticking hands that progressively allow a bidimensional image of the earth to appear in the background as the first twenty-four-hour round is complete. This background remains the same for one minute and seventeen seconds while a verbal message appears and music plays. The verbal message contains strings such as 'We have 7 years, 102 days, 13 hours, 29 minutes, 48:92 seconds to save the world', 'We can only burn 306 billion, 511 million, 548 thousand, 823 hundred tones more carbon to avoid famine, drought, floods, displacement, conflict, suffering, disaster' and 'the earth as a deadline'. The video devotes the last thirty seconds to try and change the narrative. This is done with both a) verbal means, with the string 'let's make it a lifeline' following the statement about the earth having a deadline and the hashtag #actintime appearing towards the end; and b) visual means, with the colour red used to highlight the negatively connoted words (famine, drought, floods, displacement, conflict, suffering, disaster), the clock edge around the image of the earth, the numbers in the countdown and the morpheme 'dead' in the word 'deadline' being replaced by green, first in the morpheme 'life' when the word 'lifeline' appears and then in the clock edge. However, most of the video is based on an underlying apocalyptic narrative conveyed through the CLOCK IS TICKING, TIME IS RUNNING OUT and EARTH IS A DYING LIVING BEING multimodal metaphors. By the same token, the homepage of the website displays the 'deadline' countdown in red at the top left-hand side (down to six years at the time of writing of this chapter) and the 'lifelines' (such as world's energy from renewables and percentage of women in parliaments globally) in blue at the top right-hand side. Right below is the phrase 'climate clock' in blocks. The letter 'o' of the world 'clock' is replaced by a round clock with ticking hands which divides the bidimensional image of the earth representing the clock background into a red section and a blue section. The website homepage, therefore, exploits the same multimodal metaphors as the video. Collectively, the communicative effect of the installation itself and its online paratext is confusing and contradictory, with the urgent call for climate action conveyed by the CLOCK IS TICKING metaphor clashing with the hopelessness possibly inspired by the TIME IS RUNNING OUT and EARTH IS A DYING LIVING BEING metaphors.

4.2.2 The ticking clock in news reports

The two case studies analysed in this subsection are the Doomsday Clock and the Cape Town water clock.

The Doomsday Clock will be analysed based on the news reports by McFall-Johnsen (2020) and Cowan (2020). This is a metaphorical clock maintained by the non-profit organization 'Bulleting of Atomic Scientists', which measures how vulnerable the world is in the face of political, nuclear and environmental threats. The clock was set to 100 seconds to midnight in January 2020, closer than ever to Doomsday in its seventy-three-year history (McFall-Johnsen 2020). While the underlining apocalyptic narrative is intrinsic in the name given to the clock itself, the two news reports selected both contain the CLOCK IS TICKING metaphor. In particular, the article by Cowan includes it in verbal terms, with the title reading '*Tick, Tick, Tick. Why the Doomsday Clock Is Moving Closer to Midnight*'. More specifically, the repeated use of the onomatopoeic lexeme 'tick' in combination with the phrases 'Doomsday Clock' and 'closer to midnight' explicitly refers to the verbal metaphor 'the clock is ticking' while, at the same time, implicitly referring to the TIME IS RUNNING OUT metaphor, since less than two minutes remain before midnight – in turn a metaphor for Doomsday – strikes. Conversely, the article by McFall-Johnsen (2020) contains the visual metaphor THE CLOCK IS TICKING, which is conflated with the verbal metaphor 'time is running out'. Indeed, the section entitled 'Time is running out to turn the clock back' opens with a picture of a human hand moving the black minute hand of a white clock clockwise, which is captioned 'Robert Rosner, chairman of the Bulletin of the Atomic Scientists, moves the minute hand of the Doomsday Clock to two minutes to midnight during a news conference at the National Press Club in Washington, January 25, 2018'. As in the previous article, the ticking of the clock and the running out of time are presented one in connection to the other, almost as if they were one and the same metaphor, which turns the call to action based on a 'we still have time' mentality into an apocalyptic narrative based on a 'we no longer have time' cognitive frame.

The Cape Town water clock will be investigated through the analysis of the news reports by Tafirenyika (2018) and Sinha (2018). In both articles, the 'ticking clock' metaphor is used verbally. Tafirenyika writes, 'As the clock ticks and the seasonal rains refuse to arrive, Cape Town has launched a flurry of measures to avert disaster.' Sinha's article is titled 'Water: The clock is ticking'. Both publications are focused on the water emergency experienced by the city of Cape Town in 2018, which led the authorities to launch the idea of a water clock, which took the form of a countdown to day zero, namely the day when the water supplies from the municipality of Cape Town would be completely consumed. Therefore, these articles present a case similar to the Climate Clock discussed earlier. Indeed, while the 'ticking clock' verbal metaphor is explicitly used in both publications, what is being referred to is not the cognitive framing of a clock but that of a countdown. In other words, while the explicit metaphorical schema presented is that of a 'ticking clock', the implicit cognitive schema is that of 'time running out'. This is even more evident in the article by Tafirenyika, entitled 'Cape Town water taps running dry', which traces a parallelism between 'time running out' and 'water taps running dry'. Incidentally, as underlined by Sinha (2018), a number of administrative restrictions and the cooperation of the citizenship allowed the deadline to day zero to be pushed forward a number of times, a localized equivalent of the Montreal Protocol discussed on page 90, demonstrating the effectiveness of collective environmental action. Just like the Montreal Protocol, this initiative was also questioned not so much because of its failure but because of its success. Chutel (2018) wrote a piece entitled 'Cape Town's drought doomsday clock has been pushed back, raising questions about its accuracy', in which the author comments on the deadline being pushed further multiple times running the risk of making city officials appear alarmist, which is strengthened by the choice of defying the initiative as 'drought doomsday clock'. While a specific agenda by Chutel cannot be excluded a priori, the scepticism might also be linked to the underbelly apocalyptic narrative created by the conflation of the 'ticking clock' and 'time running out' metaphors, as well as the water clock cognitively 'failing' as a clock – since it is, in fact, a countdown – thus leading to complacency rather than participation.

4.2.3 The ticking clock in social media

Finally, this subsection will focus on two tweets which are part of the #FridaysForFuture online protest as well as two tweets from the @WeDontHaveTime account. The intended communicative meaning of these case studies is the outcome of the interaction between different modes, given the potential of tweets of combining written text, emojis, hashtags, GIFs, pictures and videos.

With regard to the #FridaysForFuture tweets, the first one was retrieved by typing #FridaysForFuture in the search bar and looking through the top results, while the second was retrieved by typing 'clock is ticking' + #FridaysForFuture in the search bar and looking through the top results. The first tweet[22] is a combination of written text,[23] emojis and four pictures. The verbal text presents the string 'Act now, the clock is ticking' ('Handelt endlich, die Uhr tickt') combined with the emoji of a clock, thus giving rise to the multimodal (verbal + visual) metaphor (Pérez Sobrino 2017) THE CLOCK IS TICKING. While this first metaphor mainly has the communicative purpose to urge people to engage in climate action, the first of the four pictures presents a protest poster which is reminiscent of the Ice Watch discussed in Section 4.3.1 both in form and in function, in that it showcases a drawing in which twelve progressively melting ice cubes are arranged in a circle within which the words 'the clock is ticking' ('die Uhr tickt') are written. The combination of the written words and the drawing results in the metaphtonymy (ICE FOR) CLOCK (HANDS) IS (MELTING FOR) CLICKING, with the melting of the ice cubes hinting at time about to run out as well as the ticking of a clock.

Even though the search for 'clock is ticking' + #FridaysForFuture returned many tweets in which the verbal metaphor 'the clock is ticking' is explicitly used, the second tweet[24] was selected because it comprises both written text, emojis and a picture. More specifically, the written text contains the verbal metaphor 'the clock is ticking' which is combined with a picture displaying a raised hand during a #FridaysForFuture protest holding an hourglass, which, as discussed earlier (Section 4.2.3), is associated with the TIME IS RUNNING OUT metaphor. Therefore, this case study provides another example of the potentially encouraging TICKING CLOCK metaphor conflating with the tendentially discouraging TIME IS RUNNING OUT metaphor.

The account @WeDontHaveTime was selected precisely for its handle. This account is one of many devoted to raising awareness about the climate emergency and encouraging people to act. The choice of a handle which condenses the sentence 'we don't have time', therefore, appears counterproductive. While the TIME IS RUNNING OUT metaphor frames time as a rapidly decreasing resource, this sentence frames it as a resource which is extinguished altogether, which, in turn, suggests that any attempt to act is pointless. The tweets that will be analysed were retrieved by typing 'the clock is ticking' + @WeDontHaveTime in the search bar and looking through the top results. The first tweet[25] reads 'people have to wake up! The Clock is ticking! #wedonthavetime' and is quoting another tweet that only contains the link to an article entitled 'When the End of Human Civilization Is Your Day Job' accompanied by the hashtags #climate #globalwarming #divest. This case study is therefore almost exclusively made up of written words, with the sole exception of the graphic symbol #. The latter was initially used on Twitter to categorize content and facilitate searches but has undergone a functional evolution so that it is now also used as meta-commentary to communicate a user's attitude towards the content of the post (Heyd and Puschmann 2017). Therefore, analysing the text as a whole, the verbal metaphor 'the clock is ticking' is placed in a co-text with such strings as '#wedonthavetime' – which is interpretable more as meta-commentary than it is as a categorizing strategy – and 'End of Human Civilization' in connection to #climate #globalwarming. Both these strings convey meanings which are closer to the 'time is running out' metaphor than the 'ticking clock' metaphor, resulting in the two metaphors being conflated once again.

The second tweet[26] contains both a written message and a picture. The first sentence of the written post reads 'The clock is ticking ⏰ On July 22, @theclimateclock will tick over from 7 years to 6 years' while the picture shows a young activist holding a portable copy of the Climate Clock showing its countdown (see Section 4.2.1). In this case, the multimodal metaphor THE CLOCK IS TICKING is created in the written segment of the text due to the combination of the verbal metaphor 'the clock is ticking' and the emoji reproducing a clock with ticking hands. This is, however, placed in connection with the Climate Clock both in the written post ('On July 22, @theclimateclock will tick over from 7 years to 6 years') and in the picture, which, once again, reinforces the association of the TICKING CLOCK metaphor with the TIME IS RUNNING OUT metaphor.

4.3 Conclusions

In the case studies scrutinized, the TICKING CLOCK metaphor, both in its verbal and non-verbal forms, is mainly used to foreground how very limited the time left to take action is before the consequences of the ecological calamity we are facing become irreversible. Overall, its use often contributes to an apocalyptic and/or confusing communicative effect which can potentially discourage rather than encourage action. Indeed, research shows (e.g. O'Neill and Nicholson-Cole 2009, Nerlich and Jaspal 2012) that apocalyptic and/or catastrophic narratives are not effective in terms of inspiring people to take action. Foust and Murphy (2009) found two variations in the apocalyptic rhetoric: (1) tragic, which leads to believe we have no hope of survival; and (2) comic, which implies that we still have a chance to help the planet heal. They concluded that the second frame inspires readers to take action more than the first, and that it should be more extensively used in ecological discourse. By the same token, Dickinson et al. (2013) concluded that dire messages about the dangers of climate change for humanity are less effective than messages about the positive collective impact of individual behavioural changes. It is also interesting to note that Flusberg, Matlock and Thibodeau (2017) also concluded that the 'race' frame is less effective than the 'war' frame when discussing climate change while also underlining that the latter tends to become less effective over time (Flusberg, Matlock and Thibodeau 2017: 780). This is in line with recent approaches within ecolinguistics, such as Positive Discourse Analysis (Stibbe 2018), which suggest 'to search for new discourses to base society on; for example, discourses which promote being more rather than having more, well-being rather than growth and respecting rather than conquering nature' (Stibbe 2018: 165). In this respect, it is notable that a search in Google Images with the key phrase 'solar punk movement' did not return any instance of the TICKING CLOCK metaphor. This artistic movement is indeed focused on encouraging ecological action and sustainability by strengthening the connections between humans and nature, based on mutual respect and the rejection of doomsday narratives. On the contrary, in all the case studies analysed, THE TICKING CLOCK metaphor is almost always blended with the TIME IS RUNNING OUT metaphor to reinforce the idea that the amount of time left to enact positive change is minimal and/or insufficient. Therefore, against the backdrop of ever-increasing phenomena of eco-anxiety (Gregory 2021) and learned helplessness (Landry et al. 2018) and their impact on environmental behaviour, and based on the Positive Discourse Analysis approach of suggesting beneficial alternative forms of language and communication, in addition to – or in place of – critically exposing any ecolinguistic issue with current language usage (Stibbe 2018: 165), this chapter cannot but conclude that the TICKING CLOCK metaphor should be reframed when used in the context of climate change discourse. It should move away from the catastrophic undertones its frequent connection with the TIME IS RUNNING OUT metaphor conveys, being among the most negative realizations of the TIME IS A RESOURCE conceptual metaphor in terms of framing, as is carrier of the idea of an imminent and inevitable loss of a valuable resource. In other words, rather than suggesting that we are resourceless, and therefore doomed, the focus should be on underlining the fact that we can, and should, make use of the resources – including time – we still have to bring about positive change. In addition, in line with Dancygier (2023), we suggest that anyone involved in environmental communication consider that strategies such as the TICKING CLOCK metaphor, or the Hourglass frame, have by now become overexploited in the discourse about the urgency of the climate emergency and, as such, are starting to lose effectiveness due to repetitiveness and overexposure – a phenomenon Dancygier (2023: 11) defines as 'persuasion bleaching'. Future research might indeed focus on expanding the investigation by including reader/viewer response studies, in order to gauge whether the TICKING CLOCK metaphor dissociated from the TIME IS RUNNING OUT metaphor elicits a stronger engagement in respondents and how effective it actually is, possibly in comparison with alternative strategies conveying the message that TIME IS A RESOURCE that we still have, and should make the most of.

Notes

1. As is conventional in Conceptual Metaphor Theory (Lakoff and Johnson 2003 [1980]), conceptual metaphors are presented in small capital. The same convention is adopted in studies on visual and/or multimodal metaphors. These conventions will also be adhered to in this chapter. Conversely, when the metaphor analysed is verbal, it will be presented between single commas (e.g. 'the clock is ticking').
2. https://twitter.com/elonmusk/status/1563020169160851456.
3. https://twitter.com/MattWalshBlog/status/1549713211188027394.
4. https://www.dcceew.gov.au/environment/protection/ozone/montreal-protocol#:~:text=The%20Montreal%20Protocol%20on%20Substances,protect%20the%20earth's%20ozone%20layer.
5. https://www.unep.org/explore-topics/climate-action/what-we-do/climate-action-note/state-of-climate.html?gclid=Cj0KCQjwyt-ZBhCNARIsAKH1177Za-ofsWWVspOhjJRjJX0a5RQbaTdOymYszhylNOzn7CGJq_-v6cMaAmfVEALw_wcB.
6. https://climateactiontracker.org/global/temperatures/.
7. https://twitter.com/UN/status/1554995785141342208?s=20&t=w8AEGPo8YWvidYHKbl_USQ.
8. For an investigation on the relation between visual arts and ecological communication, see Amideo (this volume).
9. https://www.who.int/campaigns/world-health-day/2022.
10. https://climate.copernicus.eu/.
11. https://climateactiontracker.org/about/.
12. https://twitter.com/ClimateDad77/status/1561005902928412674.
13. https://twitter.com/ashtpmny/status/1554535227896258567?s=20&t=w8AEGPo8YWvidYHKbl_USQ.
14. See also Chapter 1 in this volume.
15. https://sites.google.com/view/reframecovid/initiative.

16 https://icewatchparis.com/.
17 https://icewatchparis.com/.
18 https://www.youtube.com/watch?v=m_NqyF9WQRk.
19 Dancygier (2023:7) also identifies the 'Hourglass frame' as one pervasive frame in multimodal communication about climate change, related to the idea of time running out. Even though she elects to investigate the issue through the lens of frame metonymy and blending rather than that of multimodal metaphor (Dancygier 2023:16), the scholar concludes that the Hourglass frame conveys an idea of time as a diminishing resource which contributes to 'climate doomism' rather than addressing the causes of the issue or suggesting possible solutions.
20 https://www.youtube.com/watch?v=m_NqyF9WQRk.
21 https://climateclock.world/.
22 https://twitter.com/fff_hamburg/status/1408417655053299714?s=20.
23 The verbal text is written in German but was analysed in the English translation made by a professional translator.
24 https://twitter.com/darioschramm/status/1175074583357136896.
25 https://twitter.com/WeDontHaveTime/status/819789952590364673.
26 https://twitter.com/WeDontHaveTime/status/1549733360116805632.

References

Aviram, R. and G. Manella (2020), 'A Metaphor That Keeps on Ticking: The "Clock" as a Driving Force in the History of Chronobiology Research', *Philosophy, Theory and Practice in Biology*, 12: 7. https://doi.org/10.3998/ptpbio.16039257.0012.006.

Barrera-Mera B. and E. Barrera-Calva (1998), 'The Cartesian Clock Metaphor for Pineal Gland Operation Pervades the Origin of Modern Chronobiology', *Neuroscience and Biobehavioral Reviews*, 23: 1–4.

Biello, D. (2012), 'Hit Them with the Hockey Stick', *Scientific American*, 306 (3): 72–75.

Caimotto, M. C. (2020), *Discourses of Cycling, Road Users and Sustainability: An Ecolinguistic Investigation*, Cham: Palgrave Macmillan.

Carter, R. and P. Simpson, eds (2005 [1989]), *Language, Discourse and Literature: An Introductory Reader in Discourse Stylistics*, London: Taylor & Francis.

Chutel, L. (2018), 'Cape Town's Drought Doomsday Clock Has Been Pushed Back, Raising Questions About Its Accuracy'. https://qz.com/africa/1215808/cape-town-drought-day-zero-pushed-to-july-when-water-runs-out (accessed 15 September 2022).

Citron, F. M. M. and A. E. Goldberg (2014), 'Metaphorical Sentences Are More Emotionally Engaging Than Their Literal Counterparts', *Journal of Cognitive Neuroscience*, 26 (11): 2585–95.

Cowan, J. (2020), 'Tick, Tick, Tick: Why the Doomsday Clock Is Moving Closer to Midnight', *The New York Times*. https://www.nytimes.com/2020/02/06/us/what-is-doomsday-clock.html (accessed 15 September 2022).

Crutzen, P. J. and E. F. Stoermer (2000), 'The "Anthropocene"', *IGBP Newsletter*, 41: 17–18. http://www.igbp.net/download/18.316f18321323470177580001401/1376383088452/NL41.pdf (accessed 12 June 2022).

Dancygier, B. (2023), 'Multimodal Media: Framing Climate Change', *Discourse Studies*, 25 (2), online first. https://doi.org/10.1177/14614456231154724.

Deignan, A. (2017), 'Metaphors in Texts about Climate Change', *Ibérica*, 34: 45–66.

Del Valle, G. (2022), '3 Years After the El Paso Shooting, "Environmental" Nativism Is Spreading', *The Nation*. https://www.thenation.com/article/society/el-paso-shooting-xenophobia/ (accessed 3 August 2022).

Dickinson, J. L., R. Crain, S. Yalowitz, and T. M. Cherry (2013), 'How Framing Climate Change Influences Citizen Scientists' Intentions to Do Something About It', *The Journal of Environmental Education*, 44 (3), 145–58.

Fairclough, N. (1992), *Discourse and Social Change*, Cambridge: Polity.

Fairclough, N. (2013 [1989]), *Language and Power*, London and New York: Routledge.

Fairclough, N. and R. Wodak (1997), 'Critical Discourse Analysis', in T. van Dijk (ed), *Discourse as Social Interaction*, 258–85, London: Sage.

Fill, A. (2001), 'Ecolinguistics: State of the Art 1998', in A. Fill and P. Mühlhäusler (eds), *The Ecolinguistics Reader. Language, Ecology and Environment*, 43–53, London: Continuum.

Fill, A. (2020), 'From Environmental Thinking to "Con-Vironmental" Awareness', *AAA: Arbeiten aus Anglistik und Amerikanistik*, 45 (2): 239–46.

Fill, A. and P. Mühlhäusler, eds (2001a), *The Ecolinguistics Reader. Language, Ecology and Environment*, London and New York: Continuum.

Fill, A. and H. Penz, eds (2018a), *The Routledge Handbook of Ecolinguistics*, London: Routledge.

Fill, A. and H. Penz (2018b), 'Ecolinguistics in the 21st Century: New Orientations and Future Directions', in A. Fill and H. Penz (eds), *The Routledge Handbook of Ecolinguistics*, 434–37, London and New York: Routledge.

Flowerdew, J. and J. E. Richardson, eds (2018), *The Routledge Handbook of Critical Discourse Studies*, London and New York: Routledge.

Flusberg, S. J., T. Matlock, and P. H. Thibodeau (2017), 'Metaphor for the War (or Race) Against Climate Change', *Environmental Communication*, 11 (6): 769–83.

Forceville, C. and E. Urios-Aparisi, eds (2009), *Multimodal Metaphor*, Berlin: Mouton De Gruyter.

Foust, C. R. and W. Murphy (2009), 'Revealing and Reframing Apocalyptic Tragedy in Global Warming Discourse', *Environmental Communication*, 3 (2): 151–67.

Fowler, R. (1986), *Linguistic Criticism*, Oxford: Oxford University Press.

Fowler, R., B. Hodge, G. Kress, and T. Trew (2019 [1979]), *Language and Control*, London and New York: Routledge.

Freedman, A., J. Samenow, R. Noak, and K. Domb Sadof (2020), 'Climate Change in the 2010s: Decade of Fires, Floods and Scorching Heat Waves', *The Washington Post*. https://www.washingtonpost.com/graphics/2020/weather/amp-stories/climate-change-in-the-2010s/ (accessed 5 June 2022).

Gayle, D. (2022), 'Climate Activists in Italy Glue Themselves to Botticelli Painting', *The Guardian*. https://www.theguardian.com/environment/2022/jul/22/climate-activists-in-italy-glue-themselves-to-botticelli-painting (accessed 22 Jul 2022).

Goatly, A. (2000), *Critical Reading and Writing: An Introductory Coursebook*, London and New York: Routledge.

Goatly, A. (2001 [1996]), 'Green Grammar and Grammatical Metaphor, or Language and Myth of Power, or Metaphors We Die By', in A. Fill and P. Mühlhäusler (eds), *The Ecolinguistics Reader: Language, Ecology, and Environment*, 203–25, London: Continuum.

Goatly, A. (2007), *Washing the Brain – Metaphor and Hidden Ideology*, Amsterdam and Philadelphia: John Benjamins Publishing Company.

Goatly, A. (2017), 'The Poems of Edward Thomas: A Study in Ecostylistics', in J. Douthwaite, D. F. Virdis, and E. Zurru (eds), *The Stylistics of Landscapes, the Landscapes of Stylistics*, 95–122, Amsterdam and Philadelphia: John Benjamins Publishing Company.

Gregory, A. (2021), '"Eco-Anxiety": Fear of Environmental Doom Weighs on Young People', *The Guardian*. https://www.theguardian.com/society/2021/oct/06/eco-anxiety-fear-of-environmental-doom-weighs-on-young-people (accessed 6 December 2022).

Halliday, M. A. K. (2001 [1990]), 'New Ways of Meaning. The Challenge to Applied Linguistics', in A. Fill and P. Mühlhäusler (eds), *The Ecolinguistics Reader. Language, Ecology and Environment*, 175–202, London and New York: Continuum.

Hansen, A. (2011), 'Communication, Media and Environment: Towards Reconnecting Research on the Production, Content and Social Implications of Environmental Communication', *International Communication Gazette*, 73 (1–2): 7–25.

Hansen, A. (2018), 'Using Visual Images to Show Environmental Problems', in A. F. Fill and H. Penz (eds), *The Routledge Handbook of Ecolinguistics*, 179–95, London: Routledge.

Hansen, A. and D. Machin (2013), 'Editors' Introduction: Researching Visual Environmental Communication', *Environmental Communication*, 7 (2): 151–68.

Hendricks, R. K., Z. Demjén, E. Semino, and L. Boroditsky (2018), 'Emotional Implications of Metaphor: Consequences of Metaphor Framing for Mindset About Cancer', *Metaphor and Symbol*, 33 (4): 267–79.

Heyd, T. and C. Puschmann (2017), 'Hashtagging and Functional Shift: Adaptation and Appropriation of the #', *Journal of Pragmatics*, 116: 51–63.

Jeffries, L. (2010), *Critical Stylistics: The Power of English: Perspectives on the English Language*, Basingstoke: Palgrave Macmillan.

Kövecses, Z. (2010 [2002]), *Metaphor: A Practical Introduction*, Oxford: Oxford University Press.

Kövecses, Z. (2013), 'The Metaphor–Metonymy Relationship: Correlation Metaphors Are Based on Metonymy', *Metaphor and Symbol*, 28 (2): 75–88.
Kövecses, Z. (2020a), 'An Extended View of Conceptual Metaphor Theory', *Review of Cognitive Linguistics*, 18 (1): 112–30.
Kövecses, Z. (2020b), 'Visual Metaphor in Extended Conceptual Metaphor Theory', *Cognitive Linguistic Studies*, 7 (1): 13–30.
Kövecses, Z. (2021), 'Standard and Extended Conceptual Metaphor Theory', in X. Wen and J. R. Taylor (eds), *The Routledge Handbook Of Cognitive Linguistics*, 191–203, London and New York: Routledge.
Lakoff, G. and M. Johnson (2003 [1980]), *Metaphors We Live by*, Chicago: University of Chicago Press.
Lakoff, G. (2010), 'Why It Matters How We Frame the Environment', *Environmental Communication*, 4 (1): 70–81.
Landry, N., R. Gifford, T. L. Milfont, A. Weeks, and S. Arnocky (2018), 'Learned Helplessness Moderates the Relationship Between Environmental Concern and Behavior', *Journal of Environmental Psychology*, 55: 18–22.
Li, L. and M. Ye (2017), 'Greenspeak: A Corpus-Based Comparative Study on the Word Green and Environmentalism', *Linguistics and the Human Sciences*, 13 (3): 221–40.
Lynas, M., B. Z. Houlton, and S. Perry (2021), 'Greater than 99% Consensus on Human Caused Climate Change in the Peer-Reviewed Scientific Literature', *Environmental Research Letters*, 16: 114005. https://doi.org/10.1088/1748-9326/ac2966.
Mann, M. E. (2012), *The Hockey Stick and the Climate Wars: Dispatches from the Front Line*, New York: Columbia University Press.
Mann, M. E. (2021), *The New Climate War: The Fight to Take Back our Planet*, New York: PublicAffairs.
Mann, M. E., R. S. Bradley, and M. K. Hughes (1999), 'Northern Hemisphere Temperatures During the Past Millennium: Inferences, Uncertainties, and Limitations', *Geophysical Research Letters*, 26 (6): 627–810.
McFall-Johnsen, M. (2020), 'The 'Doomsday Clock' Has Jumped Closer to Midnight than Ever as Nuclear Weapons and Climate Disasters Turn the World into a "Pressure Cooker"'. https://www.businessinsider.com/doomsday-clock-moves-closer-to-midnight-than-ever-2020-1?IR=T (accessed 30 September 2020).
Meijers, M. H. C., P. Remmelswaal, and A. Wonneberger (2019), 'Using Visual Impact Metaphors to Stimulate Environmentally Friendly Behavior: The Roles of Response Efficacy and Evaluative Persuasion Knowledge', *Environmental Communication*, 13 (8): 995–1008.
Moss, J. H. and J. K. Maner (2014), 'The Clock Is Ticking. The Sound of a Ticking Clock Speeds Up Women's Attitudes on Reproductive Timing', *Human Nature*, 25: 328–41.
Moynihan, C. (2020), 'A New York Clock That Told Time Now Tells the Time Remaining', *The New York Times online*. https://www.nytimes.com/2020/09/20/arts/design/climate-clock-metronome-nyc.html (accessed 30 September 2020).

Mühlhäusler, P. (2022), 'Time and Ecolinguistics', *Printed Key-Note Lecture for the 6th International Conference on Ecolinguistics*, University of Graz, 21–24 September 2022.

Nerlich, B. and R. Jaspal (2012), 'Metaphors We Die By? Geoengineering, Metaphors, and the Argument from Catastrophe', *Metaphor and Symbol*, 27: 131–47.

O'Neill, S. and S. Nicholson-Cole (2009), '"Fear Won't Do It": Promoting Positive Engagement With Climate Change Through Visual and Iconic Representations', *Science Communication*, 30 (3): 355–79.

Penz, H. (2018), '"Global Warming" or "Climate Change"?', in A. Fill and H. Penz (eds), *The Routledge Handbook of Ecolinguistics*, 277–92, London and New York: Routledge.

Pérez Sobrino, P. (2013), 'Metaphor Use in Advertising: Analysis of the Interaction Between Multimodal Metaphor and Metonymy in a Greenwashing Advertisement', in E. Gola and F. Ervas (eds), *Metaphor in Focus. Philosophical Perspectives on Metaphor Use*, 67–82, Cambridge: Cambridge Scholars Publishing.

Pérez Sobrino, P. (2016), 'Shockvertising: Conceptual Interaction Patterns as Constraints on Advertising Creativity', *Círculo de Lingüística Aplicada a la Comunicación*, 65: 257–90.

Pérez Sobrino, P. (2017), *Multimodal Metaphor and Metonymy in Advertising*, Amsterdam and Philadelphia: John Benjamins Publishing Company.

Piltz, R. (2008), 'The Denial Machine', *Index on Censorship*, 37 (4): 72–81.

Polzenhagen, F., Z. Kövecses, S. Vogelbacher, and S. Kleinke, eds (2014), *Cognitive Explorations into Metaphor and Metonymy*, Frankfurt am Main: Peter Lang Pub Inc.

Simpson, P. (2005 [1993]), *Language, Ideology and Point of View*, London: Routledge.

Sinha, B. (2018), 'Water: The Clock Is Ticking'. https://www.downtoearth.org.in/blog/water/water-the-clock-is-ticking-61277 (accessed 15 September 2022).

Solnit, R. (2021), 'Big Oil Coined 'Carbon Footprints' to Blame Us for Their Greed. Keep Them on the Hook', *The Guardian*. https://www.theguardian.com/commentisfree/2021/aug/23/big-oil-coined-carbon-footprints-to-blame-us-for-their-greed-keep-them-on-the-hook (accessed 30 January 2022).

Steen, G. J., ed (2019), *Visual Metaphor. Structure and Process*, Amsterdam and Philadelphia: John Benjamins Publishing Company.

Steen, G. J., A. G. Dorst, J. B. Herrmann, A. A. Kaal, T. Krennmayr, and T. Pasma (2010), *A Method for Linguistic Metaphor Identification: From MIP to MIPVU*, Amsterdam & Philadelphia: John Benjamins Publishing Company.

Stibbe, A. (2018), 'Positive Discourse Analysis. Rethinking Human Ecological Relationships', in A. F. Fill and H. Penz (eds), *The Routledge Handbook of Ecolinguistics*, 165–78, London: Routledge.

Stibbe, A. (2021 [2015]), *Ecolinguistics: Language, Ecology and Stories We Live By*, New York and London: Routledge.

Tafirenyika, M. (2018), 'Cape Town Water Taps Running Dry', *Africa Renewal*. https://www.un.org/africarenewal/magazine/april-2018-july-2018/cape-town-water-taps-running-dry (accessed 15 September 2022).

Thibodeau, P. H., R. K. Hendricks, and L. Boroditsky (2017), 'How Linguistic Metaphor Scaffolds Reasoning', *Trends in Cognitive Sciences*, 21 (11): 852–63.

Thibodeau, P. H., C. McPherson Frantz, and M. Berretta (2017), 'The Earth Is Our Home: Systemic Metaphors to Redefine Our Relationship with Nature', *Climatic Change*, 142: 287–300.

van Dijk, T. (2008), *Discourse and Power*, Basingstoke: Palgrave MacMillan.

Virdis, D. F. (2022), *Ecological Stylistics: Ecostylistic Approaches to Discourses of Nature, the Environment and Sustainability*, Basingstoke: Palgrave MacMillan.

Welch, C. (2022), 'Earth Now Has 8 Billion People—And Counting. Where Do We Go from Here?', *National Geographic*. https://www.nationalgeographic.com/environment/article/the-world-now-has-8-billion-people (accessed 15 November 2022).

Yus, F. (2009), 'Visual Metaphor versus Verbal Metaphor: A Unified Account', in C. J. Forceville and E. Urios-Aparisi (eds), *Multimodal Metaphor*, 147–72, Berlin and New York: De Gruyter Mouton.

Zarin, C. (2015), 'The Artist Who Is Bringing Icebergs to Paris', *The New Yorker*. https://www.newyorker.com/culture/culture-desk/the-artist-who-is-bringing-icebergs-to-paris (accessed 11 November 2022).

Zurru, E. (2017), 'The Agency of *The Hungry Tide*: An Ecostylistic Analysis', in J. Douthwaite, D. F. Virdis, and E. Zurru (eds), *The Stylistics of Landscapes, the Landscapes of Stylistics*, 191–231, Amsterdam and Philadelphia: John Benjamins Publishing Company.

Zurru, E. (2022), 'Social Movements and Metaphor: The Case of #FridaysForFuture', in M. Prandi and M. Rossi (eds), *Researching Metaphors: Towards a Comprehensive Account*, 224–44, London and New York: Routledge.

Online references

https://twitter.com/fff_hamburg/status/1408417655053299714?s=20 (accessed 13 June 2022).

https://twitter.com/darioschramm/status/1175074583357136896 (accessed 13 June 2022).

https://twitter.com/ashtpmny/status/1554535227896258567?s=20&t=w8AEGPo8YWvidYHKbl_USQ (accessed 2 August 2022).

https://twitter.com/ClimateDad77/status/1561005902928412674 (accessed 20 August 2022).

https://twitter.com/elonmusk/status/1563020169160851456 (accessed 26 August 2022).

https://twitter.com/MattWalshBlog/status/1549713211188027394 (accessed 20 July 2022).

https://twitter.com/UN/status/1554995785141342208?s=20&t=w8AEGPo8YWvidYHKbl_USQ (accessed 4 August 2022).

https://www.dcceew.gov.au/environment/protection/ozone/montreal-protocol#:~:text=The%20Montreal%20Protocol%20on%20Substances,protect%20the%20earth's%20ozone%20layer (accessed 20 July 2022).

https://www.youtube.com/watch?v=m_NqyF9WQRk (accessed 4 August 2022).

https://climate.copernicus.eu/ (accessed 1 April 2022).

https://climateactiontracker.org/about/ (accessed 1 April 2022).

https://icewatchparis.com/ (accessed 4 August 2022).

https://climateclock.world/ (accessed 4 August 2022).

https://www.unep.org/explore-topics/climate-action/what-we-do/climate-action-note/state-of-climate.html?gclid=Cj0KCQjwyt-ZBhCNARIsAKH1177Za-ofsWWVspOhjJRjJX0a5RQbaTdOymYszhylNOzn7CGJq_-v6cMaAmfVEALw_wcB (accessed 13 June 2022).

https://climateactiontracker.org/global/temperatures/ (accessed 4 June 2022).

https://www.who.int/campaigns/world-health-day/2022 (accessed 1 April 2022).

https://sites.google.com/view/reframecovid/initiative (accessed 19 March 2023).

5

Unreliable Narratives and Social-Ecological Memory in Kara Walker's *A Subtlety*

Emilio Amideo

Following the ode 'Rule, Britannia!' – which was to become a famous patriotic song most resoundingly associated with the Royal Navy but also used by the British Army – the closing section of James Thomson's *Alfred: A Masque* (1740)[1] presents a strong celebration of British imperialism. An excerpt of the section, which particularly emphasizes the political and economic control of the British empire over its colonial territories scattered around the globe, reads:

> I see thy Commerce, *Britain*, grasp the world:
> All nations serve thee; every foreign flood
> Subjected, pays his tribute to the *Thames*.
> Thither the golden South obedient pours
> His sunny treasures: thither the soft East
> Her spices, delicacies, gentle gifts:
> And thither his rough trade the stormy North.
> See, where beyond the vast *Atlantic* surge,
> By boldest keels untouch'd, a dreadful space!
> Shores, yet unfound, arise! in youthful prime,
> With towering forests, mighty rivers crown'd!
>
> (Thomson [1740] 2007: 43)

The North, South, and East, as part of 'the empire on which the sun never sets', are represented as subjecting to and pouring their treasures (precious metals and gems, fruits, flowers, plants, and animals) in the form of 'gifts' onto the motherland, thus establishing the wilful subjection of the colonial territories and the mastering of tropical nature through the 'potential for agricultural productivity' as key concepts in the formation of British imperial identity (Tobin [2005] 2015: 310).

A few hundred years later, in a 2019 video produced by the Tate Modern for Kara Walker's installation *Fons Americanus*, the artist reflects on our unavoidable and ongoing implication with the history of imperialism and the slave trade. Pondering over how both interlacing systems have profoundly shaped not only our individual and collective lives – through their cultural, economic and power-related manifestations – but also the ecosystem that our lives depend on and on how this enmeshment is negotiated in her work, Walker affirms:

> I wondered how to return the *gift* of having come to be through the mechanics of finance, exploitation, murder, rape, death, ecological destruction, co-optation, coercion, love, seafaring feats, bravery, slavery, loss, injustice, excess, cruelty, tenacity, submission, and progress, conceived in the U.S. to live in this time and place, with this opportunity, this ability. (Walker in Tate 2019 [italics mine])

While best known for her cut-paper silhouettes (usually black figures against a white wall) used to confront the realities of history to reflect on the contemporary legacies of slavery, I believe that Walker's desire to return a 'gift' to Western history is particularly evident in two of her most recent monumental installations, namely *A Subtlety* (2014, USA) and *Fons Americanus* (2019, UK).[2]

If these large-scale sculptures appear to be at least partly inspired by a monumental and power-saturated Western grammar of visual representation (O'Toole 2011; see also Abasnnouga and Machin 2013), a closer look reveals the cracks in this idealized iconography in the form of an infinite amount of symbolic and material layers operating as a counter-discourse. Symbols reflecting on and reinscribing colonial history and its legacies abound in both installations with the most obvious examples being the use of sugar to coat the sculptures of *A Subtlety* and of water for the monumental fountain of *Fons Americanus*, recalling the plantation system for the production of sugar and the triangular slave trade across the Atlantic, respectively. Similarly, both Walker's use of recyclable materials for the installations and their subsequent dismantling reject the colonial logic of permanence and invasiveness that has largely affected the planet.

My aim in this chapter is therefore to reflect on an often overlooked aspect of Walker's work, namely the emergence of a social-ecological memory (Barthel, Folke and Colding 2010: 256) that, by recognizing the political imbrication of history, race, and gender with the environment (not only in terms of representation but also in terms of materiality), points to a different understanding of the human relationship with the 'con-vironment' (Fill 2001; this volume), that is, the environment that encompasses living and non-living beings. The chapter is divided into four sections: Section 5.1 introduces the impact that colonialism has had on the con-vironment and delineates the emergence of a social-ecological memory with a particular focus on the African American tradition; Section 5.2 discusses the theoretical approach which mainly draws on Multimodal Critical Discourse Analysis (MCDA) with a focus on sculptures and the language of displayed art; Section 5.3 contextualizes Kara Walker's *A Subtlety* and offers an analysis of the installation and the video performance *An Audience*; and, finally, Section 5.4 offers some concluding remarks highlighting the role of Walker's installation in raising awareness of the political imbrication of history, race, and gender with the environment.

5.1 The environmental impact of colonialism and the emergence of a social-ecological memory

Ever since humans have become a numerous species, they have largely affected the environment (White [1966] 2015: 39) often led, at least in Western history, by a conception of nature as something to exploit for their benefit. As Lynn White Jr explains, this conception can be mostly attributed to the victory of Christianity over Paganism and the technological development of European nations. The former not only separated humans and nature in dualistic terms but also 'insisted that it [was] God's will that man exploit nature for his proper ends' (43). Erasing the presence of the guardian spirits (or *genius loci*) of Paganism from the natural environment, Christianity thus established the right to 'exploit nature in a mood of indifference to the feelings of natural objects' (43). The technological superiority of the European nations by the end of the fifteenth century, on the other hand, enabled them to prepare to spread across the rest of the world to conquer, violate, steal, and colonize in the process (41).

Indeed, colonialism largely reshaped the con-vironment through the transplantation of people, animals, crops, and even pathogens (that contributed to the decimation of indigenous populations) between Europe, America, Asia, Africa, and Oceania.[3] The colonial infiltration in the new territories often caused the desertification of large forest areas which were cleared to make space for slave crops- mainly the monocultures of sugar and cotton (Nixon [2005] 2015) in the Caribbean, and Pacific, and the cotton, tea, and indigo estates of India (Tobin [2005] 2015: 316). The desertification of the once well-wooded Caribbean island of Antigua, for example, is the result of a process of deforestation meant to create space for sugar and cotton plantations. As a result of this colonial-induced drought, as Rob Nixon highlights, not only has Antigua lost its capacity to retain water and is therefore forced to import it but also has had to heavily rely on tourism for its economic sustenance ([2005] 2015: 202). This situation has produced a paradox which is sadly quite common in the Caribbean: a place scarred by the trauma of slavery and violence has become a sort of garden of Eden for European and North American tourists, thus paving the way to subtler forms of ongoing exploitation.

While the consumption of the newly acquired products derived from tropical crop plants (e.g. sugar, tea, and chocolate) started to profoundly shape British national identity (Tobin [2005] 2015: 316), a pseudoscientific discourse seeking to associate colonized people with animals and the natural world emerged as an attempt to justify forms of violence, domination, and exploitation (Amideo 2021b: 437–41). In fact, not only did colonial texts define people of African descent as constituting a hybrid life form between humans, animals, objects, and sometimes even plants (what Monique Allewaert calls 'parahuman'), but the tropical climes were believed to be responsible for irrationality and moral degeneracy in the populations living in the American tropics 'with symptoms including excessive passion, sensuousness, and indolence' (Allewaert 2013: 5). At the same time, as Allewaert suggests, the life on the plantation enabled the slaves to familiarize themselves with the properties of non-human and plant life, with the result that several diasporic religions developed by the slaves and the communities of fugitive slaves known as Maroons show traces of botanical medicine and healing (7) combining elements of African, Native American, and European cosmologies.

Similarly, often within the Black diasporic cultural tradition (especially in African American literature), nature emerges not as a *locus amoenus* but rather, to use Anissa Janine Wardi's words, as a 'politically charged racialized topography' in which natural sites, in their interrelation with Black bodies, embody history, trauma, and collective memory (2011: 12–13). Wardi traces this politically charged racialized topography in different natural sites imprinted with the history of slavery, racism, and violent practices, the African and American rivers that were used to transport slaves and which occasionally aided their flight to freedom, the wide Atlantic ocean with its triangular slave trade, the swamps as deathly sites where the Maroons would gather to organize rebellions, or the woods as secluded places where the lynching of Black people would later become a common practice. Considering that the association of wilderness and historical haunting is a constitutive part of this collective memory, the separation of nature from slavery and the legacy of colonialism seems thus profoundly unnatural.[4]

This is precisely what leads to the emergence of a 'social-ecological memory' (Barthel, Folke and Colding 2010: 256), that is, the way our social and historical awareness of past and present ecological crises informs our current behaviour towards the con-vironment. I will explore the way this social-ecological memory informs Walker's *A Subtlety* from ideation to material realization by drawing on MCDA with a particular focus on the application of Halliday's social semiotics model to the analysis of the visual arts.

5.2 MCDA of art installations

In his introduction to MCDA, David Machin (2013: 347) reminds us of the way discourses are communicated through several semiotic resources and how their reiteration across different genres is responsible for their naturalization across wide segments of society. In other words, political speeches, news, film, music, architecture, fashion, and so on are inevitably permeated and shaped by values, power relations and ideological implications which are not communicated by language alone but through a complex interaction of signs in a multimodal environment, that is to say in a context in which different semiotic resources, such as spoken and written language, still and moving images, gestures, sound, music, and so on, are co-deployed and contribute to the construction of meaning.

Since in every communicative event different semiotic resources or 'modes' of communication are co-deployed, multimodality is 'the normal state of human communication' (Kress 2010: 1). At the same time, the different semiotic resources have a distinctive potential for meaning – what are referred to as affordances (see, for instance, Kress 2011: 38) – that enables them to be more effective in certain communicative tasks rather than others, not least because they 'allow certain qualities to be glossed over and others communicated more specifically' (Machin 2013: 351). As van Leeuwen (1999: 190) explains, different semiotic resources have different metafunctional configurations which are neither universal nor a reflection of the nature of the medium but cultural, since they reflect their use and the values attached to them. So, for example, sculpture functions in a different way when compared to other forms of visual communication especially if we consider the fact that it makes us 'acutely and immediately aware of our *body*' (O'Toole 2011: 32). This is possible due to its size (e.g., we might feel dwarfed by massive forms or we might feel we dominate miniature ones); its three-dimensionality, which makes the reconstruction of the whole figure a physical as much as an intellectual exercise; and its 'numinous' quality originating from our bodily relation to it, not only in the way we can walk around it and feel that it is worth doing so but also through the fact that sculpture defines space itself (32–3) through its mass, palpability, plasticity, and hapticity. O'Toole writes:

> How tactile is the surface? This will depend on other qualities of the material used besides plasticity. How 'graspable' is it? This, no doubt, depends on size and on the nature of the object represented. How 'haptic' is it? Hapticity is different from palpability in that it engages our entire body in an identification with the mass and rhythms of the sculpture, not just our hands and fingers in the sense of touch. (35)

All these elements influence our physical, psychical, and emotional response to the object we encounter, even more so with (certain) sculpture(s) that are parts of monuments or of art installations and that usually symbolize rather than show, with symbolic choices in design being deeply political and ideological (Abasnnouga and Machin 2013: 4).

This is precisely when MCDA enters the picture since it concentrates on an investigation of both denotational and connotational meanings in discourse. In other words, it focuses both on the processes that contribute to the literal message and on the sociocultural and ideological values that it engenders (O'Halloran et al. 2011), the latter representing a 'second layer of semiotic meaning construction' (Kress and van Leeuwen 2021: 96). As Ledin and Machin (2017) explain, it is important to consider different semiotic resources as being tightly interwoven, co-articulated in communication and developing in inter-semiotic ways: '[b]reaking this into isolated modes risks compromising this idea. Semiotic resources must be conceived of in the first place as interdependent. They have affordances, possibilities and limitations and have inherent dependencies on each other' (64).

A critical analysis of their co-articulation reveals interesting insights into how the different elements making up a social practice (i.e., participants, ideas, values, activities, social relations, objects, time, place, causality, modality, etc.) are re-contextualized in a document, a narrative, an event, therefore purporting a specific representation of cultural or social processes based on buried ideologies (Ledin and Machin 2017: 64). Partly drawing on Michael Halliday's systemic functional linguistics (Halliday 1978; Halliday and Matthiessen 2004) and Kress and van Leeuwen's grammar of visual representation (2021), my analysis will investigate Walker's installation according to a combination of representational meanings (how people, objects, and events are represented), interactional meanings (the way whatever is represented relates to the viewer) and organizational meanings (the way whatever is represented forms a coherent whole and relates to its physical context). The co-articulation of these three levels will be analysed to reflect on the way Walker's work advances a social-ecological memory, with a particular focus on the exploration of the material used for the installations, and the iconographic apparatus and specific poses used (Ravelli 2006; O'Toole 2011; Abasnnouga and Machin 2013).

The critical reflection on the co-articulation of the different semiotic resources (i.e., sculpture, materials, videos, written and spoken language, etc.) employed in Walker's installation enables an investigation of how certain identities, actions and circumstances are either foregrounded or rendered less salient. A reflection on the resulting ideological and political implications can then shed some light on the strategies adopted to restore a social-ecological memory that raises awareness of environmental matters by encouraging the viewers to critically reflect on the impact of colonial and neocolonial practices on the con-vironment.

5.3 *A subtlety*

In a famous cultural studies essay discussing the Caribbean presence in England, and his own since the 1950s, Stuart Hall writes: 'I am the sugar in the bottom of the English cup of tea' ([1991] 1997: 48), thus reminding us of the deep colonial roots shaping British identity and of the way its formation was inextricably bound to the presence of an often-silenced 'other'. As a matter of fact, as Hall explains, the fact that the British par excellence practice of tea drinking is not accompanied by the presence of any tea or sugar plantation in the UK reveals historical connections with other territories and populations – in the Caribbean, Ceylon, Sri Lanka, India – linked to the UK through a violent and often under-represented history.

Walker's 2014 monumental installation *A Subtlety* was a clear example of this connection and of her attempt to return a 'gift' (that she carefully confected as we can read from the extended title) to the West. Commissioned by the arts organization Creative Time, *A Subtlety* was a monumental installation made of a giant sphinx-like creature (35 feet high, 25 feet wide, and 75 feet long) and fifteen smaller (5 feet tall) sculptures of basket-carrying boys modelled after collectable figurines with cherubic faces (see Figure 5.2). It was exhibited in the soon-to-be-demolished Domino Sugar Refinery in Brooklyn during the summer months of 2014.

The term 'subtlety', while working as a wordplay reflecting Walker's (not so) subtle 'gift', historically indicates edible sculptures mostly made of sugar mixed with oil, crushed nuts, and vegetable gums that originated in North Africa in the eleventh century and that spread to Europe where they used to be served to mark intervals between the different courses of a court banquet (Mintz 1986: 88; Abbott 2011: kindle location 336). Due to the preciousness of their ingredients, these 'soteltes' (subtleties) – which were made in the form of animals, objects, buildings, and so on – were meant to be admired and eaten by the royals, the nobles, the knights, and the church. Initially displayed for their beauty, they soon became infused with political undertones and most certainly became a symbol of power, even when in the sixteenth century they ceased to be the prerogative of royals and nobles and began to be within the reach of ambitious merchant families (Mintz 1986: 88–91).

Considering the representational meaning (Kress and van Leeuwen 2021; O'Toole 2011; Abousnnouga and Machin 2013) of the installation, the combination of sweetness and power through the concept of the subtlety is reflected by Walker in the highly sexualized features of the woman-sphinx. The sphynx encapsulates two main stereotypical representations of Black women in the West that can be traced back to the period of slavery: the promiscuous and hypersexual Jezebel – through the sexualized pose and nakedness – and Mammy, i.e., the nurturing nanny symbolized by the handkerchief over the head (West 2012; van den Bergh 2018; on Jezebel see also Lomax 2018). This way, reflecting on the interactional meaning, the viewer is invited to partake in the voyeuristic 'consumption' of the main figure of the installation – important in this sense is also the video performance *An Audience* which will be explored later – as a way of reminding of the impossibility of disentangling oneself from the legacy of a violent history of exploitation of both (Black) women and nature.[5]

The combination of the sexual aspect and the nurturing one is also present in the sphinx's hand gesture (Figures 5.1 and 5.2, left hand). Known as the 'fig sign', the gesture (consisting of a fist with the thumb thrust between the index and middle fingers) has acquired multiple meanings across time and cultures (dating from ancient Greece and Rome into the modern era in Southern Europe, the Mediterranean region, but also in North-western Europe, Latin America, etc.). It goes from being a rude sign similar to the verbal expression 'fuck you' (through a symbolic representation of the encounter between a penis and a vagina) to possessing magical properties as an emblem of fertility and protection against the evil eye. Among the various meanings, it also came to symbolize the acquisition of freedom by the slaves, especially in the context of the Candomblé religion of

Figure 5.1 Kara Walker, *A Subtlety, or the Marvelous Sugar Baby, an Homage to the unpaid and overworked Artisans who have refined our Sweet tastes from the cane fields to the Kitchens of the New World on the Occasion of the demolition of the Domino Sugar Refining Plant*, 2014. Polystyrene foam, sugar. Approx. 35.5 × 26 × 75.5 feet (10.8 × 7.9 × 23 meters). Installation view: Domino Sugar Refinery, A project of Creative Time, Brooklyn, NY, 2014. Photo: Jason Wyche. Artwork © Kara Walker, courtesy of Sikkema Jenkins & Co. and Sprüth Magers.

Brazil which originally developed among Afro-Brazilian communities amidst the Atlantic slave trade between the sixteenth and nineteenth centuries.

After the installation was disassembled – and both the installation and the Domino Factory were destroyed: as an 'emblem of some bygone 500-year era [that] must never be here again [that] can only live as a memory' (Walker 2017: [29:00]) – the sphinx's fig sign became part of the 2017 installation *Figa*, hosted on the Greek island of Hydra by the Deste Foundation Project Space.[6]

The demolition of both the sugar factory and the installation is highly symbolic, as is the choice of the materials used, all pointing to transience as opposed to the permanence typical of historical monuments, almost as if to suggest that the stories told have been partly erased from the historical archive thus leaving only traces and memories behind, while at the same time suggesting a different way of memorializing altogether: one that refuses to violently impose itself as the permanent and everlasting truth.[7] The final result of Walker's

Figure 5.2 Kara Walker, *A Subtlety, or the Marvelous Sugar Baby, an Homage to the unpaid and overworked Artisans who have refined our Sweet tastes from the cane fields to the Kitchens of the New World on the Occasion of the demolition of the Domino Sugar Refining Plant*, 2014. Installation view: Domino Sugar Refinery, A project of Creative Time, Brooklyn, NY, 2014. Photo: Jason Wyche. Artwork © Kara Walker, courtesy of Sikkema Jenkins & Co. and Sprüth Magers.

gesture seems to echo Toni Morrison's famously ambiguous sentence that she uses towards the end of her 1987 novel *Beloved*: 'This is not a story to pass on' (Morrison [1987] 2004: 324). The sentence encapsulates the double meaning of a story that is too unpleasant or painful to be passed on (as in being transmitted to future generations) and its opposite, that is, a story not to pass on, meaning not to ignore. Walker is able to play with this double meaning both through her decision to dismantle the installation and the use of the materials.

Considering the organizational meaning of the installation, the main woman-sphinx figure was made of polystyrene blocks coated with sugar, while the smaller figures (see Figure 5.2) were constructed through an assemblage of molasses and wire. As the days went by, the temperature of the factory in the summer months of the exhibition mixed with respiration and perspiration from the audience contributed to the decay of the installation, especially of the smaller figures that slowly turned into liquid pools:

> As the weeks went on, the sphinx shed layers of her sugary skin, and the sugar babies, bent, bled red-black blood, and then broke, losing lollipops and limbs that were dutifully gathered each night and placed into the baskets that those babies left standing humbly proffered out to the public the next weekend. Starting empty, the baskets thus gradually filled with the sticky, sickly detritus of their siblings' disintegration – reversing the usual disappearing act of racial capitalism – and literalizing a metaphor of 'refinement' accomplished through violence, maiming, and death. (Nyong'o 2019: 119–20)

As Tavia Nyong'o words emphasize, the deterioration of the sculptures – with the loss of limbs and the bleeding in the form of candies and molasses respectively (representing other metaphors for the 'consumption' of Black bodies) – materializes the violence inherent in the history of sugar production from the colonial period (when slaves' death and loss of limbs either through the use of pieces of machinery or as a result of punishments were a daily occurrence) up to more contemporary forms of exploitation of both child and forced labour (Poppenheimer 2019a).[8]

While the sculptures that are part of monuments tend to normalize and legitimize certain discourses (e.g., war monuments portray and celebrate certain values and ideals of masculinity and heroicness rather than the actual destruction or killing caused by the war; see Abasnnouga and Machin 2013: 2) thus portraying elements that pose no threat to the 'overall set of values dominated by nation, industry and capitalism' (3), Walker's installation follows a different logic. The artist poses herself as an 'unreliable narrator' in the sense that her visual and material narrativization does not follow the normativity of a necessarily selective historiographic account but enables the emergence of otherwise silenced narratives through a process of critical fabulation (Hartman 2008: 11–12).[9] In fact, Walker uses a range of resources for her work, mixing historical documents and personal experiences and drawing on nineteenth- and twentieth-century literary and visual cultures (Peabody 2016: 1). As Rebecca Peabody recognizes, her visual retellings raise several urgent questions:

> [W]hen is it appropriate to use fantasy to fill the empty spaces left by the historical erasure of real lives and experiences? What happens when historical fiction becomes 'truer' than historical fact? Why are some contemporary depictions of racialized, sexualized violence considered noncontroversial – even heroic – while others are deeply unsettling? What are the unstated but understood narrative structures that govern the 'appropriate' alignment of race with agency and desire? How is 'whiteness' constructed to be invisible in historical fiction? (5)

By mixing reality and fabulation, Walker's counter-discourse shows *while* symbolizing: together with several symbolic layers it makes the violence of history visible, even tangible, working by addition rather than subtraction and deletion as common historiographic accounts necessarily do.

The narrative offered by the installation is not static – literally not set in stone – but continually shifts as the representational meaning oozes into the interactional and organizational ones, forcing the audience to confront their perceptions and misconceptions of what they see and eventually touch, once they are left free to interact with the installation, as demonstrated by the video recording *An Audience* (see Figure 5.3).

The public is asked to contemplate the gigantic size of the woman-sphinx feeling dwarfed and in awe in its presence, while simultaneously engaging on an equal level with the sculpted boys that are slightly bigger than the natural scale, thus experiencing vulnerability and a sense of relationality, respectively. The monumentality and aloofness of the main figure of the installation are nevertheless disrupted both by the fact that the sphinx is exposed (literally, through its nakedness and potential to circle around it to view it from all angles) in an offer image[10] that disturbingly recalls the human exhibitions/circuses of the nineteenth century (the sphinx appears almost like a modern-day Saartjie Baartman)[11] and by the possibility of interacting with it by taking selfies and touching it. Towards the end of the trailer video of *An Audience* a guy embraces

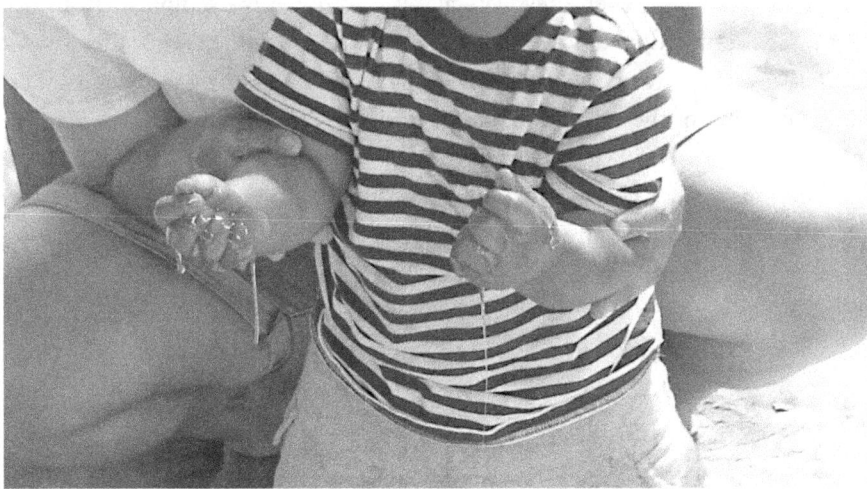

Figure 5.3 Kara Walker, still from *An Audience*, 2014. Digital video with sound, 27:18 minutes. Artwork © Kara Walker, courtesy of Sikkema Jenkins & Co. and Sprüth Magers.

the side of the sphinx and says 'I feel safe' somehow reflecting the cathartic effect of the representation of pain with the awareness of partaking in a collective experience of resilience and survival: naked and embodying stereotypes, the majestic Goddess-like sphinx stands still, seraphic, enduring, as a symbol of strength in unfavourable times.

The sense of vulnerability and transience is again emphasized by the material used (not only the organic sugar in the form of crystals or molasses) but also the polystyrene that, as opposed to solid and cold stone, invites proximity (Abasnnouga and Machin 2013: 45) and a sense of 'pliability or weakness' (49), not to mention that the use of plastics suggests something 'cheaper as a commodity' (135) – again recalling the idea of the expendability of both sugar and Black bodies. A similar discourse applies to the meaning potential of curvature characterizing the lines of the sphinx – something that suggests concepts like 'soft', 'emotional', 'nature', 'fluidity', 'organic', and even 'femininity' as opposed to the angularity that tends to be associated with 'harsh', 'technical', 'masculine', 'objectivity' (46) – something that again might recall the association and consequent common exploitation of women and nature in Western patriarchal discourses.

Between the overpowering smell of the molasses melting and dripping from the walls of the factory as described by some of the visitors and a sort of anticipation of the taste of sugar, the sensory experience of the public found its climax during the last hour of the last day of the exhibition when they were allowed to interact with the sculptures and with each other, especially during the last five minutes when they were allowed to touch the sculpture. Recorded in the above-mentioned video *An Audience* and together with the website *Digital Sugar Baby* which collected photos and videos taken by the visitors at the different stages of the exhibition, this experience remains the only trace of the installation, apart from individual memories and any article or brochure that has been written or produced about it.[12] *An Audience* remains an interesting experiment that records also much criticized behaviours, especially when people photographed themselves pinching the sphinx's rear or its breasts, or they stuck their tongues out close to its vulva. As Walker declared in an interview, such behaviour was to be expected and was meant to be part of the installation itself:

> I put a giant 10-foot vagina in the world and people respond to giant 10-foot vaginas in the way that they do. It's not unexpected. [. . .] Human behavior is so mucky and violent and messed-up and inappropriate. And I think my work draws on that. It comes from there. It comes from responding to situations like that, and it pulls it out of an audience. I've got a lot of video footage of that [behavior]. I was spying. (Walker in Miranda 2014)

As the tangible experience of the sensory interaction of the audience with the sculptures of *A Subtlety* is rendered intangible through its transposition onto another medium, we witness the openness of the installation (with its message and stories) to contamination, to the multiplication of meaning across different semiotic resources. The salvaging of the traces via recordings, or as in the case of *Figa*, by giving new life to pieces of the installation, reflects a process of recycling that in the case of Walker's installation is as metaphorical as it is factual (something that characterizes also, and perhaps to a greater extent, the installation *Fons Americanus*) and that is a manifestation of the social-ecological aspect of her most recent work.

5.4 Conclusions: Compos(t)ing history

As many critics and the public have noted, the use of a material like sugar, which is so entrenched in the history of slavery and contemporary exploitation, remains controversial. Carol Diehl (2014) traces the connection of Domino Sugar – which donated the 80 tons of sugar that were partly used for the installation – to the mega-corporation that owns the plantation Central Romana involved in allegations of forced and child labour, asking: 'I wonder how they feel about the ironic possibility that Walker's sculpture might have been enabled by slave labor', while for the same issue Tavia Nyong'o comments: 'what sort of bitter pill does this heaping spoonful of sugar help us swallow?' (2019: 119). Indeed, the production of sugar continues to have a deep impact on the environment (Poppenheimer 2019b) such as the alarming rate at which rainforests, grasslands, and wetlands are being destroyed to clear the space for those monocultural crops; the use of pesticides and fertilizers that harm numerous animal species while altering their natural habitat; and the massive use of water (e.g., as Linda Poppenheimer highlights, 1 kilogram of sugar necessitates the same amount of water that a person drinks in slightly more than two years!), so one could wonder about its use for an art installation. Yet, Walker's choice remains undoubtedly a powerful one, in the way it made us all aware of our complicity in the history of violence and of both human and natural exploitation that is part of sugar production and consumption. She did so by involving our very bodies and sensory apparatuses (at different levels of physical or virtual engagement) in that history: the voyeuristic spectacle of the vulnerability of Black women's bodies mixed with power and resilience, the anticipation of the taste of the sweetness of sugar, the tactile involvement with the viscous molasses or with the rough, crystal-like surface of the sphinx's body, up until the digital involvement through the photograph and video recording of the public's interaction with the installation while the artist remained there, as an invisible onlooker/voyeur: 'I was spying' (Walker in Miranda 2014). While controversial, Walker's choice remains true to her art, which does not 'sugar coat' (not unless it is in a material sense) the objects of her representation but remains truthful to the complexity and ambiguity of life itself.

While the sugar used for the installation could not be recycled *strictu sensu*, its decomposition (already started during the exhibition) contributed to its environmentally friendly disposal. Particular attention was also posed to the environmental impact of the disposal of the blocks of expanded polystyrene foam that constituted the main body of the sphinx (ICA 2014). This commitment to sustainability is also present in her later installation *Fons Americanus* which 'avoided the use of large quantities of non-recyclable materials and harmful substances' (Morris 2019: 28) favouring the use of cork and wood coated in jesmonite designed to be recyclable (apart from the necessary metal parts).

The attention to the environmental impact of her art – as expressed also in her way of reusing pieces of installations (as in the case of *Figa* featuring a piece from *A Subtlety*) and her focus on a different process of 'impermanent' (and as such less environmentally impactful) memorialization – points to a peculiar creative process that seems to be characteristic of Walker's work, especially her latest monumental installations. She seems to 'compost' (Hamilton and Neimanis 2018) history, in the sense that she uses the 'remains' (or 'ruins' as she would say) of history to create something new: a fertile ground for a critical reflection on social-ecological memory guiding future actions towards a more sustainable relationship between the human and the more-than-human world – one that recognizes the political imbrication of history, race, and gender with the environment, not only in terms of representation but also in its materiality.

While monuments tend to idealize and edulcorate (no pun intended) while portraying what society values and celebrates (Abasnnouga and Machin 2013: 2–3) for posterity,[13] Walker is not afraid of showing the rough edges, appearing controversial or making her audience feel uncomfortable even. Her monumental installations not only materialize the violence that traditional monuments and historical accounts in the West hide in plain sight but also compel us to face it and recognize our involvement in it. In her words: 'I don't think that my work is actually effectively dealing with history [. . .] I think of my work as subsumed by history or consumed by history' (Walker in Smith 2019: 47), and as Zadie Smith rightly points out: 'The difference between Walker and so many of us is that she knows' (Smith 2019: 47).

Notes

1. Co-written with David Mallet and set to music by Thomas Arne, *Alfred: A Masque* is a piece about the figure of Alfred the Great and was first performed at Cliveden House, South East England, in 1740.
2. Interestingly, the complete title of *A Subtlety* reads *At the behest of Creative Time Kara E. Walker has confected: A Subtlety or the Marvelous Sugar Baby, an Homage to the unpaid and overworked Artisans who have refined our Sweet tastes from the cane fields to the Kitchens of the New World on the Occasion of the demolition of the Domino Sugar Refining Plant*. The longer title recalls again the idea of making a 'gift' not only a metaphorical one to Western history in the way it forces it to confront its violent past but also to the lives of the unnamed and silenced histories of thousands of African people forcibly removed from their countries and compelled to work (and often die, due to overworking, malnutrition, and absence of medical care) in the American plantations. While I believe that both monumental installations reflect Walker's desire to return a 'gift' to the Western tradition and the emergence of a social-ecological memory in her work, for space constraints I will only focus on *A Subtlety* in this chapter anticipating an exploration of *Fons Americanus* in a forthcoming essay focusing on decolonizing the language of displayed art.
3. For a reflection on how colonialism and the slave trade created numerous contact zones that influenced cultural, political, culinary, and economic practices see, among others, Mintz (1986: xvi); Gabaccia (1998: 25); Spillers (2003: 50); Amideo (2021a).
4. See, among others, Melvin Dixon (1987) on the African American cultural tradition and Jamaica Kincaid (1988; 1994; 1999) on the Caribbean one.
5. For a reflection on the way both women and nature are objectified and devaluated through the dualistic representation of men/culture versus women/nature, which is the result of a patriarchal language system, see, among others, Berman (2001) and, more recently through an intersectional lens, Amideo (2021b).
6. For an image of the installation see https://deste.gr/hydra/kara-walker/.
7. While aware of the differences between an installation and a monument, my association here is mainly due to the 'monumental' aspect of *A Subtlety* both in terms of size and as a symbol ('a homage') acting as a reminder (however fleeting) of a specific event.
8. In a post on her website *Green Groundswell: Home of the Unlikely Environmentalist*, Linda Poppenheimer (2019a) reports: 'The U.S. Department of Labor estimates that as of 2018 there were 152 million child laborers and 25 million forced laborers being exploited worldwide. [. . .] Some of these children

and adults are forced to work in the sugar industry where they endure unsafe working conditions, toil for long hours with inadequate food, water, and rest, are not paid what they are owed, and may have been trafficked or are in debt bondage.'

9   By 'critical fabulation', Saidiya Hartman (2008) means a narrative/reconstructive process that consists of 'playing with and rearranging the basic elements of [a] story, by re-presenting the sequence of events in divergent stories and from contested points of view' in order to 'jeopardize the status of the event, to displace the received or authorized account, and to imagine what might have happened or might have been said or might have been done' (11). In other words, by mixing historical accounts and fictive reconstructions, a critical fabulation not only contests the transparency of sources showing how history is itself fiction but enables as well the emergence of otherwise silenced stories (erased from historical accounts because deemed unworthy) of disposable lives, especially the ones connected with the Atlantic slave trade.

10 It is an 'offer image' (Kress and van Leeuwen 2021) since there is no eye contact with the viewer (which would characterize a 'demand image') and so the represented participant is simply offered as an item of information for the viewer's scrutiny.

11 Saartjie Baartman was a Khoikhoi woman who was exhibited under the name of Hottentot Venus as a freak show attraction across Europe at the beginning of the nineteenth century. Baartman was exhibited for her steatopygic body type which was uncommon in Western Europe and was perceived both as a curiosity and, through the racist and pseudoscientific discourse of the time, as linked with moral degeneracy and hypersexuality.

12 The website *Digital Sugar Baby* can be accessed here: https://creativetime.org/karawalker/digital-sugar-baby.

13 As Abasnnouga and Machin (2013) explain, war monuments, for example, normalize and legitimize war by representing heroic and aestheticized male soldiers rather than portraying the reality of wars made of maiming, starvation, terror, pain, separated families, and so on (2). Similarly, in portraying what societies value and celebrate, they usually depict soldiers and capitalists, rather than humanitarian acts, unless these pose no threat to 'the overall set of values dominated by nation, industry and capitalism' (3).

References

Abasnnouga, G. and D. Machin (2013), *The Language of War Monuments*, London: Bloomsbury.

Abbott, E. (2011 [2008]), *Sugar: A Bittersweet History*, London: Duckworth Overlook (e-book).

Allewaert, M. (2013), *Ariel's Ecology: Plantations, Personhood, and Colonialism in the American Tropics*, Minneapolis: University of Minnesota Press.

Amideo, E. (2021a), 'Language, Memory, and Affect in Diasporic Food Discourse: Austin Clarke's Barbadian Culinary Memoir', *The Journal of Transcultural Studies*, 12 (1): 63–80.

Amideo, E. (2021b), 'Rethinking the Human: The Use of Animal Metaphors to Language the Utopianism of the Black Queer Existence', in R. Coronato, M. Parlati, and A. Petrina (eds), *Thinking Out of the Box in Literary and Cultural Studies: Proceedings of the XXIX AIA Conference*, 433–53, Padova: Padova University Press.

Barthel, S., C. Folke, and J. Colding (2010), 'Social-Ecological Memory in Urban Gardens – Retaining the Capacity for Management of Ecosystem Services', *Global Environmental Change*, 20: 255–65.

Berman, T. (2001), 'The Rape of Mother Nature? Women in the Language of Environmental Discourse', in A. Fill and P. Mühlhäusler (eds), *The Ecolinguistics Reader: Language, Ecology and Environment*, 258–69, London: Continuum.

Diehl, C. (2014), 'Dirty Sugar: Kara Walker's Dubious Alliance with Domino', *Carol Diehl's Art Vent: Letting the Fresh Air in*. Available online: https://artvent.blogspot.com/2014/06/dirty-sugar-kara-walkers-dubious.html (accessed 11 November 2022).

Dixon, M. (1987), *Ride Out the Wilderness: Geography and Identity in Afro-American Literature*, Champaign: University of Illinois Press.

Fill, A. (2001), 'Ecolinguistics: State of the Art 1998', in A. Fill and P. Mühlhäusler (eds), *The Ecolinguistics Reader: Language, Ecology and Environment*, 43–53, London: Continuum.

Gabaccia, D. R. (1998), *We Are What We Eat: Ethnic Food and the Making of Americans*, Cambridge: Harvard University Press.

Hall, S. (1997 [1991]), 'Old and New Identities, Old and New Ethnicities', in A. King (ed), *Culture, Globalization and the World System: Contemporary Conditions for the Representation of Identity*, 41–68, Minneapolis: University of Minnesota Press.

Halliday, M. A. K. (1978), *Language as Social Semiotics: The Social Interpretation of Language and Meaning*, London: Edward Arnold.

Halliday, M. A. K. and C. M. I. M. Matthiessen (2004), *An Introduction to Functional Grammar*, 3rd edn, revised by C. M. I. M Matthiessen, London: Hodder Arnold.

Hamilton, J. M. and A. Neimanis (2018), 'Composting Feminisms and Environmental Humanities', *Environmental Humanities*, 10 (2): 501–26.

Hartman, S. (2008), 'Venus in Two Acts', *Small Axe*, 12 (2): 1–14.

Insulation Corporation of America (ICA) (2014), 'EPS Foam and The Sugary Sphinx'. Available online: https://insulationcorp.com/kara-walker-eps-foam-sphinx/ (accessed 11 November 2022).

Kincaid, J. (1988), *A Small Place*, New York: Farrar, Strauss and Giroux.

Kincaid, J. (1994), 'Alien Soil', in T. Kidder (ed), *The Best American Essays*, 210–7, Boston: Houghton Mifflin.

Kincaid, J. (1999), *My Garden (Book)*, New York: Farrar, Strauss and Giroux.

Kress, G. (2010), *Multimodality: A Social Semiotic Approach to Contemporary Communication*, London: Routledge.

Kress, G. (2011), 'Multimodal Discourse Analysis', in J. P. Gee and M. Handford (eds), *The Routledge Handbook of Discourse Analysis*, 35–50, London: Routledge.

Kress, G. and T. van Leeuwen (2021), *Reading Images: The Grammar of Visual Design*, 3rd edn, London: Routledge.

Ledin, P. and D. Machin (2017), 'Multi-Modal Critical Discourse Analysis', in J. Flowerdew and J. E. Richardson (eds), *The Routledge Handbook of Critical Discourse Studies*, 60–76, London: Routledge.

Lomax, T. (2018), *Jezebel Unhinged: Loosing the Black Female Body in Religion and Culture*, Durham: Duke University Press.

Machin, D. (2013), 'What Is Multimodal Critical Discourse Studies?', *Critical Discourse Studies*, 10 (4): 347–55.

Mintz, S. (1986), *Sweetness and Power: The Place of Sugar in Modern History*, New York: Viking-Penguin.

Miranda, C. A. (2014), 'Q&A: Kara Walker on the Bit of Sugar Baby She Saved, Video She's Making', *Los Angeles Time*, 13 October. Available online: https://www.latimes.com/entertainment/arts/miranda/la-et-cam-kara-walker-on-her-sugar-sphinx-the-piece-she-saved-video-shes-making-20141013-column.html (accessed 11 November 2022).

Morris, F. (2019), 'Foreword', in *Kara Walker: Fons Americanus*, The curator of the catalogue is Clara Kim, 27–9, London: Tate Publishing.

Morrison, T. (2004 [1987]), *Beloved*, London: Vintage.

Nixon, R. (2015 [2005]), 'Environmentalism and Postcolonialism', in K. Hiltner (ed), *Ecocriticism: The Essential Reader*, 196–210, London: Routledge.

Nyong'o, T. (2019), *Afro-Fabulations: The Queer Drama of Black Life*, New York: New York University Press.

O'Halloran, K. L., S. Tan, B. A. Smith, and A. Podlasov (2011), 'Multimodal Analysis Within an Interactive Software Environment: Critical Discourse Perspectives', *Critical Discourse Studies*, 8: 109–25.

O'Toole, M. (2011), *The Language of Displayed Art*, 2nd edn, London: Routledge.

Peabody, R. (2016), *Consuming Stories: Kara Walker and the Imagining of American Race*, Oakland: University of California Press.

Poppenheimer, L. (2019a), 'Health and Social Consequences of Sugar: Where Do We Go from Here?', *Green Groundswell: Home of the Unlikely Environmentalist*. Available online: https://greengroundswell.com/health-and-social-consequences-of-sugar/2019/07/29/ (accessed 11 November 2022).

Poppenheimer, L. (2019b), 'Environmental Impact of Sugar: What Is Our Sweet Tooth Costing the Planet?', *Green Groundswell: Home of the Unlikely Environmentalist*. Available online: https://greengroundswell.com/environmental-impact-of-sugar/2019/07/22/ (accessed 11 November 2022).

Ravelli, L. (2006), *Museum Texts: Communication Frameworks*, London: Routledge.

Smith, Z. (2019), 'Kara Walker: What Do We Want History to Do to Us?', in *Kara Walker: Fons Americanus*, The curator of the catalogue is Clara Kim, 32–53, London: Tate Publishing.

Spillers, H. (2003), 'Introduction. Peter's Pans: Eating in the Diaspora', in *Black, White, and in Color: Essays on American Literature and Culture*, 1–64, Chicago: The University of Chicago Press.

Tate (2019), 'Look Closer: Kara Walker's *Fons Americanus*. Delve Deeper into 2019's Hyundai Commission by Kara Walker'. Available online: https://www.tate.org.uk/art/artists/kara-walker-2674/kara-walkers-fons-americanus (accessed 11 November 2022).

Thomson, J. (2007 [1740]), *Alfred: A Masque. Represented before Their Royal Highnesses the Prince and Princess of Wales, at Cliffden*, on the First of August, 1740. Available online: https://ota.bodleian.ox.ac.uk/repository/xmlui/bitstream/handle/20.500.12024/K030406.000/K030406.000.html (accessed 11 November 2022).

Tobin, B. (2015 [2005]), 'Troping the Tropics and Aestheticizing Labor', in K. Hiltner (ed), *Ecocriticism: The Essential Reader*, 310–21, London: Routledge.

van den Bergh, L. A. (2018), 'Exhibitions of the Stereotype in Kara Walker's *A Subtlety*', *Journal of Cultural Analysis and Social Change*, 3.2, Article n. 08: 1–11. https://doi.org/10.20897/jcasc/3989.

van Leeuwen, T. (1999), *Speech, Music, Sound*, London: Macmillan.

Walker, K. (2017), 'FIGA on "Epohi ton Ikonon", interview with Kara Walker, DESTE Foundation for Contemporary Art'. Available online: https://deste.gr/hydra/kara-walker (accessed 11 November 2022).

Wardi, A. J. (2011), *Water and African American Memory: An Ecocritical Perspective*, Gainesville: University Press of Florida.

West, C. M. (2012), 'Mammy, Jezebel, Sapphire, and Their Homegirls: Developing an "Oppositional Gaze" Toward the Images of Black Women', in J. C. Chrisler, C. Golden, and P. D. Rozee (eds), *Lectures on the Psychology of Women*, 4th edn, 286–99, Long Grove: Waveland Press.

White, Jr. L. (2015 [1966]), 'The Historical Roots of Our Ecologic Crisis', in K. Hiltner (ed), *Ecocriticism: The Essential Reader*, 39–46, London: Routledge.

6

(Un)welcome Waters for Multispecies Hospitality in the Anthropocene

Gavin Lamb

Introduction

In this chapter[1] I explore the fraught human relations taking shape with threatened pinnipeds (walruses and seals) in the Anthropocene. As a powerful environmental discourse, the Anthropocene depicts human beings as a collective species increasingly interwoven with the Earth's landscapes and seascapes in both potentially beneficial and damaging ways. At the same time, through an anthropocentric logic of appropriation through destruction, collective human transformation of environmental places and processes is viewed as 'authorizing' ever greater management and control of the Earth, albeit with conservationists embracing radically competing visions for what ethical human-wildlife relationships should look like now and in the future. 'Welcome to the Anthropocene', as one famous headline in *The Economist* (2011) glibly captured this new human era, reveals how new modes of global environmental management often work through a discourse of hospitality, placing (some) humans in a position to decide who (human and non-human) is welcome and who is not. Drawing on a body of work in multispecies studies exploring human-wildlife entanglements through the lens of 'hospitality' in the Anthropocene (Van Dooren 2016), this chapter compares how a discourse of hospitality is enlisted across various news and social media channels to make sense of human relations with threatened pinnipeds. In particular, I offer a comparative analysis of media discourse around two human-pinniped encounters that generated wide media coverage and public debate during the summer months of July and August of 2022: when Rocky the Hawaiian monk seal attacked a tourist swimming in the nearshore waters of Honolulu, Hawai'i, and Freya, an Atlantic walrus, was killed by wildlife management officials in Oslo harbour. I explore how these human-pinniped interactions were communicated through the language of hospitality, with certain beings positioned as welcoming 'hosts' and other beings treated as (un)welcomed 'guests'. In doing so, I suggest some conceptual and analytic directions for scholars in ecolinguistics to investigate how a discourse of hospitality increasingly mediates human entanglements with wildlife in the Anthropocene.

6.1 Hospitality in the Anthropocene

In this chapter, I build on an emerging body of work in multispecies studies that draws on Derrida's (2005) discussion of the paradoxes of hospitality to investigate how people are learning, or not, to share the world with wildlife in the Anthropocene (van Dooren 2016). On the one hand, Derrida explores 'unconditional hospitality' in which

> you don't ask the other, the newcomer, the guest, to give anything back, or even to identify himself or herself. Even if the other deprives you of your mastery or your home, you have to accept this. It is terrible to accept this, but that is the condition of unconditional hospitality: that you give up the mastery of your space, your home, your nation. (Derrida 1998: 70, cited in Candea 2012: 38)

At the same time, the very act of welcoming another unconditionally in this way is only possible if one assumes a prior ownership and control over a place to welcome others to. Recognizing this paradox, to achieve unconditional hospitality becomes impossible, since one would have to abdicate the status of the host, annihilating the possibility to ever be in a position to welcome others now or in the future. For Derrida, then, only by carefully working through this paradox of hospitality by threading a path through the violent extremes of xenophobia, on one end, and the 'self-annihilating openness' of unconditional hospitality, on the other, can we hope to find more democratic, just and sustainable modes of living together in a time of immense and interwoven social and ecological challenges.

Building on Derrida's discussion of hospitality, research in the interdisciplinary field of animal studies has pointed to a discourse of 'non-hospitality' that increasingly mediates public discourse about human relations with animals. This work shows how human relations with animals are often expressed through 'unconditional non-hospitality' that objectifies and de-individualizes non-human beings (Lawlor 2007). This dominant mode of non-hospitality is rooted in a Western tradition of human exceptionalism, involving a strategic denial of human interrelatedness with other earthly beings and processes, enabling a pre-emptive refusal to ever be called into alternative forms of mutual coexistence since these would be relationships that threaten human exceptionalism, requiring a willing loss of control and embrace of uncertainty. In contrast, hospitality, according to Derrida, embraces this future-oriented uncertainty (Oliver 2009), opening us to ethical bonds with other beings and their diverse lifeways that we cannot anticipate in advance of the encounter. 'What we call hospitality,' writes Derrida (2000: 11), 'maintains an essential relation with the opening of what is called to come [à venir]. When we say that "We do not yet know what hospitality is," we also imply that we do not yet know who or what will come' (cited in Van Dooren 2019: 232).

In picking up these various lines of thinking about hospitality, multispecies scholar Thom van Dooren (2016) notes that while the notion of hospitality and the figures of the host/guest have been prominent in research on human-animal relations, less explored is Derrida's emphasis on the territorial underpinnings of hospitality. As van Dooren explains,

> to welcome is itself sometimes an act of appropriation, while in other contexts one is simply able to welcome because of a prior, more or less violent, appropriation (although perhaps these two moments are never so neatly divided . . .) *whether we actively welcome or exclude, to assume the power to do so is to appropriate to oneself a place*, it is to claim the right to decide who comes and who goes. (van Dooren 2016: 197, emphasis in original)

Beings deemed 'invasive species' are the prototypical unwelcome guest: uninvited trespassers whose presence impinges on valued natures. This has been the case with a small community of house crows in Hoek van Holland, as van Dooren explores. While small in number, for wildlife management officials the house crow represents a threat to the 'natural balance' of the city's ecology that must be defended: 'Dutch authorities imagined a future overrun by crows and they said "you are not welcome".' Yet, what if instead 'the presence of crows might have become an invitation to some other, some more demanding, form of responsibility for our changing world' (van Dooren 2016: 198). In the following sections, I take up these concerns with hospitality in the Anthropocene to ask how the presence of a rather different pair of threatened species – the Hawaiian monk seal and the Atlantic walrus – is inviting people to envisage new, more demanding forms of responsibility, curiosity and care in a changing and shared world.

6.2 Background and discourse analysis

This chapter examines and brings into comparative analysis two widely mediatized events in July and August 2022 involving two very different but problematic human interactions with pinnipeds on opposite sides of the planet: (1) when Rocky the Hawaiian monk seal attacked a tourist swimming near her and her pup on 25 July 2022 in Honolulu, Hawai'i, and (2) the killing of Freya by the Norwegian Fisheries Directorate on 14 August 2022, in Oslo, Norway. Drawing on two small, specialized English- and Norwegian-language corpora of media discourse of these events, I explore how (in)hospitality emerged as an object of contention and debate before, during and after these events. I selected these two events of interspecies encounter for discourse analysis, in part because of my own experience living in and familiarity with human-pinniped relations in Hawai'i and Norway. I have researched problematic human relations with endangered species in Hawai'i for several years and have had multiple opportunities to observe Rocky as she slept at different beaches in Hawai'i, most recently in 2017 when she weaned her tenth pup at Kaimana Beach in Waikīkī. In the summer of 2022, I was living in Oslo, Norway, and followed news about Freya the walrus closely as well as the controversy surrounding the decision by wildlife officials to euthanize her on 14 August 2022.

The data from the study consists of a relatively small, specialized corpus I created consisting of newspaper articles, transcribed news broadcasts, government press releases, opinion essays and social media posts from Facebook and Twitter that were cited in these news articles as part of the reporting on the events leading up to, during and after the two focal events mentioned earlier. In building these specialized event-based corpora, I sought to capture the crescendo and subsequent dissipation of news media about these two events over the course of several months from June 2022 to January 2023 (see Table 6.1). I used Sketch Engine (Kilgariff et al. 2014) as a corpus-building tool to facilitate the collection, organization and querying of concordance lines in the two corpora for lemmas containing both 'monk seal' (154 tokens) and 'Rocky' (102 tokens) in the REC corpus and 'hvalross' (walrus) (180 tokens) and 'Freya' (301 tokens) in the FNC corpus. The analytic aim was to identify which social actors/institutions invoked Rocky and Freya as a matter of concern and how these actors enlisted certain discourses (see later in the text) to construe human action taken in relation to the monk seal and walrus in question.

Methodologically, the chapter explores how ecolinguists can fruitfully examine a relatively small corpus or set of corpora through the construction and analysis of news media corpora of wildlife controversies. As 'generative events' (Whatmore 2009), wildlife controversies disrupt the taken-for-granted social fabric of human-wildlife interaction, thrusting new ethical possibilities for multispecies relationships into public scrutiny and debate. This approach draws inspiration in part from Poole's (2022: chapter 5) analysis of animal representations in the media to illustrate the value of using relatively small, specialized corpora to examine 'salient discursive spaces of ecolinguistic interest which may not be represented by copious data but which nevertheless may be fruitfully analyzed with CADS [Corpus-Assisted Discourse Studies] techniques' (2022: 111). However, this study diverges from – but seeks to compliment – CADS approaches in ecolinguistics theoretically grounded in corpus linguistics, instead using specialized corpora to address overlapping methodological concerns in nexus analysis and Actor-Network Theory with mapping the discourse-action links composing environmental controversies (Scollon 2012; Venturini and Munk 2021). The notion of *controversy mapping* refers to how knowledge claims *about the world* (or discourses) are always connected to arguments for taking action *in the world*, revealing how discourses primarily serve in public controversies as *reasons* for taking collective action to realize certain future worlds and not others. In other words, this approach seeks to trace not only *what* discourses come to dominate in a given wildlife controversy but also *how* key social actors (and actor-networks) enlist such discourse(s) in their arguments, both to advance particular courses of action and to position themselves and others in relation to 'competing philosophies of nature' (Thompson 2002). Table 6.1 provides an overview of the media sources this study draws on that were compiled in the two pinniped corpora. The 'Rocky' English-language corpus (REC) consists of 14,018 words, and the 'Freya' Norwegian-language corpus (FNC) consists of 19,444 words (see Table 6.1):

In examining two highly mediatized public debates involving controversial human-pinniped interactions that occurred over the course of several months in Hawai'i and Norway in the summer of 2022, in the later sections I explore how the prominent social actors in these debates advanced or challenged certain proposals for enacting relationships of (in)hospitality with Rocky the monk seal and Freya the walrus. In tracing how different actors mobilized a discourse of hospitality in these public debates to shape these human-pinniped interactions, I argue for the importance of attending to the *anticipatory* (future-oriented) and *retrospective* (past-oriented) discursive tactics (de Saint-George 2013) social

Table 6.1 Media sources contained in the two pinniped corpora

Rocky EnglishLanguage Corpus (REC) (22 July 2022–25 August 2022) 14,018 words	Freya Norwegian-Language Corpus (FNC) (22 June 2022–13 January 2023) 19,444 words
ABC News (abcnews.go.com)	Aftenposten (www.aftenposten.no)
Daily Mail (www.dailymail.co.uk)	Agderposten (www.agderposten.no)
DLNR Blog (dinr.hawaii.gov)	Bergens Tidene (www.bt.no)
Hawaii News Now (www.hawaiinewsnow.com)	Dagavisen (www.dagsavisen.no)
Honolulu Civil Beat (www.civilbeat.org)	Dagbladet (www.dagbladet.no)
Honolulu Star Advertiser (www.staradvertiser.com)	Faktisk (www.faktisk.no)
KHON2 News (www.khon2.com)	Fiskeridirektoratet (www.fiskeridir.no)
KITV 4 Island news (www.kitv.com)	NRK (www.nrk.no)
New York Post (nypost.com)	TV2 (www.tv2.no)
NOAA Blog (pifscblog.wordpress.com))	Varden (www.varden.no)
Spectrum Local News (spectrumlocalnews.com/hi/Hawaii)	VG (www.vg.no)

Excerpts above are referenced with both the corpora followed by the news source they are extracted from (e.g. REC-ABC).

actors use to facilitate or hinder, challenge or justify competing visions for multispecies communities in the Anthropocene.

6.3 Data analysis

Freya the walrus

In the fall of 2021, an Atlantic walrus began descending south from her home in the Arctic, likely the Norwegian island of Svalbard where a population of around 30,000 walruses make their home. The Norwegian Biodiversity Information Centre has categorized this walrus population as 'vulnerable', meaning 'a high risk of collapse for the ecosystem type in Norway'. Arctic ice melt due to climate change, along with increasing oil exploration, and noise pollution from human activity (e.g. planes, ships and sonar) threatens the future of these walruses. On 21 October, a walrus hauled out onto a stationed submarine in the Netherlands, the first time a walrus had been seen in the country in over twenty years, biologists said. She was about five years old and 600 kilos of concentrated ocean energy. Freya, as the walrus soon came to be known, then embarked on a tour of northern Europe, visiting Germany, the UK, Denmark, Sweden and finally Norway, making her way up the Oslofjord right into the heart of urban Oslo. 'Walruses are coastline embodied', writes environmental historian Bathsheba Demuth (2019: 75). 'They cannot eat without the sea, feeding a hundred or more feet underwater, where they root beds of clams and benthic worms from the mud. But they must breed and birth in the air.' They also enjoy sleeping in the air too, especially on small, expensive boats, as it turns out.

Rune Aae, a Norwegian biologist, created a Google Map to track Freya's movements, and each time the walrus was sighted at different places along the Oslofjord, news of her presence circulated and people would flock to catch a glimpse of the famous walrus. 'Big story in Norway this summer is a walrus we've named Freya has made it to our shores and is touring the country, laying around and sinking boats', said a viral tweet posted on 19 July 2022.[2] Now a media sensation, Freya was also causing concern for the Norwegian Fisheries Directorate (in Norwegian: Fiskeridirektoratet), the agency tasked with managing marine wildlife and enforcing conservation laws for threatened species like the Atlantic walrus: we aim 'at maximizing the long term sustainable yield of the living marine resources and at the same time protecting biodiversity and the functioning of ecosystems', says their English-language website.[3] But when a walrus showed up in Oslo during the busy summer vacation season, the agency found itself also tasked with managing the large crowds gathering around Freya. Towards the end of July, the agency posted a statement on its website: 'euthanasia is out of the question'[4] (FNC-Fiskeridirektoratet) due to the species protected status. However, as crowds continued to gather, with some close encounters with the walrus in the water, and reports that onlookers had even thrown rocks at her, the Fisheries overt discourse about Freya began to shift.

The statements made by the Norwegian Fisheries prior to their decision to kill Freya reveal a steady amplification of an *anticipatory discourse* (de Saint-George 2012). By invoking a future imaginary of Freya endangering people's safety, coupled with claims that people were also endangering Freya's own welfare, and therefore the capacity for the agency to secure Freya's well-being, the agency argued that euthanizing the walrus could be necessary to secure the well-being of both people and the walrus. Not killing Freya, according to the Fisheries, depended on whether a curious public could keep a safe distance. As de Saint-George argues, anticipatory discourses involve two categories of stance-taking towards the future: *epistemic stances* claiming more or less knowledge about what will happen in the future (with statements ranging on a spectrum from agnostic or oracular) and *agentive stances* claiming more or less power to affect the future (on a spectrum from fatalistic to agentive). In practice, social actors' agentive and epistemic stances about the future are both tactfully interwoven and interactionally oriented in efforts to construe how much (or little) control one has over future events and therefore how much (or little) one should be held responsible for what could happen. For example, in the case of the Fisheries Directorate's official statements on their website leading up to their killing of Freya, we can see a steady shift in epistemic stance over several weeks from oracular to agnostic ('euthanasia is out of the question' → 'If the animal has to be euthanised, this is our responsibility') (FNC-Fiskeridirektoratet). Through this incremental epistemic shift from certainty to uncertainty, as I discuss in more detail later, the Fisheries prepared the ground for a future world in which their (agentive) responsibility to kill Freya is a result of the public's (fatalistic) irresponsibility in refusing to keep a distance from her. Analysis of anticipatory discourse, as de Saint-George (2012) further notes, 'also includes consideration of who gets to be the primary definer of the future, how it gets to be defined, and what power relations are involved in this definition' (2). Along these lines, defining the future also enables the definer to take certain interactional 'footings' (Goffman 1981) in discourse that distribute responsibility for courses of action: the more control one can be said to have for *authoring* and *animating* an action, the more one, as the *principal* of an action, can be praised or blamed for its realization and consequences. In this case, for the Norwegian Fisheries Directorate, their (agentive) killing of Freya would be an unfortunate but necessary consequence of the public's (fatalistic) irresponsibility. As Freya approached ever closer to Oslo at the end of July 2022, the Directorate of Fisheries began issuing statements warning the public that 'If people keep a good distance [*god avstand*] from Freya the walrus, dangerous situations will not arise ... A walrus needs 18–20 hours of rest a day. When it is disturbed by humans and does not get the rest it needs, it may feel threatened and attack. Nearby people can provoke dangerous situations' (FNC-Fiskeridirektoratet).

During this time, Rune Aae, a biologist and research fellow at the University of South-Eastern Norway, had been following Freya's international travels for over a year. Every time the famous walrus popped up in a new location to lounge on boats, piers and even a submarine, Aae pinned her location along with all the social media and news stories covering her visit on a public Google Map so that others could follow her journey. As Freya approached ever closer to Oslo at the end of July, another anticipatory discourse was circulating in news media, expressed in particular by Per Espen Fjeld, a senior adviser to the Norwegian

Environmental Agency which conserves and manages wildlife populations on land. In an opinion piece entitled 'Shoot Freya!'[5] published on the NRK (Norwegian Broadcasting Corporation) on 27 July 2022, Fjeld argued that while threatened marine animals like Freya are normally protected, the public had fallen under the spell of a 'pure Bambi effect' [ren Bambi-effekt] (FNC-NRK) that mistakenly imagined care for an individual animal as care for the species. In his op-ed, Fjeld writes:

> As a biologist and nature lover, it becomes almost parodic to see how much emotion and concern we manage to mobilise around a single individual, which strictly speaking doesn't have the slightest importance for the future of the species. Why are we not as concerned that climate change could destroy the habitat of hundreds of thousands of arctic animals within a few years? . . . If we really care about the walrus we should look to the north, where thousands of Freya's relatives live. The sea ice they live on is melting away due to climate change. Dozens of oil-platform leases are to be allocated near the ice edge, close to the walruses' vulnerable home. It is a gigantic paradox that these challenges receive hardly any attention, while a solitary walrus is protected as if it means everything. Unfortunately, not all walruses have their own name. (author's translation)

There is a lot that could be unpacked here in Fjeld's statement, but I will briefly point to three key concerns relevant to the discourse of hospitality I examine in this chapter. First, this statement expresses a well-rehearsed tension between discourses of conservation science's concern with caring for a species versus animal welfare advocates' concern with caring for the well-being of individual animals. Second, in claiming that 'Not all walruses have their own name', Fjeld's framing positions conservation science as rational care, while naming an animal, in this case 'Freya', indicates an irrational form of anthropomorphic care, valuing the individual at the expense of caring about issues that negatively impact the species as a whole (e.g. 'climate change' and 'oil leases'). Last, Freya has a natural home ('a habitat'), and thus Oslo is framed as an unnatural home for a walrus. A rational multispecies hospitality means clear boundaries between spaces for humans and spaces for wildlife: when straying from her natural habitat, Freya becomes not only an unwelcome guest but also a trespasser in Oslo, just as humans are in her arctic home in 'the north'. For Fjeld, recognizing these boundaries of hospitality is the correct application of human care for walruses. In sum, a discourse of natural hospitality enables social actors to invoke 'hierarchies of care' which bind 'correct' modes of caring for wildlife with expert articulations of *knowing* wildlife in the right way (Giraud 2019).

'She's having a splendid time on her holiday down here', said biologist Rune Aae in an interview with *The New York Times* (NYT) on 12 August. 'She's not afraid of us. Maybe she thinks we're her flock.'[6] And then, in the early morning hours of Sunday, 14 August, Freya was shot and killed by the Fisheries Directorate. A few days later, another NYT article[7] appeared on 19 August describing how Freya was 'assassinated' with 'mob-like efficiency': 'when night fell, and Freya was left alone, the Fishery professionals got to work. They executed Freya with what their boss, Frank Bakke-Jensen, a former Norwegian defence minister, later called "bullets that suit this mission"', wrote the NYT journalist Jason Horowitz. 'They covered her body in a tarp, cut the ropes of the boat, and towed away their victim, returning the vessel the next day, empty and cleaned, without a trace.' Freya's killing provoked wide controversy and 'divided Norwegians' according to Horowitz's 19 August report in the NYT. Conservation organizations, animal welfare groups, academics and even famous wildlife presenters called into question the rationale behind the Norwegian Fisheries' decision to kill Freya. Some scientists and academics turned to Twitter to voice their anger and frustration at the decision. For example, in a Twitter thread,[8] animal studies scholar Jeff Sebo compared Freya to an unwelcome climate refugee:

> The world is rightly condemning the killing of Freya. Freya was a climate refugee, and humans killed her rather than welcoming her into their community . . . when human and nonhuman interests conflict and violence *is* the only option available, this lack of options is often our fault . . . It will be a long time before we know how to build multispecies communities that can be accommodating for humans and nonhumans alike. But when human activity is changing the world, we have a responsibility to try.

Frank Bakke-Jensen, the Norwegian Fisheries director who made the decision to 'euthanize' Freya, argued that Freya was becoming dangerously habituated to people, and that the public was not obeying warnings to keep a safe distance from the animal. On 14 August, he issued a statement on the Fisheries governmental website: 'Through on-site observations the past week it was made clear that the public has disregarded the current recommendation to keep a clear distance to the walrus. Therefore, the Directorate has concluded, the possibility for potential harm to people was high and animal welfare was not being maintained' (FNC-Fiskeridirektoratet). Recognizing the flood of confusion and anger the killing of Freya was generating both in Norwegian and international media, Bakke-Jensen added: 'We have sympathies for the fact that the decision can cause reactions with the public, but I am firm that this was the right call. We have great regard for animal welfare, but human life and safety must take precedence' (FNC-Fiskeridirektoratet). Jonas Gahr Støre, the Norwegian prime minister, felt compelled to publicly support Bakke-Jensen's decision: 'I support the decision to euthanise Freya. It was the right decision. I am not surprised that this has led to many international reactions. Sometimes we must make unpopular decisions' (FNC-NRK). In a widely shared Facebook post written in both Norwegian and English responding to Freya's killing,[9] and to the explanation given by Bakke-Jensen claiming it was necessary, Norwegian biologist and walrus expert Rune Aee lambasted the decision, arguing it was 'another example of a trigger-happy gun management – for which Norway is already well known. Norway is the country that killed Freya after being around for over two years around the entire North Sea. What a shame! This is just sad!' The determination that Freya was becoming too accustomed to the delicious clams in Oslofjord, suggesting her intention for a long-term stay, was the reason invoked for the need to relocate or, 'as a last resort', kill her. Yet already as Freya was approaching Oslo, killing her was already being debated by the Norwegian Fisheries as a potential future action: an anticipatory discourse setting the stage for Freya's future death to be blamed on an admiring public who disregarded the agency's warnings to stay away from the walrus.

In the retrospective discourses that circulated in Norwegian media outlets in the weeks following Freya's killing, debate in Norwegian media continued to centre on the rational forms of care that should inform the kind of (in) hospitality we extend to a wayward walrus in the city. Per Espen Fjeld, for instance, reasserted his position after Freya's killing that naming 'it' reflected an irrational and misguided 'care' for individual members of a species: 'It becomes a matter of care, it gets a name and is referred to in human terms. But taking care of this individual has nothing to do with taking care of the walrus population' (FNC-VG). Peggy S. Brønn, a professor at the Department of Communication and Culture at BI Norwegian Business School, wrote in an article seeking to temper worries that killing Freya had damaged Norway's image as a sustainability-minded, wildlife-loving nation: 'It's a talking point, [...] But there are plenty of other big things to worry about in the world than poor Freya' (FNC-Aftenposten). Brønn who is described in the article as one of 'Norway's leading reputation experts' says that she agreed with the reasoning behind the authorities' decision to kill Freya: 'Professionals make decisions based on facts. But perhaps they could show a little more understanding in their communication. In this case, there is a clash between facts and feelings. And the emotional always wins' (FNC-Aftenposten). These statements point to how claims that other actors hold illegitimate knowledge about wildlife can provide a powerful resource not only for delegitimizing others' ways of welcoming wildlife into a community. As new forms of hospitality emerge under conditions of climate change in the Anthropocene, such a discourse will be a powerful strategy for depoliticizing wildlife as a category up for contestation, shutting down alternative possibilities for sharing a changing world with wildlife otherwise.

Hospitality works by 'gathering up' discourses about different times and places to construe certain multispecies futures as more or less possible, and desirable, argues van Dooren (2016: 194). And statues are potent ways to materialize these discursive *chronotopes* of hospitality. As of this writing, a crowdfunded statue to memorialize Freya is currently being sculpted and will eventually be placed on the dock where she was killed in April 2023. The hope is that it promotes public dialogue about how to welcome walruses like Freya in the future. The sculptor, environmental artist Astri Tonoian told NRK reporters in an interview on 13 January 2023:[10] 'It doesn't surprise me if there is resistance [to more dialogue about Freya's killing] as well. But you cannot prevent wild nature from existing to protect people. We must learn to coexist with nature. I hope we can talk more about that' (FNC-NRK).

Rocky the Hawaiian monk seal

On the other side of the planet, another story of human-pinniped entanglement was also unfolding in Hawai'i. On a Sunday morning on 24 July 2022, the pup, Koalani ('heavenly warrior'), swam into the Waikīkī War Memorial Natatorium, a dilapidated former ocean water swimming pool, while her mom Rocky slept. A tourist swimming in the nearshore waters off Kaimana Beach – an elementary school teacher vacationing in Hawai'i from California – would later tell wildlife officials investigating the incident that she did not hear the dozens of onlookers on the beach yelling at her to get out of the water. As her husband recounted to wildlife enforcement officers with Hawai'i Department of Land and Natural Resources (DLNR) who interviewed the couple after the incident: 'The mother woke up and was very agitated and was barking, clearly distressed by the absence of her pup' (REC-DLNR). Over video recordings of the event taken by onlookers, a newscaster narrates: 'The two-week old pup gets closer to the woman, mother monk seal known as Rocky protecting her pup, apparently biting the swimmer' (REC-KHON2). The viewer can see the swimmer only a couple of meters from Rocky and her pup attempting to swim back to the beach, as onlookers on the beach can be heard yelling 'get to shore!' When Koalani the pup approaches the swimmer, Rocky intervenes and then appears to bite the woman. Three people come to intervene – with one in an outrigger canoe coming between the seal and the woman – and are able to bring her to shore. The swimmer's injuries require hospitalization.

The next day, in an interview with local news media, the swimmer describes the severe lacerations she received to her face, arms and back from Rocky's bites: 'Neither of us could sleep last night. Every time I closed my eyes, I was seeing the mother seal's mouth' (REC-ABC). After reviewing the video and interviewing the couple and witnesses, wildlife management officials with the Division of Conservation and Resources Management (DOCARE), a division of the DLNR tasked with enforcing infractions of endangered species laws in Hawai'i, concluded that the 'Visitor injured by monk seal didn't provoke attack, won't face state fines' (REC-HNN). Under state and federal laws protecting Hawaiian monk seals, touching, harassing, capturing, injuring or killing a Hawaiian monk seal can result in fines of up to $50,000 and/or five years in jail. 'When the Hawaiian monk seal Rocky, and her pup encountered a 60-year-old California elementary school teacher', DLNR said both on Twitter[11] and in a press release, 'a State investigation shows she [the swimmer] did nothing to provoke the incident and was not even aware the seals were in the water' (REC-DLNR). While the Hawaiian monk seal is one of the most critically endangered species in the world, consisting of only 1,500 individuals, in 2013 the species finally began to rebound after decades of decline and are beginning to make a comeback, albeit a highly uncertain one (Kittinger et al. 2012). 'There is no one to blame here', the swimmer's husband told reporters in an interview soon after. 'All my wife did was go swimming and she happened to be in the wrong place at the wrong time' (REC-ABC).

In this section, I primarily examine the *retrospective discourses* of this event told by several key social actors that were circulated in local news media outlets *after* the encounter between Rocky and the swimmer. Actors that make an appearance in this event include the wildlife officials with several agencies tasked with enforcing endangered species laws in Hawai'i, conservation volunteers who support these state and federal efforts, lifeguards stationed at Kaimana Beach, tourists, local Waikīkī residents like Larry Akiyama, the Native Hawaiian organization Kia'i (protector) and, of course, Rocky and her pup. I draw attention to how actors' retrospective discourses about this event served to construe certain social actors (human and non-human) as (un)welcome at this beach. In exploring how a heterogenous public formed around Rocky and her pup as a matter of concern and care, retrospective discourses about Rocky's presence at the beach after the incident serve to justify certain arguments for welcoming Rocky as well as unwelcome others. Indeed, one way actors exert power to shape the future is through construing a desired future goal or imaginary as the already existing circumstances from which actions should be taken (Fairclough and Fairclough 2012). Following the swimmer's encounter with Rocky, a number of discourses – legal, governmental, scientific and traditional – circulated in local news media before and after the incident. Here, I argue that understanding this incident through the lens of hospitality helps bring focus to how these myriad discourses are enlisted in retrospective narratives of the encounter to both construe different pasts and imagine different futures where humans and pinnipeds might share the world. 'The arrival of a stranger,' Van Dooren argues, 'is always haunted in this way, grounded in specific pasts and futures, imagined and/or lived' (2016: 197). In this case, the dominant discourse circulating in local media around Rocky overwhelmingly construed the swimming elementary schoolteacher as 'the stranger', the 'unwelcome guest', and Rocky as the tolerant (up to a point) host. In what follows, I explore how this discourse of hospitality worked through the multispecies relations at this beach as a powerful generator of identity and community.

Following Rocky's encounter with the Californian swimmer, there were numerous videos and news stories of people continuing to harass Rocky and the pup. 'We were very, very concerned there was going to be another incident because people were not listening' (REC-StarAdvertiser), Dana Jones told reporters. Jones is the executive director of the Hawaiian Monk Seal Preservation 'Ohana' ('family' in Hawaiian), a non-profit conservation organization that collaborates with state and federal wildlife management officials to monitor monk seals and educate visitors about them. 'Rocky was protecting her pup', she said. 'She did not attack this woman, this woman provoked it by being in *her space*' (emphasis mine) (REC-StarAdvertiser). Jones's frustration with tourists entering 'Rocky's space' further stems from knowing that it takes about four to six weeks for a mother monk seal to wean their pup, and so it was just a matter of holding the line between eager visitors and Rocky for a few more weeks. Through this statement and others, Jones expresses intimate knowledge of monk seals, and Rocky in particular, retrospective discourses that establish an interpretive frame through which to view the interaction between Rocky's actions, not as a seal 'attack' but as a human 'provocation'.

In an interview with a local television station a few days after Rocky bit the tourist, Dan Denisson, DLNR's senior communication manager, was asked by local reporters, 'what's the message that you're wanting to give to everybody?':

The basic message is we need to give this monk seal mom Rocky and her pup lots of lots of room. As we know, a week and a half ago, a lady swimming in the ocean was bit by the mom. There's been other incidents around the islands over the years where people have had encounters with monk seals that did not turn out so well. As you can see behind us the mom and the pup are resting this morning. (REC-HNN)

One of the challenges for DLNR is that there is no legal basis to close a beach to the public in Hawai'i, as all beaches in Hawai'i are public, and the state protects the public's rights to beach access. As such, DLNR repeatedly stated in their public messaging that their enforcement efforts to cordon off the beach to protect Rocky would be temporary, as Rocky was expected to wean Koalani in two to three weeks and be on her way to a new beach. One of the challenges for wildlife management officials is the absence of legally required minimum distance to be kept from Hawaiian monk seals, as only a 'recommended distance' exists. DLNR's wildlife conservation division tasked with enforcing endangered species protections, DOCARE had never guarded a monk seal for several days, let alone several weeks, before. However, as DLNR chair Suzanne Case said in a statement to local media after Rocky had finally weaned her pup and left the beach at the end of August, 'While this duty [to protect Rocky] certainly taxed DOCARE resources to the limit, we felt law enforcement presence was called for to prevent any further encounters, which could well have ended tragically' (REC-DLNR). Retrospective discourse, as this instance shows, also provides a resource for pre-emptive action, in this case to prevent a 'tragic' incident, presumably meaning a human being seriously injured or even killed in an encounter with Rocky.

In addition to DOCARE, another key actor involved in this event was the Hawai'i Marine Animal Response (HMAR), a non-profit partner with NOAA that responds to protect sleeping and nursing monk seals as well as provides educational outreach to the public. HMAR 'were constantly monitoring and moving the physical cordon [of 50 meters] as Rocky and Koalani became more and more active', Case said. 'People are again reminded that Hawaiian monk seal moms with pups are protective, can be dangerous, and have inflicted serious wounds on nearby swimmers', HMAR told reporters in a statement circulated in local media. 'We continue to warn people not to engage in in-water activities when a monk seal mother with a pup are in the area and to stay at least 150 feet from mother seals with pups . . . Continued vigilance is advised for several more weeks until the mother monk seal weans her pup' (REC-DLNR).

On 7 August, Hawai'i media reported that Native Hawaiian kia'i (protectors) had arrived at Kaimana Beach to assist in the effort to protect Rocky and her pup Koalani. A local newscast on KHON2 News Honolulu interviewed several kia'i, who are also part of Kū Kia'i Mauna (Protectors of Mauna Kea), which a few years earlier had established a pu'uhonua (place of refuge) on Mauna Kea to protect the sacred mountain from construction of the Thirty-Meter-Telescope. In the video, the camera shot pans over Kaimana Beach showing the sign and rope perimeter around the seals but now with several inverted State of Hawai'i flags: upside-down flags are a sign of protest to the US government, an internationally recognized symbol of a nation in distress, in this case the Hawaiian Nation. Over this shot, the newscaster narrates: 'The kia'i are not at Kaimana beach to cause trouble. They say they're acting hand in hand with officials' (REC-KHON). In the interview, a kia'i wearing a red T-shirt that reads 'protector' explains: 'We have more eyes than them [DLNR]. So if we see something, and we're like, "Hey, get out of the water!" and they [tourists] don't listen. We're like, "DLNR!"' Another kia'i member interviewed later in the segment says, 'You know, we are here to assist [DLNR] to help keep all these people basically out of the water. You know, it's not only for Rocky and the pups protection. It's also for the people who come to visit Kaimana.' The newscaster then says, 'The kia'i point out that monk seals have been in the islands for a lot longer than we have. Rocky first found Kaimana [beach] five years ago.' The kia'i then tells the newscrew: 'She's had her pups here since 2017. This is her 'āina before me, before them [pointing to kia'i behind her], certainly before them [pointing to tourists]' (REC-KHON).

'The Hawaiian word for "land" is 'āina, which translates as "that which feeds," and can also be considered as "origin," "mother," "inspiration," and "environment"', writes Native Hawaiian scholar Karen Amimoto Ingersoll (2016: 33), citing Manulani Alulu Meyer's (2001: 128) scholarship on Hawaiian epistemology. In Ingersoll's exploration of Kānaka Maoli 'seascape epistemology', she writes that '[w]hen I refer to Hawaiian "land" or 'āina, I will be referring to both land and ocean, because although land and sea are distinguished areas, Kānaka Maoli epistemologically perceive them as connected'. It is in this sense that I understand the kia'i's use of the word 'āina in the earlier interview, which recognizes 'the fact that activities that take place on the land always affect the sea, just as oceanic activities have effects on the health of the land'. Monk seals' presence on the beach unsettles the divide we might imagine between land and sea, as beings who seamlessly traverse watery and terrestrial habitats from their foraging grounds in deeper reefs to the nearshore and beach spaces they frequent for weaning, pupping and sleeping (Kittinger et al. 2012; Rose 2017). Returning to the language of hospitality, the kiaʻi's statement that 'This is her [Rocky's] 'āina before me', or any human for that matter, 'āina decentres human entitlement to the world, as well as the anthropocentric pretence that the world was ever 'ours' to control (van Dooren 2016: 204). In doing so, such an epistemology suggests possibilities for less appropriative and anthropocentric modes of inhabiting the earth grounded in an expanded sense of 'response-ability' to other species' needs, that is, respectful of a seal's project to get on with her life in the face of an uncertain future.

While the kiaʻi were at Kaimana Beach helping DOCARE protect Rocky and her pup, a news segment covering the story also interviewed local resident Larry Akiyama. Newscaster: 'Larry Akiyama is at Kaimana every day. He's happy to see locals protecting the creatures and says those who are unfamiliar with island regulations just need to show some respect.' Larry: 'No need for go Harvard for read the sign. Just read the sign and listen, abide by it. So, everybody's my friend. I mean, you know, I love everybody. But show more respect. I feel really good when all these Hawaiian flags out. I feel like part of Hawaiʻi again.' Before the kiaʻi arrived, Larry told a reporter that

> Nothing works over here. Tourists will never listen to anybody. They just ignore everything. They just take things into their hands. They just don't care ... They yell at the lifeguards, this and that. They yell at us guys. 'Why can't we see the seals?' They chase one guy off the beach over there ... 'Oh I'm a taxpayer, I can sit anyplace I like'. (REC-KHON)

Larry's reported speech of a recalcitrant tourist here who claims to be able to 'sit anyplace I like', or his declaration of 'feeling good' and 'like Hawaiʻi again' in seeing the kiaʻi's Hawaiian flags on the beach, points to the scale-shifting nature of hospitality. In other words, zooming in and out on the context of hospitality enables one to strategically swap host-guest relationships, shifting the power relations for deciding who has the right to (un)welcome who. Candea argues that this scale-shifting affordance in the language of hospitality is what makes it such a potent object of public debate, explaining why people can 'draw a very different meaning from hospitality, while ostensibly talking about the same thing' (2012: 37).

6.4 Discussion and conclusion

On 22 August 2022, in the aftermath of Freya's killing, Christian Ytteborg, the marina worker who had called Norwegian Fisheries officers to protect Freya from crowds the night before she was killed, and instead discovered it would be those same officers who were instructed to kill Freya early the next morning, wrote an op-ed about his experience in one of Norway's largest news outlets, *Aftenposten*:

> The fear and curiosity of the people in the area was kept under control with the help of young people with walkie-talkies. They reported when Freya got out of the boat and into the water, and when she got out of the water and back on board the boat. Which meant that humans could swim when Freya was sunbathing, and when Freya was swimming, the humans would stay on land and sunbathe.

In this retrospective discourse, Ytteborg describes how an experimental mode of hospitality emerged for a brief time while Freya was visiting Oslo, with people and the walrus exploring more welcoming and less lethal ways to live together. As Ytteborg concludes: 'the decision to euthanise Freya feels wrong. And because we have to look ahead, so as not to become bitter and sour people, we would like to be told that we would be happy to welcome more walruses, and the like, at this marina the next time an interesting foreign guest comes to visit the Oslofjord' (FNC-Aftenposten). Ytteborg's comments are a call to hold open possibilities for a less human-centred hospitality: a multispecies hospitality that demands a willingness to learn from and make room for other species' experiments to explore new ways of living in the Anthropocene.

At the same time, Rocky's story, and the alliances of human care that took shape around her and her pup, suggests possibilities for alternative modes of sharing the world with others that work 'outside the logic of host'. As Thom van Dooren (2016: 206) argues, 'on a world that is for all of its diverse creatures [and not just "ours"], futures must be constructed by fragile collectives that cannot claim absolute knowledge, power or authority'. Such multispecies collectives, he argues, can only emerge by challenging the drive to find immediate and 'practical' solutions to environmental problems, without interrogating the underlying models of the world causing these ecological problems in the first place. As an increasingly dominant model, the Anthropocene often underpins an ecologically destructive and appropriative world view that the Earth is 'ours' to order and control. By taking a closer look at this discourse, and how the language of hospitality is enlisted to address problematic human-wildlife entanglements, this chapter suggested ways for ecolinguists to interrogate the anticipatory discourses that till the soil for solutions to be realized, as well as the retrospective discourses enlisted to justify or contest their realization. 'Analysis of such discourses,' as Stibbe (2012: 6) reminds us, 'can expose and critique the models of the world that they are based on, and act as a first step toward opening up alternatives.'

Notes

1. This work was partly supported by the Research Council of Norway through its Centres of Excellence funding scheme, project number 223265 (MultiLing).
2. Available online: https://twitter.com/steinkobbe/status/1549470090030202885 (accessed 21 February 2023).
3. Available online: https://www.fiskeridir.no/English/Coastal-management/Marine-protected-areas.
4. Unless otherwise noted, all extracts from the FNC corpus were analysed in their original Norwegian but with English translations provided here. URLs are provided when the original media source was also analysed.
5. Available online: https://www.nrk.no/ytring/skyt-freya_-1.16048109 (accessed 21 February 2023).
6. Available online: https://www.nytimes.com/2022/08/12/world/europe/freya-walrus-norway.html (accessed 21 February 2023).
7. Available online: https://www.nytimes.com/2022/08/19/world/europe/norway-walrus-freya-killed.html (accessed 21 February 2023).
8. Available online: https://twitter.com/jeffrsebo/status/1559214790052118531 (accessed 21 February 2023).
9. Available online: https://www.facebook.com/rune.aae/posts/pfbid05ncKAAaH1EWfTdabTCA44KoZpUaM45eF421csJ5wTKx526Yj44XoaZYfdTeSJ6aJl (accessed on February 2023).
10. Available online: https://www.nrk.no/video/slik-vil-de-hedre-freya_350f3981-2fe8-48f8-86f2-53a50b723bab (accessed 21 February 2023).
11. Available online: https://twitter.com/dlnr/status/1551702984907583488 (accessed 21 February 2023).

References

Anonymous (2011), 'Welcome to the Anthropocene', *The Economist*, 26 May. Available online: http://www.economist.com/node/18744401 (accessed 20 February 2023).

Candea, M. (2012), 'Derrida en Corse? Hospitality as Scale-Free Abstraction', *The Journal of the Royal Anthropological Institute*, 18 (1): 34–48.

de Saint-Georges, I. (2012), 'Anticipatory Discourse', in C. A. Chapelle (ed.), *The Encyclopedia of Applied Linguistics*, 118–24, Oxford: Wiley-Blackwell.

Demuth, B. (2019), *Floating Coast: An Environmental History of the Bering Strait*, New York: W. W. Norton & Company.

Derrida, J. (1998), 'Hospitality, Justice and Responsibility: A Dialogue with Jacques Derrida', in R. Kearney and M. Dooley (eds), *Questioning Ethics: Contemporary Debates in Philosophy*, 65–83, London: Routledge.

Derrida, J. (2000), 'Hostipitality', Angelaki: Journal of the Theoretical Humanities 5.3: 3–18.

Derrida, J. (2005), 'The Principle of Hospitality', *Parallax*, 11 (1): 6–9.

de Saint-George, I. (2013), 'Anticipatory Discourse', in C. A. Chapelle (ed), *The Encyclopedia of Applied Linguistics*, 101–9, Oxford: Wiley-Blackwell.

Fairclough, I. and N. Fairclough (2012), *Political Discourse Analysis: A Method for Advanced Students*, London: Routledge.

Giraud, E. H. (2019), *What Comes after Entanglement?: Activism, Anthropocentrism, and an Ethics of Exclusion*, Durham: Duke University Press.

Goffman, E. (1981), *Forms of Talk*, Philadelphia: University of Pennsylvania Press.

Ingersoll, K. A. (2016), *Waves of Knowing: A Seascape Epistemology*, Durham: Duke University Press.

Kilgarriff, A., V. Baisa, J. Bušta, M. Jakubíček, V. Kovář, J. Michelfeit, P. Rychlý, and V. Suchomel (2014), 'The Sketch Engine: Ten Years on', *Lexicography*, 1: 7–36.

Kittinger, J. N., T. M. Bambico, T. K. Watson, and E. W. Glazier (2012), 'Sociocultural Significance of the Endangered Hawaiian Monk Seal and the Human Dimensions of Conservation Planning', *Endangered Species Research*, 17 (2): 139–56.

Lawlor, L. (2007), *This Is Not Sufficient: An Essay on Animality and Human Nature in Derrida*, New York: Columbia University Press.

Poole, R. (2022), *Corpus-Assisted Ecolinguistics*, London: Bloomsbury Publishing.

Oliver, K. (2009), *Animal Lessons: How They Teach Us to Be Human*, New York: Columbia University Press.

Rose, D. B. (2017), 'Monk Seals at the Edge: Blessings in a Time of Peril', in D. B. Rose, T. van Dooren, and M. Chrulew (eds), *Extinction Studies: Stories of Time, Death, and Generations*, 117–48. New York: Columbia University Press.

Scollon, R. (2012), *Analyzing Public Discourse: Discourse Analysis in the Making of Public Policy*, London: Routledge.

Stibbe, A. (2012), *Animals Erased: Discourse, Ecology, and Reconnection with the Natural World*, Middletown: Wesleyan University Press.

Thompson, C. (2002), 'When Elephants Stand for Competing Philosophies of Nature', in J. Law and A. Mol (eds), *Complexities*, 166–90. Durham: Duke University Press.

van Dooren, T. (2016), 'The Unwelcome Crows: Hospitality in the Anthropocene', *Angelaki*, 21 (2): 193–212.

van Dooren, T. (2019), *The Wake of Crows: Living and Dying in Shared Worlds*, New York City: Columbia University Press.

Venturini, T. and A. K. Munk (2021), *Controversy Mapping: A Field Guide*, Cambridge: Polity.

Whatmore, S. J. (2009), 'Mapping Knowledge Controversies: Science, Democracy and the Redistribution of Expertise', *Progress in Human Geography*, 33 (5): 587–98.

Identity Representation of Plants in Relation to Humans and the Lifescape

Maria Bortoluzzi

Introduction

The chapter[1] focuses on the representation of plants in the lifescape (Bortoluzzi and Zurru, this volume). Vegetation and plant life include the overwhelming majority of the living mass on our planet. Animal life (human and non-human animal) would not exist without plants, whereas most plants could still exist or adapt to a life without animals (Baluška and Mancuso 2020: 1).

In ecolinguistics studies, research about animal representation constitutes a relevant subfield (see Section 7.1), while discourses about plants need further exploration. This chapter is part of an ongoing research project which focuses on plant representation in a variety of genres and text types. The overarching research questions are: How are plants represented in connection with the environment they belong to and contribute to creating? How are plants represented in relation to humans and other animals? In the present chapter, these questions will be investigated in selected multimodal texts that recognize the value of plants and ecosystems and promote environmental protection (Section 7.2). Since verbal and multimodal communication tends to be inevitably anthropocentric, this is the dominant outlook for plant representation even in texts promoting ecosustainable solutions to climate issues and the protection of life on the planet.

In this study, 'text' is meant in its sense of 'multimodal text in its discourse context' whereby a variety of modes (verbal and visual) contribute to meaning-making (Bezemer and Kress 2016). The theoretical framework draws on Critical Discourse Studies (Fairclough 2003, 2014; Reisigl and Wodak 2009), the socio-semiotic approach in multimodal discourse studies (Kress and van Leeuwen 2021; van Leeuwen 2022; Moschini and Sindoni 2022) and ecolinguistics (Fill and Mühlhäusler 2001; Steffensen and Fill 2014; Fill and Penz 2018; Stibbe 2021). The outlook offered by these studies is used to investigate the specificities of plant representation in discourse and reveal underlying ideologies and beliefs that influence and are influenced by sociocultural conventions.

The chapter is organized as follows: Section 7.1 presents the theoretical framework; Section 7.2 introduces data selection and methodology; Section 7.3 is a summary and discussion of the findings; and Section 7.4 offers some concluding remarks and scope for further research.

7.1 Theoretical framework

In academic publications and popularization of their research, botanists, plant biologists and other experts underline how we humans tend to undermine the relevance of plants giving priority to human and non-human animals, whereas in fact animal life is only possible thanks to plants. The sheer scale of plant life is overwhelming: around 90 per cent of all that is living on the earth (biomass) consists of plants (Baluška and Mancuso 2020: 1; Mancuso 2017: 144). However, plants are often considered passive participants of life events:

> Earth is a planet dominated by plants. Tundra, forests, prairies and jungle are all words that describe the easily dominant organisms. Oxygen, 20% of the atmosphere, testifies to the power and dominance of photosynthesis. Despite this dominance, plants in our time frame seem to do nothing. But when time lapse is used, movement becomes obvious. In reality, with just a few exceptions, plant movement is growth and growth is slow in all organisms. (Calvo and Trewavas 2021: 78)

Discoursal representations of concepts such as identity, movement and action tend to suit physical and sociocultural human conventions, while their suitability for other animals or plants is not without problems. However, even within the human domain, representations of identities are complex sociocultural constructs instantiated in discourse and igniting endless debates (and controversies) (Benwell and Stokoe 2006; Caldas-Coulthard and Iedema 2008; McEntee Atalianis 2019).

Plant scientists Baluška and Mancuso write: 'Self-identities allow vascular plants to act as individuals enjoying sociality via their self/non-self recognition and kin recognition' (Baluška and Mancuso 2021: 1). In their view, research clearly demonstrates that vascular plants have 'perception and awareness of the physical self' and 'act as individualities having both plant-specific agency and cognition' (Baluška and Mancuso 2021: 3). Plants are also crucial protagonists in the preservation of the planet: 'As our survival on planet Earth is completely dependent on plants [. . .], we should change our attitudes to plants and start to study them as cognitive and intelligent organisms [. . .] endowed with lots of behavioural and cognitive competencies' (Baluška and Mancuso 2021: 6).

Plants are represented by these scientists as active networks of living beings that improve their environment as ecological actors: plants 'provide' for their existence, 'choose' how to grow, 'sequester' carbon dioxide and chemicals, 'enjoy' features considered specific to animals, 'influence' how animals around them behave (see Gagliano, Ryan and Vieira 2017). Plants are presented as initiators and active participants of '(social) action' in the sense that plants actively interact with their context, other plants and animals in complex networks that are sometimes called 'wood-wide-webs' (Baluška and Mancuso 2020; Calvo 2022).

The question, then, is what frameworks can be used to analyse (identity) representations and interactions of plants in discourse? Representation of identity, action and interaction are mostly related to studies of human groups in human-centred disciplines, such as anthropology, sociology, linguistics and so on, or in groups of animals as in ethology. Social action, for instance, refers to human groups when representing themselves and 'others' and interacting among themselves and with 'others' (van Leeuwen 2008). Brubacker and Cooper (2000: 14 ff) define (dis)identification as a dynamic and multifaceted act of human positioning towards 'self' and 'others'. It is a balancing act between 'personal', 'relational' and 'collective' identities (Brewer and Gardner 1996: 83–4).

Investigating human identities from a socio-semiotic point of view, van Leeuwen states that social identity 'relates people, not only to other people but also to things, places, animals and their spiritual values' (2022: 7). The list does not mean to be exhaustive, but it is remarkable that plants are not mentioned. Are they implicitly included as 'things' or elements of 'places'?

Language and other semiotic systems we humans use for communicating are inevitably anthropocentric due to their nature and origin (Heuberger 2018) and to our bio-sensory perception of nature as being 'around us' as 'environment' rather than 'us' (Jung 2001). This anthropocentrism is instantiated in linguistic and socio-semiotic outcomes that can powerfully influence the way we experience our relation with the lifescape (see Bortoluzzi and Zurru, this volume). Latour calls this phenomenon (found also in scientific discourse) 'pseudo-realism', because it is perceived as 'realistic', even though it gives salience to humans against the background of the natural world (Latour 2020: 96).

Plant specificity has been discussed in some fields of discourse studies such as MG crops (Cook 2004). Literary criticism has a long tradition of dealing with plants representation in literature (see Critical Plant Studies by Woodward and Lemmer 2019) and so does research focusing on First Nations' traditions and communication; the latter two fields are beyond the scope of this chapter. At the time of writing, plant relevance seems to be under-represented in ecolinguistics (Poole and Micalay-Hurtado 2022 is an exception), whereas discourse on non-human animals has been widely investigated (among many others, Freeman 2009; Stibbe 2012; Forte 2015; Jacobs 2016; Cook and Sealey 2018; Zhdanava, Surinderpal and Kumaran 2021; Lamb this volume and 2024).

The literature focusing on non-human animals (their treatment and the discourses of respect or exploitation) shows that (critical) discourse frameworks developed for human groups and individuals tend to be applied to the relation between human and non-human animals. Stibbe writes: 'The way that animals are socially constructed influences how they are treated by human society' (Stibbe 2012: 20) and '[t]he relationship between humans and other animals is, therefore, partially constructed by the language used to talk to and about them' (Stibbe 2012: 64–5). These remarks derive from a Hallidayan view of language whereby 'our "reality" is not something ready made and waiting to be meant – it has to be actively construed; and [. . .] language evolved in the process of, and as the agency of, its construal' (Halliday 2001: 179).

This view of language and communication also informs the present study. All texts and artefacts influence, reproduce and transform social practices; discourses are a recontextualization of social practices (Fairclough and Wodak 1997; Fairclough 2003). Within this framework, van Leeuwen (2008, 2022) draws up 'sociosemantic inventories' of the ways in which human social actors can be represented in language and other modes: 'Activation occurs when social actors are represented as the active, dynamic forces in an activity, passivation when they are represented as "undergoing" the activity, or as being "at the receiving end of it"' (van Leeuwen 2008: 33).

In Actor-Network Theory, Latour (2005) goes beyond the dichotomy animate/inanimate and includes the effects of animate and inanimate participants in social action and interaction. In socio-semiotic studies, meaning is achieved by and through the interaction between animate and inanimate participants in the process of communication (Bezemer and Kress 2016; Kress and van Leeuwen 2021; van Leeuwen 2022). In multimodal studies, the term 'participant' is used to encompass a variety of elements in visual compositions (Kress and van Leeuwen 2021: 47) which are related to one another through processes;

participants are defined according to their positioning in the composition (Kress and van Leeuwen 2021). In critical discourse analytical methodology the representation of social actors includes 'objects/phenomena/events and processes/actions' which are discoursally construed 'more or less positively or negatively' (Reisigl and Wodak 2009: 95). Drawing on these studies, the present research focuses on the positioning and the representation of plants as actors/participants in relation with human and non-human (social) actors/participants in (multimodal) discourse. Issues of representation of individual and collective identities, 'animacy' and 'agency' in multimodal texts will be presented and discussed in the data analysis, reflecting on the (inevitable) human perspective (van Leeuwen 2008, 2022). The analysis adopts a social-semiotic multimodality framework to discuss the orchestration of modes in the selected texts (Baldry and Thibault 2006; Kress 2010; Bezemer and Kress 2016; Kress and van Leeuwen 2021; Moschini and Sindoni 2022).

7.2 Data selection and methodology

Whereas the human point of view is unavoidable in texts that humans have created for other humans, my working hypothesis to investigate plant representation is that plants are backgrounded or represented as passive participants even in texts which seemingly focus on their environmental relevance and role. The follow-up hypothesis is that plants are represented as serving purposes for humans rather than as key ecological protagonists of the planet ecosystems.

For this study, the working definition of the hypernym 'plant' is very broad and based on the entry of the Encyclopedia Britannica (2022): plants are eukaryotic life forms that mostly (but not in all cases) present characteristics which range from the capacity to produce chemical energy through photosynthesis (for green plants), cells that contain cellulose, the absence of organs of motions and nervous system.

The texts selected as data are addressed to a variety of publics, encompassing expert and non-expert communities of addressees. The criteria for selecting the first three texts follow Reisigl and Wodak (2009: 98): they belong to similar if widespread language communities; they are present-day reports of international authoritative organizations; they are based on research; they are agenda setting and therefore they belong to specific fields of action related to the formation of public attitudes and opinion; they can be found open access online; they are Reports or Summaries of Reports by the United Nations and UNESCO. The publics addressed are local, national and global policymakers, educators, expert and non-expert citizens. The main purpose of these texts is promoting a better quality of life and the protection of the environment. The addressers tend to influence and guide environmental policies and educational programmes. These reports are part of institutional discourse (Mayr 2008) that informs policymaking and agenda setting at global and local levels.

The analysis is complemented by two short videos about positive environmental awareness and action. *Nature Now* is an awareness-raising and fund-raising video promoting natural sustainable actions. The second video is the official trailer of the BBC documentary series *The Green Planet* by David Attenborough. Both videos address international English-speaking publics, mostly in the Global North; the first addresses non-experts and the second both expert and non-expert publics.

The three reports and two videos are so authoritative and influential (in different ways) that their evaluations, explanations, causal representations and call for action become advisable and desirable.

The data analysis is qualitative and offers reflections for further research, as mentioned in the concluding remarks (Section 7.4). The label 'participant' is used for entities socioculturally construed in discourse which are part of the convironment (Fill 2001) or lifescape (Bortoluzzi and Zurru, this volume): human and non-human animals, plants, inanimate objects, events and situations that contribute to and interact with plant representation in context.

The main categorization is based on Social Actors by van Leeuwen (2008, 2022) and adapted to capture the different ways in which plants can be construed as participants. The categories Inclusion and Exclusion[2] are seen as a cline rather than a dichotomy. Exclusion can be instantiated as Suppression or Backgrounding (van Leeuwen 2008: 28 et passim; Stibbe 2021: 139 et passim). Suppression is rather problematic to detect since the participant is completely absent from the text. By default, texts and discourses are a selection of semiotic (and linguistic) features (van Leeuwen 2008: 30); therefore, a participant can be considered suppressed only when it is expected it should be present but it is not. However, different publics might have different expectations influenced by sociocultural conventions. In Backgrounding, participants are 'de-emphasized, pushed into the background' (van Leeuwen 2008: 29; Stibbe 2021). Linguistically this is instantiated in a variety of ways (some cases of agentless passive use, non-finite clauses, nominalizations, etc.; see Fairclough 2003, 2014; van Leeuwen 2008; Stibbe 2021). In visual modes, participants can be blurred, unidentifiable, peripheral elements (see Kress and van Leeuwen

2021). In this study, Backgrounding is part of the cline between Exclusion and Inclusion.

Inclusion can be expressed verbally and represented visually in a great variety of ways. Two main subcategories used here are Activation and Passivation. Van Leeuwen (2008: 33) writes: 'Activation occurs when social actors are represented as the active, dynamic forces in an activity, passivation when they are represented as "undergoing" the activity, or as being "at the receiving end of it."' This will be adapted to plant behaviour and to the relationship plant-animal (human or non-human) taking into account that plant participants activate themselves differently from animals (see Section 7.1). Other subcategories (Personalization and Impersonalization, for instance) emphasize human-related aspects which are not suitable for plant representation. Zhdanava, Surinderpal and Kumaran (2021) adopt Social Actor Theory to 'identify whether nonhuman animals are presented as human equals to human beings, and if so, how' (2021: 8). The present study does not take 'equality' with humans as a benchmark feature to represent plants but rather recognition and respect for multispecies diversity.

For images and videos, the analysis draws on the socio-semiotic approach elaborated, among others, by Kress and van Leeuwen (2021), van Leeuwen (2008, 2022) and Baldry and Thibault (2006). Van Leeuwen (2008: 147) summarizes the strategies to represent human others vis-à-vis the viewer as 'visual actor network': Inclusion includes three levels: Involved in Action (as Agent or Patient), Generic (Cultural categorization or Biological categorization) or Specific, and Individual and Group (Homogenization and Differentiation).

The qualitative data-driven analysis will show how these variables can be adapted to suit plant representations in a variety of contexts and modes. More specifically, variables as 'Involved in action' can mean doing what plants normally do (such as producing oxygen or storing carbon) and the categories of Generic and Specific, Individual and Group assume a different meaning for living beings who can be represented as 'individuals' but generally exist in networks of plants and other beings (including animals).

7.3 Data analysis and discussion

7.3.1 The 2030 Agenda for Sustainable Development

The 2030 Agenda for Sustainable Development by the United Nations is a document that has been having a great impact in policymaking, education and social action of charity work at local and global levels (Valvason 2019/2020; Stibbe 2021: 150 et passim). The official version of the Resolution A/Res/70/1 was published on 21 October 2015 (2030ASDG2015).

The document defines itself as 'an Agenda of unprecedented scope and significance' which aims at a world 'free from poverty, hunger, disease and want where all life can thrive' (2030ASDG2015-6-7).[3] The Preamble sets the priority for the whole document: 'This Agenda is a plan of action for people, planet and prosperity' (2030ASDG2015-3). The alliterative three-part list of the topic sentence clarifies who the beneficiaries are: humans are singled out while all ecosystems are included in the hypernym 'planet'. 'Prosperity' refers to economic and cultural aspects of human society. The agenda focuses on human well-being: 'the three dimensions of sustainable development' are 'the economic, social and environmental' (2030ASDG2015-5) whereby the priority of humans and their economy is explicitly set. Within this human-centred document, how is the world of plants represented, given that it sustains the planet's well-being and its lifescape?

In her corpus-assisted analysis of the text, Valvason (2019/2020: 155–6, 380) categorizes the occurrence of tokens (percentage of single occurrences of lexemes) as follows: natural elements (56 per cent), humans (38 per cent), non-human animals (3 per cent), plants (3 per cent). Only one positive keyword[4] explicitly refers to plants: 'forests' (ranking 206 in the keyword list). In terms of quantitative presence, both plants and non-human animals are definitely backgrounded.

A close qualitative reading of the report shows that the natural habitats to protect ('the planet and its natural resources') are viewed as 'resources' for human needs (see a critique of this document in Stibbe 2021: 150 et passim). In the text, plant life is either implied in highly generic and all-encompassing terms, such as 'biodiversity', 'nature', 'wildlife and other living species' and 'biological system of the planet' (2030ASDG2015-7-9), or it is implicit in generic terms of human activities such as 'agriculture' or human categories such as 'farmers' (and their specifications) as in Example 1:

1. 2030ASDG2015-11 'We will devote resources to developing rural areas and sustainable agriculture and fisheries, supporting smallholder farmers, especially women farmers, herders and fishers in developing countries, particularly least developed countries.'

The explicit mention of plant life as 'forests' occurs in text structures where humans are the agents that 'conserve and sustainably use' 'natural resources' whereas plants are undergoing the process (Example 2):

2. 2030ASDG2015-13 'We are therefore determined to conserve and sustainably use oceans and seas, freshwater resources, as well as forests, mountains and drylands and to protect biodiversity, ecosystems and wildlife.'

In the document, plants are either implied in non-specific metonymic relation to their hypernyms ('biodiversity', 'ecosystems') or mentioned as generic 'resources' for human needs ('forests', 'plants'). Both plants and non-human animals are backgrounded and represented in generic terms as beneficial for humans. Given the policymaking aims for improving human life quality on the planet, it could be argued that backgrounding other than human life might be expected. The counterargument, however, is that humans would benefit from establishing a more respectful relation with all aspects of the lifescape especially in globally influential agenda-setting texts.

7.3.2 Restoring life to the land and heritage forests

Two reports released by prestigious international organizations in 2021 were selected as data because they focus on the protection of plant ecosystems and forests: *Restoring Life to the Land. The Role of Sustainable Land Management in Ecosystem Restoration* (RLL2021, 21,442 words) was co-published by United Nations Convention to Combat Desertification (UNCCD) and World Overview of Conservation Approaches and Technologies (WOCAT); *World Heritage Forests. Carbon sinks under pressure* (WHF2021, 13,404 words) was published by the United Nations Educational, Scientific and Cultural Organization (UNESCO). They belong to the genre of institutional reports which summarize wide-ranging research for publics of policymakers at global and local levels, international charities and NGOs, academia and educational institutions. They are authoritative, research-based and agenda-setting reports. Both texts are freely accessible online and rich in colour images, photos and diagrams. Due to the similarities in text type, purpose, authorship and publics addressed, these two texts form a small corpus.

The #Lancsbox corpus tools (Brezina, Weill-Tessier and McEnery 2021) were used for basic data extraction and context retrieval. The data were qualitatively analysed and manually checked to eliminate occurrences with a different meaning (e.g. industrial 'plant' and surnames); header and footer occurrences were also excluded.

Some frequent collocations confirm the focus on land protection: 'world heritage sites', 'sustainable land management', 'ecosystem restoration', 'world heritage forests', 'heritage forests'. In these collocations, a close relation between humans and other participants (land, ecosystems and forests) is established through the human-centred concepts of 'restoration' and 'heritage' (respectively occurring also in the titles of the two reports). Heritage is, in this context, a metonymic extension of passing on valuable assets from (human) generation to generation. However positive and respectful, the concept is mapped onto human ownership and framed as such (Entman 1993 and Lakoff 2010 for a definition of frames). The collocations 'sustainable land management' and 'ecosystem restoration' are nominalizations in which the head noun implies human agency. In the complex nominalization 'Heritage forests carbon sinks' (WHF2021), 'heritage forests' are modifiers of 'carbon sinks' whereby human responsibility for carbon in excess is obfuscated. Interestingly, however, the nominalization 'carbon sinks' also implies the active role of the forest in holding on to carbon that would otherwise be dangerous for the planet.

Table 7.1 reports the raw occurrences of the most frequent generic search terms related to plants. All occurrences were qualitatively analysed in their wider discoursal context of occurrence, and findings are summarized later in the text. Specific plant names (coffee, Casuarina Equisetifolia, etc.) rarely occur in the two texts. The asterisk means that the term includes all types of the relevant lemmas.

In RLL2021, the definition of sustainable land management clearly defines 'plants' as one of the 'land resources' for human needs (Example 3):

3. RLL2021-5 'land resources including soils, water, animals and plants, for the production of goods to meet changing human needs'.

The occurrences of the verb 'to plant' and the term 'plantation' (included in the analysis) imply human agency.[5] In most contexts where the lemma 'plant' occurs as noun or modifier, the active agent in the clause is human, even when only implied, as in the agentless passive of Example 4:

4. RLL2021-16 'in developing countries many medicinal drugs are derived from local plants'.

Table 7.1 Occurrences of generic terms related to plants in RLL2021 and WHF2021

	plant*	tree*	vegetation*	forest*
RLL2021	56	23	17	86
WHF2021	3	31	4	260

In the very few occurrences in which plants are overtly active participants, the result of their action is, without exception, a positive outcome for humans. Among these occurrences, I included the following instance of nominalization: 'dynamic development of plant synergies' presented as part of 'dynamic agroforestry' (RLL2021-13). In nominalizations, processes are presented as noun phrases and agency in the process is only implied, not explicitly expressed. Thus, plant agency and animacy is discoursally obfuscated and backgrounded even when implied, and it is usually represented as driven by human agency (see Example 4).

The only contexts in which plants are not directly related to human well-being are in diagrams, as in the categorization 'plant diversity' (RLL2021-12). In a few instances plants become problematic for other organisms as in the generic statement: 'Invasive aquatic plants are a threat' (RLL2021-20).

In one occurrence plants are beneficiaries of human action which protects them from other animals (indirectly implied in 'grazing areas') in order to restore 'indigenous plant cover' without further specification of direct advantage for humans (RLL2021-31).

Only exceptionally, plants are represented as active agents:

5. 'Mangroves are propagated through cigar-shaped "propagules", produced by mature plants.' (RLL2021-27)

In Example 5, the passive structure thematizes these specific plants that are also presented as producing what propagates themselves. If this is common to all plants, here the concept is rendered salient in a context where plant reproduction is generally viewed as triggered by human action.

In summary, in RLL2021, plants are represented in relation to human needs and dependent on human action and agency. Similarly, the term 'tree*', in its singular or plural form, occurs as undergoing human action or contributing to human needs or well-being (Example 6):

6. RLL2021-17 'Coffee is originally a forest species, and when the first commercial plantations were created, tall shade trees were planted amongst the coffee.'

In one only occurrence (Example 7) human action, implied in the infinitival form 'mixing', is reported as beneficial to crops and trees:

7. RLL2021-13 'Mixing trees and crops can be mutually beneficial.'

In two occurrences, tree action is mentioned because beneficial to human activities and animals related to them ('cattle'):

8. RLL2021-19 'The trees Parashorea s: , Taxus s: and Nyssa s: have intrinsic value- while shading the ground and depressing weeds.'

In Example 8, the trees mentioned by their species names seem to have 'intrinsic value', but in fact, their actions facilitate the healthy growth of the rubber plant as economic crops.

In WHF2021 trees are places for carbon storage (circumstantial):

9. WHF2021-7 'Carbon in forests is mainly stored in trees (aboveground biomass), roots (belowground biomass) and soils.'

'Tree' is often used as attributions in nominalizations such as 'tree cover loss', 'lack of tree cover gain' and 'tree mortality and reduced resilience to climate change'. The implied process is represented as an environmental threat to the well-being of the tree and the planet. In this sense, WHF2021 moves beyond the framing of plants as beneficial for human needs (as crops or grazing land) as in RLL2021, and it establishes the connection between the health of plant biomass and the health of the planet.

A similar discoursal situation can be seen for the term 'vegetation*': vegetation tends to be either part of the general setting (circumstantial), passivated or viewed as a resource. However, in two occurrences out of twenty-one 'vegetation' (as noun or adjective) is presented as just 'existing' (in existential process clauses), and in three instances out of twenty-one, vegetation is an active participant (two occurrences in WHF2021 and one in RLL2021).

'Forests' and 'forest' are, respectively, the fourth and ninth keyword of the mini-corpus.[6] Forests are also one of the eight main ecosystems in RLL2021 and the central topic in WHF2021.

In RLL2021, the *Take Away Message* states:

10. RLL2021-vii 'FORESTS are in the public eye – with dramatic images of degradation stemming from deforestation. Protection of forest areas is only a partial answer: there is growing experience of successful community management. Furthermore, productive agroforestry systems can effectively mimic forests and forest function.'

In Example 10, forests are represented metaphorically 'located' in the global infosphere ('the public eye') and needing human protection and community management; the third sentence entails that they can be successfully replaced by human-made environments, which does not sound promising for a *Take Away Message*.

RLL2021 represents forests as providers for human needs or needing human action. Even when a completely different vision of life is endorsed (forests as sacred places), they are still presented only as participants in need of human protection (Example 11):

11. RLL2021-17 'Sacred groves comprize islands of original forest, protected by the traditional authorities through a system of taboos and restrictions.'

In four instances out of eighty-six occurrences, forests are given a clear active role: 'as protectors against storm surges and filters from sediments' (RLL2021-26) or animals (RLL2021-27): 'Mangrove forests are highly biodiverse and act as breeding grounds for fish and other marine creatures.' However, one of these four occurrences is agroforestry, which means heavily managed ecosystems.

In all other eighty-two occurrences in RLL2021, forests undergo processes instigated by humans (directly or indirectly) or are viewed through a human perspective as in the following instance (Example 12), where the predicative adjective 'simple' sounds rather incongruous in the Conclusion of a report on global complexity:

12. RLL2021-40 'Forest ecosystems may appear to be simple, but forests vary enormously.'

In WHF2021, instead, forests are identified through complexity and presented as active participants in carbon storage (Example 13):

13. WHF2021-iii 'Forests are some of the most biodiverse habitats on Earth and play a crucial role in climate regulation by absorbing carbon dioxide (CO_2) from the atmosphere.'

They need human protection (this is the purpose of the document), but they are key participants through their active role and their value in environmental processes. They are represented not only in function of human needs but also as intrinsically valuable for the crucial processes they carry out. As suggested in Example 14, they need protection due to large-scale human-made damage:

14. WHF2021-3 'World Heritage forests provide critical climate benefits only if safeguarded from threats.'

As already mentioned, in RLL2021 the written text construes the identity and the role of plants as closely related to human priorities and the passive participant of human actions (positive or negative). Also, non-human animals connected to plants are mentioned or implied in relation to human needs (see, for instance, 'grazing'). In a nutshell, the title of RLL2021 summarizes the key viewpoint of the report: the action of 'restoring life to the land' is performed by humans through sustainable land management: it is humans that give life to the land and not vice versa. The colour images in the report are aligned with this, as shown in Table 7.2:

In the photos, local people belonging to a variety of ethnicities are represented working on the land or planning together in different natural settings. In Table 7.2, humans are categorized as backgrounded when only human artefacts and not people are present in the photo; images clearly represent the relevance of local communities on the land (seventy-three out of seventy-seven photos), empowering them. The implicit message is that life on land can only be restored by humans, or, more positively, it can only exist if humans relate to it respectfully as many native people do.

There is a tension between the representation discussed so far (in written text and photos) and the visual representation of the eight ecosystems excluded from the count in Table 7.2 because it is a mosaic of images and drawings forming a visual refrain which signposts each section in the document[7] and dominates the cover. The same composition of eight photos and eight drawings representing the main eight ecosystems can be also found in the copyright page and at p. 11. At the end of the report (RLL2021-39) the drawings only (without the photos) form a jigsaw puzzle, visually implicating the necessity of interrelation between these ecosystems. The key issue here is that this composite image seems to contradict the idea that all life-giving restoration powers are in human hands: only two images (out of eight) include humans (working the land or as human-made artefacts in urban areas). Non-human animals are erased and plant ecosystems are salient, both in the drawings and in the photos. Thus the most representative visual feature of the report is not aligned with the general message of the text.

In the written text of WHF2021, the ecosystems of the forests are represented as multifaceted and complex: their intrinsic qualities, values and activities are acknowledged and highlighted, along with human needs and factors that

Table 7.2 Images in RLL2021

Vegetation – no visible animal	3
Vegetation + non-human animal	1
Vegetation + human and/or non-human animals – humans backgrounded	31
Vegetation + human and/or non-human animals – humans foregrounded	41
Only humans no vegetation	1
Total	77

damage the environment. Plants, especially the collective entity of forests, are activated through both the powerful and unique activities they carry out on the planet and the forests' position in relation to human needs and values. This report clearly states the need for humans to repair the damage done to ecosystems that prevents forests from performing their irreplaceable active role on the planet.

The cover of the WHF2021 report is a drawing that represents an idyllic, fairy-tale-like forest without humans; stylized birds cross the sky as the only animals. The drawing, in the dominant colours that have metonymically come to represent the planet (green and blue), includes waving lines connecting sky and soil and evoking either carbon emissions or their sequestration by the forest. The report includes diagrams and drawings that visually expose the complexity of the issues, give agency to forests using arrows as action vectors indicating absorption of carbon (WHF2021-7) and represent trees including what is hidden to the human eye (root system and its effects) (WHF2021-12). The photos are only thirteen (including three headers); the images of forests are mostly taken from above in panoramic bird's-eye view (eleven out of thirteen) to give the impression of the extension of these forested areas and the thickness of the canopy. Humans are only physically present in three photos out of thirteen as watch guarding the forest from above and as firefighters. In other four photos the human presence is implied in images of deforestation and degraded land. The forest is represented as an imposingly powerful yet fragile ecosystem.

7.3.3 'Nature Now' video and 'The Green Planet' trailer

Two additional examples of plant representation are taken from two short videos. The first is *Nature Now* (NN2019[8]) released in 2019 and narrated by climate activists Greta Thunberg and George Monbiot; it is a social promotional video to raise awareness and funds for Natural Climate Solutions (NCS), namely solutions based on the healing power of natural events. The two protagonists address the viewers directly by looking into the camera (level direct gaze) from what looks like rooms in their respective homes. Medium/close-up shots establish a friendly, informal and equal relation between them and the viewers.

Greta Thunberg mentions the core problem and George Monbiot provides a natural solution (Examples 15 and 16, respectively):

15. Thunberg: 'Our Climate is breaking down [...] But we can still fix this. You can still fix it.' (NN2019: 00'12"–00'17")

16. Monbiot: 'There is a magic machine that sucks carbon out of the air, costs very little and builds itself. It is called . . . a tree. The tree is an example of NATURAL CLIMATE SOLUTION. Mangroves, peatbogs, jungles, marshes, seabeds, kelp forests, swamps, coral reefs. They take carbon out of the air and lock it away. Nature is a tool we can use to repair our broken climate.' (NN2019: 00'38"–01'08")

Both verbally and visually, trees are given emphasis and activated as offering a solution to the climate crisis: the scene shifts from Monbiot's medium/close-up shot to the image of a forest (while we can hear Monbiot's voice-over) in which a tree trunk is foregrounded in a close-up shot level with the gaze of the viewer while the background is the deep green shadowy forest floor and undergrowth. After this, plant ecosystems are represented in successively fast-edited shots while Monbiot's voice mentions them. These plant ecosystems are viewed in panoramic shots from above, which enhances their vastity and beauty. Visually, therefore, trees and plants are seen as individual participants forming complex collective ecosystems in which the network of relations is fundamental. The tension (Fill, this volume) arises between these edited images and the extended verbal metaphor of the tree as a human-made mechanism ('machine', 'tool', Example 16) to repair ('fix') another complex mechanism, the climate that 'is breaking down' (Example 15). In a video promoting Natural Climate Solutions, this tension is probably meant to give salience to trees and plants as agents of positive action. However, the implications of these verbal metaphors are that the climate crisis is represented as a linear problem solution that can be repaired as a human-made mechanism. Trees are a solution without the negative side effects of human artefacts ('it costs very little' and 'builds itself', Example 16). These metaphors reinforce the interpretative frame that human artefacts are powerful and effective to counteract a human-made crisis,[9] which is not aligned with the promotion of natural solutions.

The second short video is one of the official BBC trailers for the five-documentary series *The Green Planet* (TGP2022); the series, presented by the world-famous documentarist David Attenborough and produced by the BBC, was broadcast in spring 2022. The analysis only focuses on the ensemble of the written captions, the soundtrack and moving images edited using clips from the series episodes. The written text appears subdivided into sections in different edited shots of the trailer; it is rendered salient by its central position and the contrast of the white block capitals superimposed on the dark or colourful moving images, as shown in Example 17:

17. 'THERE IS A SECRET WORLD / THAT IS ALMOST HIDDEN FROM US / BREATHING LIFE / INTO OUR WORLD'.

Towards the end, the series title (THE GREEN PLANET) appears in the centre of the shot enclosed in a circle while small leaves are sprouting in time lapse towards the title; title and leaves are bright against the dark brown soil in the background: this gives them salience and connects them conceptually as the vector of the leaves points towards the series title within the circle that looks like a water drop. The soundtrack of the trailer (music and sounds) evokes the environments in which plants live; sounds are associated with the movements of the plants filmed in time lapse. The filming techniques magnify both moving images and sounds to recreate for the viewer plant movements that are mostly imperceptible to humans. Thus, the 'secret world that is almost hidden to us' (Example 17) is verbally represented as powerfully active through the transitive use of the process 'breathe': 'breathing life into our world' implies a near divine power of giving life. The multimodal correlation between moving images, soundtrack and written captions orients the interpretation towards recognizing the powerful energy of plants in creating living habitats for themselves and animals (human and non-human). The magnifying techniques of moving images and sounds, and time lapse video recording, bring plant organs, shapes and action to human perception and comprehension (the complexity of time perception is beyond the scope of the present chapter; see Adam 1990, 1998). Thus, the metaphorical and literal expression 'breathing life into our world' is instantiated by the ensemble of soundtrack and moving images within a multimodal orchestration that orients the viewers towards an attitude of recognition, marvel and awe.

7.4 Concluding remarks and scope for further research

Plant representation in ecolinguistics is vastly underexplored even though plants are at the core of all ecosystems. This chapter has raised some methodological issues within a vast field that needs investigation and critical reflection.

The data analysed reveal tension between the purposes of the texts and their discoursal realizations. In agenda setting and widely influential 2030ASDG2015 plants are backgrounded, as are non-human animals, due to the emphasis of the report on basic human priorities and rights, which, however, would profit from a better alignment between humans and the lifescapes they belong to.

RLL2021 and WHF2021 posit the relevance of plants at their core since their purpose is taking action against the deterioration of ecosystems and positively promote their protection through plants. In the two reports plants are mostly represented as resources related to human needs and framed as means to repair ecosystems damaged by humans. In the institutional discourse of the two reports, there is a disalignment between the relevance of plants per se and as resources to repair the effects of human-inflicted climate crisis. However, there are instances, especially in WHF2021, that reveal the overwhelming power and energy of plants: it is mainly expressed through images and drawings and only partly in written discourse.

In the video *Nature Now*, tension arises between the promotion of natural solutions for the climate crisis and the discourse framing trees and nature as machines and tools, while images offer the complexity of natural plant environments as collective connections in ecosystems. It is in *The Green Planet* trailer that the multimodal orchestration between modes (written captions, sound and moving images) offers its viewers a coherent (if surprising) representation of plants as active and independent collectivities of participants who allow our world to exist through their action of 'breathing life' into it. It is an evocative and memorable representation of a scientifically sound concept.

In this study, ecolinguistics and critical multimodal studies have been adopted as frameworks; further reflection is needed on the analytical framework to be adopted for a variety of genres and text types. Some principles and categories were drawn from Social Actor Analysis and adapted to the aims of the study. Some categories used in the analysis of plant representations need adaptation: the notions of 'collectivity' and 'genericity' in plants acquire new meaning due to their close interrelation among themselves and with the lifescape; the concepts of 'individual' and 'collectivity' intertwine and overlap; categories such as 'generic' and 'specific' change their meaning when representing plants; the verbal and multimodal representation of action and movement (processes), existence, animacy, agency and time, among other variables, need to be reassessed. In visual representation, for instance, a panoramic view from above gives the viewer the sense of vastity and power of the collective being called 'forest', rather than the impression of human domination from above. The 'body' of plants tends to be partly (or mostly) hidden to human sight or perception and so are the relationships among plants, and among plants and animals. This gives drawings and diagrams in reports the key role of revealing what we cannot otherwise perceive. Capra writes: 'Because living systems are nonlinear and rooted in patterns of relationships, understanding the principles of ecology requires a new way of seeing the world and of thinking – in terms of relationships, connectedness, and context – that goes against the grain of traditional Western science and education' (Capra 2007: 4).

This study confirms the necessity of investigating a variety of different genres and subgenres multimodally in order to reflect on ways of representing the world of plants for a variety of cultural contexts, communicative purposes and for different discourse communities. Public response to different multimodal texts would also contribute to revealing human reactions to plant representation.

Stibbe (2012: 150 et passim) writes that animals and plants are presented as agents and sensers in haiku just by leading their lives; in Japanese this is captured in the concept of 'sonomama: the way things are'. In the texts analysed in this chapter, plant action and agentivity are often instantiated through the way they lead their life acting on their environment. Studying the way plants are represented multimodally in discourse can help us establish a relation with beings who are extremely different from us, and adapt our methodological frameworks to understand – and, ultimately, represent – them better.

Whereas critical discourse studies (including multimodal critical discourse studies) are generally concerned with expressing solidarity with the powerless and at-risk individuals and groups, this contribution focuses on a powerful and widespread group of diverse living beings on the planet. Some plants will most likely survive and regenerate life after a human-inflicted, pollution-driven animal mass extinction. Rather than erasing, neglecting, backgrounding, disempowering plants from our discourses, we would need to explore the extraordinary energy they share with the lifescape and learn from that. Latour (2014: 15–16) writes: 'The point of living in the epoch of Anthropocene is that all agents share the same shape-changing destiny, a destiny that cannot be followed, documented, told, and represented by using any of the older traits associated with subjectivity or objectivity. [. . .] Living with a world that has not been previously deanimated will make a great difference for the Earthbound.'

Notes

1 I am deeply grateful to the scholars who kindly read parts of this chapter, discussed issues and offered me their encouragement and feedback. Among them, Barbara Cauzzo read an early draft of this chapter; Alwin Frank Fill, Barbara Adam, Federica Pedriali and Matt Drury offered me suggestions and ideas; Emile Bellewes gave me

detailed comments on the final draft of the chapter. I also thank the anonymous reviewers for their observations.
2   The capital letter is used only when present in the literature it refers to. The category adaptation used in this study is without capital letter to indicate that the investigation is ongoing and categories will be further refined.
3   Quotes from the data are identified with title initials, date of publication and page numbers of the open access texts.
4   Keywords in corpus linguistics are the statistically more frequent words in one corpus as compared to a reference corpus (Baker 2006: 125; Poole, this volume).
5   Emile Bellewes noticed that 'there is almost a co-agency that happens or a joint process whereby the human is the instigator and the plant continues the growth as the agent of its own development' (personal communication).
6   The LOB corpus was used as reference corpus.
7   https://www.unccd.int/sites/default/files/documents/2021-10/211018_RestoringLifetotheLand_Report%20%282%29.pdf.
8   Examples refer to video time stamps in minutes and seconds.
9   See the 'machine' metaphor in Adam (1990: 76 et passim).

References

Adam, B. (1990), *Time and Social Theory*, Oxford: Polity Press.
Adam, B. (1998), *Timescapes of Modernity*, London: Routledge.
Baker, P. (2006), *Using Corpora in Discourse Analysis*, London: Continuum.
Baldry, A. and P. Thibault (2006), *Multimodal Transcription and Text Analysis*, London: Equinox.
Baluška, F. and S. Mancuso (2020), 'Plants, Climate and Humans', *EMBO Reports*, 21 (e50109): 1–5.
Baluška, F. and S. Mancuso (2021), 'Individuality, Self and Sociality of Vascular Plants', *Philosophical Transactions - Royal Society: Biological Sciences Online*, 376 (1821): 1–11.
Benwell, B. and E. Stokoe (2006), *Discourse and Identity*, Edinburgh: Edinburgh University Press.
Bezemer, J. and G. Kress (2016), *Multimodality, Learning and Communication*, London: Routledge.
Brewer, M. B. and W. Gardner (1996), 'Who Is 'We'? Levels of Collective Identity and Self-Representations', *Journal of Personality and Social Psychology*, 71 (1): 83–93.
Brezina, V., P. Weill-Tessier, and A. McEnery (2021), #LancsBox v. 6.x [software package].
Brubacker, R. and F. Cooper (2000), 'Beyond "Identity"', *Theory and Society*, 29 (1): 1–47.

Caldas-Coulthard, R. and R. Iedema, eds (2008), *Identity Trouble: Critical Discourse and Contested Identities*, Basingstoke: Palgrave Macmillan.

Calvo, P. with N. Lawrence (2022), *Planta Sapiens: Unmasking Plant Intelligence*, London: The Bridge Street Press.

Calvo P. and A. Trewavas (2021), 'Cognition and Intelligence of Green Plants: Information for Animal Scientists', *Biochemical and Biophysical Research Communication*, 564: 78–85.

Capra, F. (2007), 'Sustainable Living, Ecological Literacy and the Breath of Life', *Canadian Journal of Environmental Education*, 12 (1): 9–18.

Cook, G. (2004), *Genetically Modified Language: The Discourse of Arguments for GM Crops and Food*, London: Routledge.

Cook, G. and A. Sealey (2018), 'The Discursive Representation of Animals', in A. F. Fill and H. Penz (eds), *The Routledge Handbook of Ecolinguistics*, 311–24, London: Routledge.

Encyclopedia Britannica (2022), Available online: https://www.britannica.com/plant/plant (accessed 18 February 2022).

Entman, R. M. (1993), 'Framing: Toward Clarification of a Fractured Paradigm', *Journal of Communication*, 43 (4): 51–8.

Fairclough, N. (2003), *Analysing Discourse: Textual Analysis for Social Research*, London: Routledge.

Fairclough, N. (2014), *Language and Power*, London: Routledge.

Fairclough, N. and R. Wodak (1997), 'Critical Discourse Analysis', in T. A. Van Dijk (ed), *Discourse as Social Interaction*, 258–84, London: Sage.

Fill, A. (2001), 'Ecolinguistics: State of the Art 1998', in A. Fill and P. Mühlhäusler (eds), *The Ecolinguistics Reader: Language, Ecology and Environment*, 43–53, London: Continuum.

Fill, A. F. and P. Mühlhäusler, eds (2001), *The Ecolinguistics Reader: Language, Ecology and Environment*, London, New York: Continuum.

Fill, A. F. and H. Penz, eds (2018), *The Routledge Handbook of Ecolinguistics*, London: Routledge.

Forte, D. (2015), 'Nonhuman Animal Legislation and Speciesist Discourse: Argentina's Pet Responsibility Act: Anti-Cruelty Law or Death Row Pardon?', *Language and Ecology*, 1–19. Available online: https://www.ecolinguistics-association.org/_files/ugd/ae088a_517a3863157641a1b6dd997dd1b0b3b0.pdf (accessed 31 May 2022).

Freeman, C. P. (2009), 'This Little Piggy Went to Press: The American News Media's Construction of Animal in Agriculture', *Communication Review*, 12: 78–103.

Gagliano, M., J. C. Ryan, and P. Viera, eds (2017), *The Language of Plants: Science, Philosophy, Literature*, Minneapolis: University of Minnesota Press.

Halliday, M. (2001), 'New Ways of Meaning: The Challenge to Applied Linguistics', in A. Fill and P. Mühlhäusler (eds), *The Ecolinguistics Reader: Language, Ecology and Environment*, 175–202, London: Continuum.

Heuberger, R. (2018), 'Overcoming Anthropocentrism with Anthropomorphic and Physiocentric Uses of Language?', in A. Fill and H. Penz (eds), *The Routledge Handbook of Ecolinguistics*, 342–54, London: Routledge.

Jacobs, G. (2016), 'The Presentation of Animals in English as an Additional Language Coursebooks', *Language and Ecology*, 1–9. Available online: https://www.ecolinguistics-association.org/_files/ugd/ae088a_43d39bc18b0b43f9ac1ab11ac4af8339.pdf (accessed 31 May 2022).

Jung, M. (2001), 'Ecological Criticism of Language', in A. Fill and P. Mühlhäusler (eds), *The Ecolinguistics Reader: Language, Ecology and Environment*, 270–85, London: Continuum.

Kress, G. (2010), *Multimodality: A Socio-Semiotic Approach to Contemporary Communication*, London: Routledge.

Kress, G. and T. van Leeuwen (2021), *Reading Images: The Grammar of Visual Design*, London: Routledge.

Lakoff, G. (2010), 'Why It Matters How We Frame the Environment', *Environmental Communication*, 4 (1): 70–81.

Lamb, G. (2024), *Multispecies Discourse Analysis*, London: Bloomsbury Academic.

Latour, B. (2005), *Reassembling the Social: An Introduction into Actor-Network Theory*, Oxford: Oxford University Press.

Latour, B. (2014), 'Agency at the Time of the Anthropocene', *New Literary History*, 45 (1): 1–18.

Latour, B. (2020), *La Sfida di Gaia* (1st French edn, 2015), Milano: Meltemi Press.

Mancuso, S. (2017), *Plant Revolution. Le Piante Hanno già Inventato il Nostro Futuro*, Firenze: Giunti Editore.

Mayr, A. (2008), 'Introduction: Power, Discourse and Institutions', in A. Mayr (ed), *Language and Power: An Introduction to Institutional Discourse*, 1–25, London: Continuum.

McEntee Atalianis, L. (2019), *Identity in Applied Linguistics Research*, London: Bloomsbury Academic.

Moschini, I. and M. G. Sindoni, eds (2022), *Mediation and Multimodal Meaning Making in Digital Environments*, London: Routledge.

Poole, R. and M. A. Micalay-Hurtado (2022), 'A Corpus-Assisted Ecolinguistic Analysis of the Representations of Tree/s and Forest/s in US Discourse from 1820–2019', *Applied Corpus Linguistics*, 2 (3). https://doi.org/10.1016/j.acorp.2022.100036

Reisigl, M. and R. Wodak (2009), 'The Discourse-Historical Approach (DHA)', in R. Wodak and M. Meyer (eds), *Methods of Critical Discourse Analysis*, 2nd edn, 87–121, London: Sage.

Steffensen, S. V. and A. Fill (2014), 'Ecolinguistics: The State of the Art and Future Horizons', *Language Sciences*, 41: 6–25.

Stibbe, A. (2012), *Animals Erased*, Middleton: Wesleyan University Press (kindle edition).

Stibbe, A. (2021), *Ecolinguistics: Language, Ecology and the Stories We Live By*, 2nd edn, London: Routledge.

Valvason, E. (2020 [2019]), *The Semantics of Sustainable Development: A Corpus-Assisted Ecological Analysis of Discourse Across Languages*. Unpublished PhD Thesis. University of Pavia, Italy.

van Leeuwen, T. (2008), *Discourse and Practice*, Oxford: Oxford University Press (Kindle edition).

van Leeuwen, T. (2022), *Multimodality and Identity*, London: Routledge.

Woodward, W. and E. Lemmer (2019), 'Introduction: Critical Plant Studies', *Journal of Literary Studies*, 35 (4): 23–7.

Zhdanava, A., K. Surinderpal, and R. Kumaran (2021), 'Representing Nonhuman Animals as Equals: An Ecolinguistic Analysis of Vegan Campaigns', *Journal of World Languages*, 7 (1): 26–57.

Data

Natural Climate Solutions (NCS), #Nature Now [video]. Available online: https://www.naturalclimate.solutions (accessed 30 March 2022).

The Green Planet Trailer (2022) [trailer], Dir. David Attenborough, BBC. Available online: https://www.youtube.com/watch?v=FcnLPH11qJw&list=PL50KW6aT4UgzTQ7vRFo1VXzbKnWjiJv2y&index=1 (accessed 3 June 2022).

UNESCO, WRI, IUCN (2021), *World Heritage Forests: Carbon Sinks Under Pressure*, Paris: UNESCO.

United Nations (2015), 'The 2030 Agenda for Sustainable Development'.
Available online: https://www.un.org/ga/search/view_doc.asp?symbol=A/RES/70/1&Lang=E (accessed 31 May 2022).

UNCCD and WOCAT (2021), 'Restoring Life to the Land: The Role of Sustainable Land Management in Ecosystem Restoration'. Available online: https://www.unccd.int/sites/default/files/documents/2021-10/211018_RestoringLifetotheLand_Report%20%282%29.pdf (accessed 13 November 2022).

Part III

Ecoliteracy for Citizenship Education

8

Promoting Ecoliteracy in Essayistic Media Texts through the Case of *The Anthropocene Reviewed*

Andrea Sabine Sedlaczek

Introduction

In his podcast and recent book, *The Anthropocene Reviewed* (2018–20, Green 2021a), the American author John Green rates different aspects of life in our human-centred age on Earth on a five-star scale. From marvelling at large-scale natural phenomena to examining apparently small human consumerist practices, Green's essays reflect the contradictions inherent in our current lifestyles that are at the heart of the ecological crises we are currently facing. By combining personal narratives, evocative descriptions and subjective evaluations with scientific explanations and philosophical argumentation, the essays relate our human lived experiences to the world and ascribe meaning to it. They thus invite the reader to reflect upon their own experiential relationship with the natural world they inhabit as well as some of the social and cultural practices that define our human lives. In this chapter I will argue that, by doing so, these essayistic media texts can be fruitfully understood as ecoliteracy practices.

Ecoliteracy has emerged as a concept alongside other analogous notions such as ecological literacy, environmental literacy or sustainability literacy (Orr 1992; McBride et al. 2013; Stibbe 2010) to point towards educational endeavours that want to foster the knowledge, skills and values that are deemed necessary to engender ecologically beneficial action. In Section 8.1 of the chapter, I will explore this emergent notion of ecoliteracy and its relation to traditional and new literacy concepts, as they are critically discussed in literacy studies (Kress 2003; Code 2019). Works in the field of New Literacy Studies (NLS) and multiliteracies studies (Cazden et al. 1996; Street 2003; Gee 2004; Anstey and Bull 2018) point to the need for expanding the original notion of literacy as the ability to read and write but caution against simplistic and reductive literacy concepts that are confined to prescribed functional skill sets. Instead, they conceptualize literacies as social practices of meaning-making (Street 2003) and incorporate multimodal, multimedia and multilingual 'reading' practices (Cazden et al. 1996; Anstey and Bull 2018). Following from these works, I propose a refined notion of ecoliteracy that includes the 'reading' practices involved in interpreting the signs of nature (Code 2019).

For this dynamic and holistic perspective to ecoliteracy, which I introduce in Section 8.2, I draw on a critical ecosemiotic framework based on the semiotic theory of Charles S. Peirce (Peirce 1931–58). Peirce's holistic sign theory provides an integrative framework that can account for both multimodal communicative practices of humans and the everyday interpretation of natural signs necessary for adequately understanding and assessing the relationship of humans to the world. As such, this critical ecosemiotic framework can serve both as a theoretical foundation for a concept of ecoliteracy and as a methodological framework for an ecolinguistic analysis (Sedlaczek 2018).

Complemented by methodological tools from multimodal and critical discourse analysis (Reisigl and Wodak 2016; Stibbe 2014; Sedlaczek 2016, 2017), I will use this framework in Section 8.3 to analyse the essayistic media texts of *The Anthropocene Reviewed*. In the analysis, I will examine the essayistic texts as ecoliteracy practices that construct and represent values and behaviours in relation to human life in the Anthropocene on a small and large scale. In two small case studies – one from the printed book version and one from the audiobook version of *The Anthropocene Reviewed* – I will focus on the way the essays are structured as open and hybrid genres that combine different generic patterns such as narration, argumentation, explication and description and that employ multimodal resources. In discussing the essays, I will argue that they demonstrate an acute understanding of the way meaning-making is at the heart of humans' relationship to the world – an understanding that is in line with the ecosemiotic concept of ecoliteracy that I will introduce. Following from the analyses, in the final section (8.4) I will offer some suggestions on how the essayistic media texts of *The Anthropocene Reviewed* and textual practices based on them could be fruitfully used in educational settings to foster further ecoliteracy practices.

8.1 Ecoliteracy in the expanding network of literacy concepts

The past decades have seen an expansion of the traditional notion of literacy with the proliferation of an increasing number of new literacy concepts. From health literacy to financial literacy, emotional literacy to cultural literacy, sexual literacy to computer literacy – these literacy concepts encompass a wide range of competencies associated with different fields of knowledge or areas of life (McBride et al. 2013: 4; Kress 2003: 17–18; Code 2019: 1270).

Most of these emergent literacy concepts rest on a broader, extended notion of literacy that goes beyond the original definition of literacy as being concerned with the ability to read and write. In this broader notion, fashionable in educational research and policy, literacy is seen as a tool for gaining knowledge, skills and capabilities on a cognitive, affective and behavioural level in different fields (McBride et al. 2013: 2).

At the same time, such field-specific literacy concepts and their application in educational policy and practice have met with criticism or caution among theorists in the field of literacy studies (Kress 2003: 17–18; Code 2019: 1270). Kress (2003: 17–18) warns against an undifferentiated metaphoric extension of the term of literacy to social and cultural domains that warrant different treatments and regulations than what literacy originally entails and that are restricted to narrow functional skill sets. Reviewing some popular definitions of ecoliteracy, Code (2019) similarly points to the limitations of ecoliteracy concepts that could be equated with ecological awareness or environmental education, without theoretically accounting for what is implied by 'being literate' in this context (Code 2019: 1268). I agree that while focusing on field-specific knowledge and competencies can have value, to conceptualize them as unique literacy types, their relation to foundational literacy concepts must be explored more deeply.

The problem of field-dependent literacy concepts can be exemplified by comparing ecoliteracy to two similar concepts – ecological literacy and environmental literacy – that share their focus on education for enhancing human-environment relationships. While these different terms are often used interchangeably, McBride et al. (2013) point to the different disciplinary backgrounds and corresponding theoretical frameworks behind them.

Environmental literacy emerged in the field of environmental education and takes a problem-oriented perspective on the knowledge, skills, attitudes and behaviours necessary to solve current environmental issues (McBride et al. 2013). Ecological literacy takes a broader, science-based perspective, situated in the discipline of ecology. It wants to promote knowledge about basic ecological concepts as well as systems thinking that acknowledges the complexity of the environment as a basis for informed decision-making (McBride et al. 2013).

Ecoliteracy, while sharing aspects of environmental and ecological literacy, has emerged as a concept within the broader humanities, similarly to other fields such as ecolinguistics or ecocriticism and in line with movements that promote education for sustainable development (McBride et al. 2013: 14; Orr 1992). According to common definitions, ecoliteracy wants to foster cognitive, affective and behavioural capabilities that lead to a deeper understanding of the organization of ecosystems and thus help to create sustainable human communities and societies (McBride et al. 2013: 14).

While environmental and ecological literacy are more strongly bound by their disciplinary background, the concept of ecoliteracy has been more open to incorporating different disciplinary traditions and ways of thinking – within and also going beyond modern Western science. McBride et al. (2013) point to holistic and spiritual components being incorporated into ecoliteracy, while Code (2019) advocates for connecting to Traditional Ecological Knowledge and indigenous science as a means of overcoming reductive approaches dominant in Western science (Code 2019: 1275).

Ecoliteracy thus seems a promising concept that can transcend the limitations of field-specific literacy concepts. While many of these narrow literacy concepts reinforce the dominant educational culture with their focus on functional skills, ecoliteracy has a more transformative aspiration. Recognizing that the ecological crisis is also a crisis of education, ecoliteracy wants to reorient dominant educational practices towards sustainable development (McBride et al. 2013: 14).

Rethinking traditional educational approaches and corresponding literacy notions has also been at the forefront of works in the field of NLS (Street 2003; Gee 2004) and multiliteracies studies (Cazden et al. 1996). This research recognizes the need for expanding the notion of literacy from its original narrow focus on the ability to use alphabetic writing systems. Instead, they identify a plurality of literacies while still grounding this expansion of literacy notions in its original meaning of dealing with written language.

NLS conceptualize literacies not as sets of skills to be taught and that will have direct effects on other social and cognitive practices but as situated social practices of meaning-making that are ideological and thus depend on and vary according to the culture and context (Street 2003: 77, Gee 2004: 12). While a skill-based approach to literacy can only account for the superficial ability to decode texts and to assign 'literal' meanings to them, gaining a deeper understanding of texts relies on being familiar with the context-dependent communicative resources used (Gee 2004: 12f.). NLS thus advocates for understanding literacy learning as a cultural process that is based on the socialization and enculturation in meaning-making practices of a community and their specialized forms of language (Gee 2004: 31).

A plurality of literacies is also recognized by the concept of multiliteracies first introduced by the New London Group (Cazden et al. 1996). Influenced by work in both multilingualism and multimodality, multiliteracies studies expand the traditional concept of literacy not just to incorporate different types of languages but other communicative resources as well. Against the backdrop of the changing communicative and media landscape that modern literacy practices are embedded in, multiliteracies account for multilingual, multimodal and multimedia practices (Cazden et al. 1996; Anstey and Bull 2018).

Expanding from these works, multimodal and multiliteracies studies can serve as a useful reference point for a concept of ecoliteracy that is not rooted in skills but in meaning-making, that is, semiotic practices. From a semiotic perspective, literacy practices such as reading and writing texts are fundamentally acts of semiosis, that is, of interpreting, (de)constructing and transforming signs (Kress 2003). While multimodal approaches have long applied semiotic frameworks to account for the use and understanding of a variety of semiotic modes in texts and discourse, interpreting signs and constructing meaning from them reaches beyond human communicative resources to the domain of the wider natural world.

This idea is in line with Code (2019) who advocates for centring ecoliteracy around the notion of 'reading in the book of nature' and treating nature as a text in its own right. Code, however, misses the semiotic nature of his proposal, instead suggesting Goethe's delicate empiricism as a theoretical and methodological reference point. While I find Code's deliberations on redefining ecoliteracy very compelling and inspiring, I suggest that an ecosemiotic framework based on the pragmatic and semiotic theory of Charles Sanders Peirce offers a better epistemological, theoretical and methodological foundation for a dynamic and holistic perspective on ecoliteracy. In the next section, I will introduce this critical ecosemiotic framework and point out its use as both a theoretical and methodological foundation.

8.2 A critical ecosemiotic framework for ecoliteracy and ecolinguistics

Peirce's semiotic theory is a holistic and ecological sign theory that is centrally concerned with the relation between humans, signs and the outer world. Peirce's theory, however, does not only cover signs used by humans as intentional communicative resources but also considers everything in the world as a potential sign that can be interpreted in a variety of ways (by humans but also by non-human interpreters) (Short 2007: 19). Peirce's sign concept involves a triadic relationship between three central elements: (1) the sign itself in its material manifestation, (2) the object as the sign-external reality that the sign refers to and (3) the interpretant as the effect the sign has on an interpreter in the construction of meaning (CP 2.228, 2.274).[1]

Human perception, cognition and communication rely on this triadic sign process. From an epistemological standpoint, Peirce's theory is a weak realism that acknowledges that we humans can only perceive and make sense of the reality or the world via signs (Sedlaczek 2016). The mind-independent reality that Peirce calls the 'dynamic object' cannot be grasped and understood directly but only mediated through the interpretation of signs. Peirce calls the mediated version of the object, as represented by the sign, the 'immediate object' (CP 4.536, 8.183, 8.314). While this immediate object can only ever be an incomplete approximation of the dynamic object, the dynamic object nonetheless has a reality of its own and thus has concrete material implications for humans' relationship to the world (as observable through natural, indexical signs).

The triadic form of Peirce's sign model is founded on basic phenomenological categories that give rise to further triadic distinctions and trichotomies on each of the three poles of the sign process. These different categories show the breadth of Peirce's semiotic theory (Short 2007) and can be applied as an ecosemiotic framework that can serve both as foundation for a concept of ecoliteracy as a meaning-making practice and as an analytic framework for a discourse analytical investigation of texts or sign complexes (Sedlaczek 2018):

1. The first pole is concerned with the material quality of the sign itself: Peirce distinguishes between potential signs (qualisigns/tone, i.e. anything that may become a sign), actual, instantiated signs (sinsigns/token) and habitual, rule-based signs (legisigns/type) (CP 2.244–246; 4.537).
2. The second pole is concerned with the referential relationship between sign and object: Peirce distinguishes between signs that are based on a

relationship of similarity to their objects (iconic signs, e.g. images), signs that are causally or contiguously linked to their objects (indexical signs, e.g. natural signs) and signs that rely on a conventional relationship to their objects (symbolic signs, e.g. language) (CP 2.247–249).
3. The third pole is concerned with the interpretative aspects of the sign process. Here, Peirce makes several useful distinctions. He distinguishes three types of sign effects: feelings (emotional interpretants), actions (energetic interpretants) and thoughts (logical interpretants) (CP 5.475–476), and he differentiates three stages in the interpretation process: a potential interpretation (immediate interpretant), the actual interpretation (dynamic interpretant) and an evolved, intended interpretation (final interpretant) (CP 4.536). These two trichotomous categories are not mutually exclusive but interact and build on one another. Regarding the relationship of a sign to a logical interpretant, Peirce differentiates signs further, based on their degree of complexity: signs with a possible meaning (rhematic signs, i.e. terms), signs with a fact-asserting, predicative meaning (dicentic signs, i.e. propositions) and signs that involve a complex inferential reasoning (argumentative signs) (CP 2.250–253).

Against the backdrop of this ecosemiotic framework, ecoliteracy can be understood as meaning-making practices of humans in engagement with the environment surrounding them. Like all literacy practices, as propagated by NLS, ecoliteracy practices are culturally specific and context-dependent: meaning-making in relation to the environment varies, for example, between scientists trying to understand the mechanics of ecosystems, indigenous cultures trying to navigate their subsistence in connection to their living environments or environmental activists trying to preserve endangered habitats. What all these practices have in common is that they rely on humans interpreting a variety of natural indexical signs, that these signs have different affective, behavioural and cognitive effects on them and that humans use these signs – in conjunction with other communicative signs – to construct further meanings based on them. To be considered ecoliteracy practices, I would also add the prerequisite that the meaning-making practices always have the intention of understanding the direct objects of the natural world and our human relationship to them. Thus, I follow the transformative aspiration of other ecoliteracy approaches that are oriented towards fostering sustainable human communities and practices (McBride et al. 2013: 14).

How ecoliteracy practices conceived in this way can look like, I will show in the analytic part of my chapter. The critical ecosemiotic framework based on the semiotic theory of C. S. Peirce, as introduced earlier, will serve as the central methodological framework, allowing me to analyse multimodal texts (as sign complexes) by investigating the material, referential and interpretative character of the sign process, respectively (Sedlaczek 2018). This analytic framework is complemented by methodological tools from ecolinguistics and multimodal and critical discourse analysis (Sedlaczek 2016; 2017; cf. also Stibbe 2014; Reisigl and Wodak 2016).

Analysing media texts through an ecolinguistic multimodal and critical discourse analysis sheds light on how these texts discursively construct and represent ecologically relevant issues through their use of multimodal communicative resources. The ecolinguistic perspective implies a normative ecological standpoint that is applied to critically evaluate whether the media texts and practices can help or hinder positive action that fosters harmonious relationships of humans with their environment (Stibbe 2014; Sedlaczek 2016). While critical discourse studies and ecolinguistic research have often focused on pointing out the limitations of human language and communication to adequately represent the natural world, an increasing amount of work tries to highlight positive examples of communicative practices that help to foster ecological awareness and understanding and that promote positive action in line with ecological values.

Nanson (2021), Gersie, Nanson and Schieffelin (2022) and Hofman-Bergholm (2022), for example, have investigated storytelling practices as opportunities for environmental learning. These can both foster systems thinking, that is, a holistic understanding of the complex dynamics and interrelations at play in ecosystems (McBride et al. 2013: 13; Hofman-Bergholm 2022: 8), and promote a deeper sense of connection to the natural world. The essayistic texts of *The Anthropocene Reviewed*, I will argue, can be understood in a similar light, although they transcend pure narrative storytelling, by combining narration with other generic patterns.

In line with text and discourse analytic approaches, I assume five basic generic patterns to be at play in texts and distinguish their material, referential and interpretative aspects as follows (adapted from Reisigl 2021: 377):

1. Description: aims at iconically representing objects that can be perceived by the human senses. Makes use of mainly rhematic iconic qualisigns and sinsigns and evokes both emotional and logical interpretants.

2. Explication: makes factual processes and connections comprehensible. Relies on indexical dicentic sinsigns and legisigns and the formation of logical interpretants.
3. Argumentation: wants to convince of a disputed claim of truth or normative rightness. Involves dicentic and argumentative legisigns and aims at the formation of energetic and logical interpretants.
4. Narration: constructs a meaningful story around events by structuring them in a narrative arc (orientation, complication, resolution). Weaves together iconic, indexical and symbolic sinsigns and legisigns and wants to evoke both emotional and logical interpretants.
5. Instruction: provides guidance for actions. It can make use of iconic, indexical and symbolic qualisigns, sinsigns and legisigns and mainly aims at evoking energetic interpretants.

In the two case studies at the centre of the analysis later in the text, I will reflect on both these different generic patterns at play in the essayistic media texts of *The Anthropocene Reviewed* and the multimodal resources used in them. By revealing the material, referential and interpretative aspects of the semiotic choices made in the texts, I will reflect on how these texts can be considered as instantiating ecoliteracy practices.

8.3 Promoting ecoliteracy in *The Anthropocene Reviewed*

The Anthropocene Reviewed (TAR) is a podcast series and book project of American author John Green, who has gained international popularity – especially among younger generations – through his young adult fiction novels (*The Fault in Our Stars, Turtles All the Way Down*) and through his YouTube productions together with his brother Hank Green (*Vlogbrothers* and the educational channel *Crash Course* aimed at humanities and science courses).

In the podcast *The Anthropocene Reviewed* (2018–20) and the book based on it (*The Anthropocene Reviewed: Essays on a Human-Centered Planet*, Green 2021a), Green reviews different aspects of human life on Earth on a five-star scale. The subjects of his essayistic reviews range from the small and obscure to the broad and abstract: they include natural phenomena and organisms, such as 'Sunsets', 'Canada Geese' or 'Viral Meningitis'; human consumerist products and practices, such as 'Air-Conditioning', 'Teddy Bears' or 'The Nathan's Famous Hot Dog Eating Contest'; and abstract concepts and ideas about human nature, such as 'Humanity's Temporal Range', 'Mortification' or 'Our Capacity for Wonder'.[2]

As he states in the introduction of the book, Green developed the idea behind his project through both his experience with writing book reviews for the journal *The Booklist* and his fascination with the proliferation of online reviewing practices that in the past decade have made everyone a potential reviewer as well as every aspect of our human lives a potential subject for review – from books and films to tourism sites, service professionals or medications. These online reviewing practices have also popularized the use of a five-star scale to rate the subject of review. This common feature of online reviews transforms the mainly qualitative evaluations that formed the basis of the original format of professional book reviews to a quantitative evaluation that is mainly geared towards data aggregation and artificial intelligence instead of humans (Green 2021a: 3).

By writing his own reviews of different facets of life on our human-centred planet and evaluating them with a rating on a five-star scale, Green both appropriates and subverts these modern reviewing practices and their digitalized consumerist logic. With both the form and the content of his reviews, he is thus demonstrating an acute awareness of the contradictions inherent in our modern human cultures and lifestyles and how these contradictions are connected to human meaning-making.

As a genre, Green's reviews are open and hybrid. Speaking about them both as 'reviews' and as 'essays', they best fit the broad literary genre of the essay (Chadbourne 1983), without conforming to a strict structural form. As literary essays and as a reflective take on modern reviewing practices, the essayistic texts are always personal, combining subjective evaluations and autobiographical narrations with descriptive, explanatory and argumentative parts.

In the introduction, Green makes his own positioning in his essayistic reviews explicit, acknowledging that he is engaging in meaning-making practices in them: instead of adopting the impersonal style of the classic book review genre, he likens his form of essayistic reviews to 'a kind of memoir' and justifies his use of a personal style with the premise that 'in the Anthropocene, there are no disinterested observers; there are only participants' (Green 2021a: 5). In this reflection, Green thus demonstrates an insight into the basic ecosemiotic principle that humans cannot observe the world as dynamic objects directly and objectively but only through the interpretation of signs and the mediation of an interpretant that is subject to change with both the intention of the sign interpreter and the context of interpretation.

At the same time, Green shows commitment in recognizing the dynamic objects and he explicitly rejects meaning-making practices that are not rooted in an ecological understanding of the relationship of humans to the world. In his introduction, for example, he weaves a personal story of a time when he was struck down by a sudden bout of the vertigo-inducing disease labyrinthitis into the text while reflecting on the meanings he wants and does not want to ascribe to this story (Green 2021a: 3):

> It is tempting to make labyrinthitis a metaphor: My life lacked balance and so I was devastated by a balance disorder. I spent a month drawing a straight line of a trail only to be told that life is never simple paths – only dizzying labyrinths folding in on themselves. Even now I'm structuring this introduction like a maze, coming back to places I thought I'd left. But this symbolization of disease is exactly what I've tried to write against in my novels *Turtles All the Way Down* and *The Fault in Our Stars*, where I hope at least OCD and cancer are portrayed not as battles to be won or as symbolic manifestations of character flaws or whatever, but as illnesses to be lived with as well as one can. I did not get labyrinthitis because the universe wanted to teach me a lesson about balance. So I tried to live with it as well as I could.

In the introduction, he uses the metaphor of the labyrinth as a strategic semiotic choice to tie together different narrative and explicatory parts of his text – making the structure of the text iconically resemble a labyrinth – but he is not ascribing a higher, external meaning to it: his vertigo is not a metaphoric, iconic sign of an abstract moral object, as narrative meaning-making practices are prone to purport, but it is an indexical natural sign pointing to the direct object of an illness that is caused by processes unconnected to human meaning-making. In this passage, Green thus instantiates an ecoliteracy practice that interprets natural signs as pointing to direct objects outside of human cognition. Green also offers a perspective on the kind of interpretants to be formed as a result of such an ecoliteracy practice: the energetic interpretant, that is, action, following from the interpretation of natural sign is not to 'fight' against nature but to accept and 'live with' nature 'as well as one can'. In the following two case studies, I will further highlight the way Green effectively mixes different generic patterns and uses multimodal semiotic resources in his essayistic reviews and how these texts can be considered as instantiating ecoliteracy practices. The first case study is from the book and the second from the audiobook version of TAR.

8.3.1 Case study 1: The Penguins of Madagascar

In most of the essayistic reviews of TAR, the rating on a five-star scale is only revealed in the end as an evaluative summary of Green's qualitative deliberations on the subject, which are presented throughout the main part of the essay. One exception is Green's review of *Penguins of Madagascar* (Green 2021a: 106–10), which is structured like an argumentative essay (Hyland 1990) and begins with a clear thesis statement already hinting at the final rating (of four and a half stars): 'The opening sequence of the 2014 film *Penguins of Madagascar* is one of the greatest scenes in cinematic history.'

This thesis, however, is not stated outright in the essay but is only introduced at the end of a lengthy introductory stage. This introductory stage uses a move that Hyland (1990) calls a 'gambit' or attention grabber: in a dramatic illustration that uses a direct address of the reader with the second-person pronoun 'you', Green introduces the concept of a 'Provocative Opinion Person' who likes to annoy people in everyday conversations with an unsolicited argumentative discussion about an unconventional evaluative standpoint. For his dramatic illustration, Green uses a seemingly random example that is unrelated to the following essay (the thesis 'Ringo was the best Beatle') but which he can assume is a statement that most readers will agree is unwarranted. Green concludes his dramatic illustration with the concessive: 'Most of us are not Provocative Opinion People, thank God', bridging to his own thesis statement: 'But I think everyone secretly harbours at least one provocative opinion, and this is mine'.

Framing the main thesis of his essay as a 'provocative opinion' that people may find ridiculous and doing so with a dramatic evocation in which the readers are invited to imagine themselves as the unwilling recipients of such an argumentative discussion (thus forming strong emotional interpretants) may seem an odd choice, as it mitigates the persuasiveness of the following argumentation. This mitigating effect, however, can be seen as an intentional strategy that shows an ecoliterate awareness for an important distinction between types of argumentative claims: Green's argumentation is not concerned with claims of truth or normative rightness connected to external dynamic objects of the natural or social world but with an evaluative judgement that is internal and personal. Thus, the energetic interpretant Green aims for in his essay is not to convince the audience to agree with his judgement but just to understand his reasoning for the judgement. This becomes apparent in the argument stage of his essay where Green does not present his arguments in a traditional argumentative way but frames them as explanatory reasons connected to his own interpretative act in watching the movie and his personal connection with it.

The argument stage begins with a description of the opening sequence of the animated children's movie *Penguins of Madagascar* (PoM) to be reviewed (Green 2021a: 107–8):

> The movie begins as a faux nature documentary. 'Antarctica, an inhospitable wasteland,' the famous documentary filmmaker Werner Herzog intones with his trademark gravitas. But even here, he tells us, 'We find life. And not just any life. PENGUINS. Joyous, frolicking, waddling, cute, and cuddly life.'

> A long line of penguins marches mindlessly behind an unseen leader. As Herzog calls penguins 'silly little snow clowns,' we follow the line back to the three young penguins at the center of the movie, one of whom announces, 'Does anyone even know where we're marching *to*?'

> 'Who cares?' an adult penguin responds. 'I question nothing,' another adds.

> Soon thereafter, the three young penguins are bowled over by an egg rolling downhill. They decide to follow the egg, which tumbles off the edge of a glacier to a shipwrecked boat below. These three little penguins now stand on the edge of a cliff, looking down at an egg about to be devoured by a leopard seal. The penguins must decide: Risk it all to save this egg, or watch as it gets eaten?

> At this point, the camera zooms out, and we see the documentary crew following the penguins. 'Tiny and helpless,' Herzog says, 'the babies are frozen with fear. They know if they fall from this cliff, they will surely die.' And then there is a moment's pause before Herzog says, 'Günter, give them a shove.'

> The sound guy uses a boom mic to whack the penguins from behind, forcing them into the great unknown. It's a children's movie, so of course the penguins survive and go on to great adventures. But every time I watch *Penguins of Madagascar*, I think of how almost all of us are invisible to penguins almost all of the time, and yet we are nonetheless their biggest threat – and also their best hope. In that respect, we are a kind of god – and not a particularly benevolent one.

This iconic description serves to make the audiovisual opening sequence imaginable to the audience (in lack of seeing the dynamic object themselves) so that they can form immediate emotional and logical interpretants about it. At the same time, the description is already an interpretative act that presents a specific immediate object to the audience through its topical and semiotic choices. Thus, the audience is enabled to form more evolved dynamic logical interpretants from this description that support the following argumentation.

In the argument stage, Green gives two main arguments in support of his main thesis. Both are concerned with the metaphoric quality of the opening sequence of PoM and are introduced as his own associations while watching the movie (as dynamic logical interpretants): The first argument is given at the end of the earlier descriptive passage ('Every time I watch [PoM], I think of'). With a more abstract argumentative reconstruction, this argument can be paraphrased as: PoM metaphorically mirrors the relationship of humans to the non-human animal world (such as penguins) as that of not very benevolent gods, being invisible to them and having power over them.

The second argument is introduced in the beginning of the next paragraph with another associative statement ('I also find myself thinking about the lemming'). This argument is detailed in an extended discussion in the remainder of the essay and can be summarized as: PoM subverts the widespread myth of lemmings committing mass suicide by metaphorically showing that the myth reveals more about human nature than the nature of lemmings. The argument is split into two sub-arguments that can be paraphrased as follows:

1. PoM parodies the 1958 Disney nature documentary *White Wilderness* that perpetuated the myth of lemmings committing mass suicide by jumping from oceanside cliffs, while in reality the documentary filmmakers threw the lemmings from the cliffs themselves for the camera.
2. PoM makes fun of humans acting like what we have long claimed lemmings to do: mindlessly following a leader, unaware of the precipice we are approaching.

In his discussion, Green presents both these sub-arguments as explanatory reasons why he loves the opening sequence of PoM: firstly, because he learned the story about the *White Wilderness* scam that the sequence metaphorically (iconically) mirrors, from his father, who is a documentary filmmaker himself; secondly, because the sequence makes him reflect on his own problematic tendency of unquestioningly following rules ('it captures, and makes the gentlest possible fun of, something about myself I find deeply troubling').

In the short conclusion stage of the essay, Green iterates his mitigated thesis statement from the beginning, by conceding that PoM overall is 'an exceptionally silly movie', but concludes that often silliness is needed 'to confront the absurdities of the Anthropocene' – thus finally giving the opening sequence a rating of four and a half stars.

Green's argumentative essay is a prime example of an ecoliteracy practice that reflects on humans' relationship to the environment and the role of meaning-making, basing this reflection on a text from popular culture that – as Green argues – shows the same kind of ecoliterate awareness and that presents it as a satire through metaphorical means and with a variety of intertextual allusions.

8.3.2 Case study 2: 'The Kauaʻi ʻōʻō'

As essays, Green's reviews in TAR rely mainly on linguistic modes for meaning-making. This, however, does not imply that there are no multimodal aspects to the essays. Most of the essays were first written to be read in an audio format, thus already bridging between the modes of written and spoken language. In the podcast and audiobook renditions of his essays, the cadence of Green's slightly monotonic and distinctly melancholic baritone voice adds a significant layer to the essays, affecting the emotional interpretants formed in the audience. Additionally, in the podcast series – beside the strategic use of atmospheric background music – many reviews were annexed with a short audio recording (either historic footage or a personal recording), connected to the subject of review. In the book and audiobook versions, these audio snippets are mostly lost. Only one of the bonus essays included in the audiobook, 'The Kauaʻi ʻōʻō' (Green 2021b),[3] retains an audio recording, which is used in a very deliberate, strategic way as an integral part of the meaning-making process.

The audio essay 'The Kauaʻi ʻōʻō' is mostly structured in a documentary narrative form, telling the story of the last Kauaʻi ʻōʻō, a bird that was native to the Hawaiian island of Kauaʻi and that went extinct in the late twentieth century as the last of four ʻōʻō species. The essay begins with an explicatory and descriptive style, giving an iconic description of the bird, its phenotype, habitat and mode of life, detailing its genus and tracing its relationship to humans, from the first indigenous Hawaiian people to the arrival of European settlers, and explaining the causes for the ʻōʻō's eventual extinction through the introduction of invasive diseases and species.

Throughout this first stage of the review, Green mixes his descriptions and explications with personal reflections and evaluations, following the usual form of his essayistic reviews. At the same time, these personal reflections also demonstrate an ecoliterate consideration of the way we humans can only ever approach the dynamic objects of our environment through the interpretation of signs. Wondering at the function of the ornate plumage found in many bird species, Green, for example, cites different explanations discussed in evolutionary biology but ultimately acknowledges that he cannot know the real reason for the plumage but only the meaning given by humans, for example, the indigenous people of Hawaii who used the feathers of the Kauaʻi ʻōʻō as decoration and as currency for their own purposes.

In the second stage of the review, Green switches from the small to the big scale (i.e. from the sinsigns to the legisigns), relating the extinction of the ʻōʻō species to wider biodiversity loss in the Anthropocene and reflecting on the power and powerlessness of humans in this development: as a species, humans are a powerful force that is the cause for mass extinction of other species on Earth, while on the social and individual level we have no power to reverse this development. Green ends this stage with an evocative passage: 'Anyone who has ever lived with loss knows what it is like to stand on the shore and see water out in front of you, water not just as far as you can see but much farther. We all know what it's like to feel alone. We will all call out some day to someone who cannot answer us.' This evocation of a shared human experience of loneliness elicits emotional interpretants that serve as an interpretative frame for the last stage of the essay.

In this stage, Green turns to a documentary narrative of the – ultimately unsuccessful – preservation efforts around the last pair of Kauaʻi ʻōʻōs at the beginning of the 1980s. The essay culminates in a retelling of an encounter with the last remaining male of the Kauaʻi ʻōʻō species, which had been previously told in an essay in the online literary magazine *The Rumpus* (Shattuck 2018). The documentary narrative uses direct quotation and an original tape recording of the call of the Kauaʻi ʻōʻō (Green 2021b):[4]

> In 1986, an ornithologist named Jim Jacobi was with a group when they heard the last surviving Kauaʻi ʻōʻō begin to sing. Jacobi later described the encounter to Ben Shattuck in *The Rumpus*: 'I took out my tape recorder, clicked it on,' he said. 'The bird sang again, then flitted away. I quickly rewound the tape. I played it again to see what I got, and I turned up the volume so John and Pete could hear it. And then, bam! All of a sudden, the bird came right back. I thought, this is great, it came back! And then it hit me: the reason it came back is it heard another bird. And it hadn't heard another bird in, you know, how long. And it turns out this was probably the last one there was.'
>
> <Original tape recording: acoustic noise of old tape recorder, a bird begins to sing in phrases with pauses in between, sound of wind hitting the microphone>
>
> That's the song. It's supposed to be a duet. You can hear the silences, where the ʻōʻō still waits for a reply.
>
> <Original tape recording, repeated>
>
> We cannot save this bird, gone now for more than three decades. All we can do is hear its call.

<Original tape recording, repeated>

I give the Kauaʻi ʻōʻō four and a half stars.

The original tape recording of the Kauaʻi ʻōʻō singing is played three times, which – as I argue – correlate with different interpretants being elicited in the audience: the first time, the recording is mainly used to illustrate the story and as a means to create authenticity (via the indexical quality of the recording), giving the audience the chance to relate to the experience told in the story. Thus, the first playback is mainly meant to evoke an immediate emotional interpretant. After explaining the significance of the pauses in the bird song, the recording is repeated, enabling the audience to form a new, more evolved logical interpretant. This interpretant is informed by a better understanding of the communicative structure and function of the bird song (as a language of its own) and in turn evokes a changed dynamic emotional interpretant as well: as the bird song is now being interpreted as an incomplete duet, the feeling of loneliness that was conjured as a frame for this stage of the essay (calling out to someone who cannot answer us) is invoked. The third recording builds on this dynamic emotional interpretant and is played to enact a final energetic interpretant: the act of listening to the recording of this now-extinct bird is itself positioned as a necessary practice – mirroring human rituals of mourning and commemoration in the face of tragedy and loss – that pays homage to the bird species and takes accountability for its loss caused by us humans.

By embedding the multimodal resource of the audio recording into the essay in this deliberate, threefold way, I thus argue that an ecoliteracy practice is enacted that encompasses affective, cognitive and behavioural components and that invites the audience to reflect on and ascribe meaning to their relationship to the natural world as humans.

8.4 Conclusion: Avenues for promoting ecoliteracy in educational settings

In an era in which human life and our social practices become progressively more removed and estranged from the environment that we are part of and that we are embedded in, and considering the numerous ecological crises we are facing, raising ecological awareness and promoting learning and education for sustainable development is an imperative necessity. Ecoliteracy has emerged as a concept that can be beneficial for such endeavours.

In this chapter, I wanted to point to the potential of a concept of ecoliteracy that goes beyond ecological awareness and a narrow view of field-specific skills and instead takes a more dynamic and holistic perspective on (eco)literacy practices. Resting on an ecosemiotic framework informed by the holistic sign theory of Charles S. Peirce, such a concept of ecoliteracy emphasizes meaning-making in humans' relationship to their environment and the dynamic objects they encounter there. I used this ecosemiotic framework as a theoretical foundation and as a methodological tool to offer cursory analyses of the essayistic texts of the podcast series and book project *The Anthropocene Reviewed* and demonstrate why I consider them to instantiate ecoliteracy practices.

Following the analysis of the two brief case studies in this chapter, I want to offer some final remarks on the way these essayistic media texts can be further used and adapted in educational settings to promote ecoliteracy as practices of meaning-making and learning. The essays – in book, audiobook or podcast form – could be used as a starting point for reflections and discussions on the subjects of review, inviting the learners to provide their own interpretations and evaluations on the basis of an ecosemiotic interpretation of the dynamic objects in question. This also includes tracking the intertextual references in Green's essays and in turn examining these texts for their ecoliteracy value.

Additionally, the form of the essayistic reviews could be used to encourage learners to write their own essays 'about some of the places where my small life runs into the large forces of the Anthropocene' (Green 2021a: 6). Learners would thus engage in their own ecoliteracy practices that require them to interpret signs of a variety of sorts, to pay attention to the dynamic objects and to recognize the role of their own meaning-making in their relationship to their environments.

Notes

1 The collected papers of Peirce (1931–58) are cited as follows: (CP Volume number. Paragraph number).
2 The original podcast series included fifty-seven reviews in thirty-five episodes between 29 January 2018 and 24 September 2020 (*The Anthropocene Reviewed* 2018–20). The printed book and e-book, released on 18 May 2021, contain forty-five essays (including the introduction), some of which were originally not featured in the podcast (Green 2021a). The book version was recorded as an audiobook by the author as well, which includes three bonus reviews not featured in the book version (Green 2021b).

3 The essay originally aired in the podcast episode 'QWERTY Keyboard and the Kauaʻi ʻōʻō' on 26 September 2019 (*The Anthropocene Reviewed* 2018–20) and is featured as the penultimate essay in the audiobook (Green 2021b).
4 Transcription adapted from the published transcript of the podcast episode (*The Anthropocene Reviewed* 2018–20) from 26 September 2019.

References

Anstey, M. and G. Bull (2018), *Foundations of Multiliteracies: Reading, Writing and Talking in the 21st Century*, London: Routledge.

Cazden, C., B. Cope, N. Fairclough, J. Gee, M. Kalantzis, J. Cook, G. Kress, A. Luke, C. Luke, S. Michaels, and M. Nakata (1996), 'A Pedagogy of Multiliteracies: Designing Social Futures', *Harvard Educational Review*, 66 (1): 60–92.

Chadbourne, R. M. (1983), 'A Puzzling Literary Genre: Comparative Views of the Essay', *Comparative Literature Studies*, 20 (2): 133–53.

Code, J. M. (2019), 'Ecoliteracy and the Trouble with Reading: Ecoliteracy Considered in Terms of Goethe's "Delicate Empiricism" and the Potential for Reading in the Book of Nature', *Environmental Education Research*, 25 (8): 1267–80.

Gee, J. P. (2004), *Situated Language and Learning: A Critique of Traditional Schooling*, New York: Routledge.

Gersie, A., A. Nanson, and E. Schieffelin, eds (2022), *Storytelling for Nature Connection: Environment, Community and Story-Based Learning*, Gloucestershire: Hawthorn Press.

Green, J. (2021a), *The Anthropocene Reviewed: Essays on a Human-Centered Planet*, New York: Random House.

Green, J. (2021b), *The Anthropocene Reviewed: Essays on a Human-Centered Planet*, Read by the Author [Audiobook], New York: Penguin Audio.

Hofman-Bergholm, M. (2022), 'Storytelling as an Educational Tool in Sustainable Education', *Sustainability*, 14 (5): 2946.

Hyland, K. (1990), 'A Genre Description of the Argumentative Essay', *RELC Journal*, 21 (1): 66–78.

Kress, G. (2003), *Literacy in the New Media Age*, London: Routledge.

McBride, B. B., C. A. Brewer, A. R. Berkowitz, and W. T. Borrie (2013), 'Environmental Literacy, Ecological Literacy, Ecoliteracy: What Do We Mean and How Did We Get Here?', *Ecosphere*, 4 (5): 67.

Nanson, A. (2021), *Storytelling and Ecology. Empathy, Enchantment and Emergence in the Use of Oral Narratives*, London: Bloomsbury.

Orr, D. W. (1992), *Ecological Literacy: Education and the Transition to a Postmodern World*, Albany: State University of New York Press.

Peirce, C. S. (1931–1958), *Collected Papers of Charles Sanders Peirce*, Cambridge: Harvard University Press.

Reisigl, M. (2021), '"Narrative!" I Can't Hear that Anymore": A Linguistic Critique of an Overstretched Umbrella Term in the Social Sciences, Discussed with Regard to the Discourse on Climate Change', *Critical Discourse Studies*, 18 (3): 368–86.

Reisigl, M. and R. Wodak (2016), 'The Discourse-Historical Approach (DHA)', in R. Wodak and M. Meyer (eds), *Methods of Critical Discourse Studies*, 23–61, London: Sage.

Sedlaczek, A. S. (2016), 'Representations of Climate Change in Documentary Television: Integrating an Ecolinguistic and Ecosemiotic Perspective into a Multimodal Critical Discourse Analysis', *Language & Ecology*. Available online: http://ecolinguistics-association.org/journal (accessed 1 July 2022).

Sedlaczek, A. S. (2017), 'The Field-Specific Representation of Climate Change in Factual Television: A Multimodal Critical Discourse Analysis', *Critical Discourse Studies*, 14 (5): 480–96.

Sedlaczek, A. S. (2018), 'Multimodal Argumentation in Factual Television', in S. Oswald and D. Maillat (eds), *Argumentation and Inference: Proceedings of the 2nd European Conference on Argumentation*, Fribourg 2017, Vol. II, 741–54, London: College Publications.

Shattuck, B. (2018), 'First and Last Songs: the Extinct Song of the Kaua'i 'Ō'Ō', *The Rumpus*, 2 July. Available online: https://therumpus.net/2018/07/02/first-and-last-songs-the-extinct-song-of-the-kauai-oo/ (accessed 1 July 2022).

Short, T. L. (2007), *Peirce's Theory of Signs*, Cambridge: Cambridge University Press.

Stibbe, A. (2010), *The Handbook of Sustainability Literacy: Skills for a Changing World*, Cambridge: Green Books.

Stibbe, A. (2014), 'An Ecolinguistic Approach to Critical Discourse Studies', *Critical Discourse Studies*, 11 (1): 117–28.

Street, B. (2003), 'What's 'New' in New Literacy Studies? Critical Approaches to Literacy in Theory and Practice', *Current Issues in Comparative Education*, 5 (2): 77–91.

The Anthropocene Reviewed (2018–2020), [Podcast series], John Green, USA: Complexly and WNYC Studios. Available online: https://www.wnycstudios.org/podcasts/anthropocene-reviewed (accessed 1 July 2022).

Picturebook Mediation for Children's Ecoliteracy in English L2

Elisa Bertoldi

Introduction: Read-aloud sessions about nature in English L2 in informal contexts

Reading aloud picturebooks in a foreign/second language with children is an activity that can be used to cross the boundaries between formal contexts (language lessons at school or after-school) and informal contexts (out-of-class activities such as events in libraries, museums, parks and playgrounds) offering children the opportunity to reflect on environmental issues from new points of view. Read-aloud sessions in English L2[1] offered in natural science museums, natural reserve parks, science centres and libraries increase children's exposure to environmental education through a language different from the native language and offer opportunities to experience positive communication about the environment, create connections with other people and with nature and provide new experiences in and with nature. They also offer children the opportunity to engage in a wide range of immersive, bodily experienced, multisensory and hands-on activities that can complement formal learning opportunities such as lessons at school. Museums, natural reserve parks, science centres and libraries contribute to bringing ecoliteracy to a broadly inclusive range of people in order to create communities that think, act and communicate for a sustainable present and future in an ecologically healthy world (Capra 2007: 9). Crossing the boundaries of formal and informal contexts through read-aloud sessions in English L2 gives the opportunities to children to reflect on natural aspects and environmental issues from local and global perspectives.

The chapter focuses on the initiative Telling And Listening to Eco-Sustainable Stories (*TALES*). *TALES* is a series of picturebook read-aloud sessions in English

L2 for children that takes place in museums and libraries of the Udine area (north-east Italy). Students of the Primary Education degree course (University of Udine) participate as volunteer storytellers and picturebook mediators: they select picturebooks and give read-alouds in English L2 for children's language and environmental education. The picturebook mediation process is aimed at offering children and adult participants tools to communicate, reflect on and interpret natural and environmental issues while catalysing positive communication and action about the environment.

The aims of the initiative *TALES* are:

1. Establish partnership and close collaboration between different educational institutions (university, museums, libraries).
2. Promote children's positive relation with the environment through picturebook read-aloud sessions in English L2.
3. Promote student teachers' reflection on reading aloud as a multimodal communicative practice for environmental education.

Taking a multimodal perspective on picturebook mediation, the aims of the present study focus on identifying which multimodal features in picturebooks about nature were considered salient by student teachers for read-aloud sessions in English L2 and to analyse multimodal ensembles of semiotic resources used by storytellers to give salience to key elements about nature during read-aloud performances. Section 9.1 of the chapter presents the theoretical framework. Section 9.2 describes the initiative *TALES* and the methodological approach for data gathering and analysis. Data from semi-structured interviews and multimodal annotation of video recordings are discussed in Section 9.3. Implications for teacher education for picturebooks in children's language and environmental education close the chapter.

9.1 Picturebooks as sources of stories about nature

At a time when one of the most urgent challenges is to find eco-sustainable ways of living on and with our planet, picturebook authors address citizenship education for children by giving salience to natural elements and devoting special attention to environmental issues (Colombo 2012). Children are fascinated by the stories about nature and by the many characters that belong to it, and in environmental education it has been suggested (Schenetti, Salvaterra and Rossini 2015) that the use of stories may help children acquire knowledge about nature and feel connected with it. As Nanson underlines, stories can be used to provide a framework for educational programmes that involve inquisitive and creative interaction with the natural environment (Nanson 2021: 24). Picturebooks about plants, animals and natural elements can empower young readers/listeners, help them become sensitive and respectful towards nature, and active and positive agents of change in relation to the environment and their own future life (Eisler 2000; Bruno 2020).

In picturebooks the story is told through the interplay between written text, illustrations and design features (Nodelman 1988; Nikolajeva and Scott 2001; Mourão 2015; Mourão 2016); they are conceived and designed as a unit in which all parts are integrated to produce meaning: peritextual features (cover, spine, dust jacket, endpapers, typographical elements, etc.) work together with the written words and illustrations to produce a unified item of manufacture (Nodelman 1988; Nikolajeva and Scott 2001; Sipe 2008). Among different types of picturebooks for children, informational picturebooks are aimed at disseminating knowledge (Goga, Iversen and Teigland 2021: 1). According to Heeks, '[i]nformation books serve as the tools which can help readers to knowledge' (1996: 428). They structure, organize, interpret facts and data and turn them into information presented in a way that it can be perceived as meaningful by the target readers/listeners. Mallett underlines that the main intention of informational picturebooks 'is to impact knowledge and ideas' (Mallett 2010: 622). They are 'an art form, designed to give pleasure, and enlightenment, to arouse wonder, and to reveal our capacity for self-awareness and understanding' (Kiefer and Wilson 2011: 291). Pictures are essential in informational picturebooks: they are aimed at triggering an intellectual, emotional, affective and aesthetic reaction in children. Non-fiction informational picturebooks are tools that allow children to access a wide range of information combining scientific knowledge with the assumptions of artistic experience. Informational picturebooks aim to entertain, inspire and amuse (Von Merveldt 2018). As Grilli states, '[w]hile often spectacular in a visual and material sense, the new generation non-fiction picturebooks perform their task of providing information about the world in a "humble" way' (2020: 14). Informational picturebooks about nature are aimed at encouraging children to reflect on environmental issues, to focus their attention on natural elements, to wander through the illustrations and the written text, to slow down and take time to observe the details and to linger on pages (Terrusi 2014). They give space to questioning and speculating infusing a sense of mystery, discovery and wonder, and most of all they allow children to experience awe (Grilli 2020: 25). Awe is a complex emotion that has beneficial effects on humans' physical and mental well-being. Experiencing awe makes humans less self-oriented and more collaborative, humble, sharing and altruistic (Allen 2018). Offering children the opportunity to experience awe through informational picturebooks about nature fosters openness towards other creatures and stimulates curiosity about the environment we belong to and sustains us.

9.1.1 The mediation of picturebooks

Even though picturebooks are addressed to children, they are also meant to be read aloud to children by parents, caregivers, teachers and storytellers. Read-aloud sessions are an effective tool to help children familiarize with a new language as they contribute to the development of verbal and non-verbal communicative competences, stimulate the interpretation of situations and events, facilitate comprehension and raise awareness on the complexity and variety of communicative contexts (see, among others, Ellis and Brewster 2014; Masoni 2019; Ellis and Mourão, 2021). As Ellis and Mourão mention, during read-aloud sessions in English L2 the picturebook is mediated by the storyteller. The mediation is 'the support or assistance, often referred to as "scaffolding"', given by the storyteller 'when sharing a picturebook with a group of children' (2021: 23). As Ellis and Mourão write (2021) the picturebook mediation process includes three stages: 'mediation begins with the picturebook selection, continues during the read-aloud itself and extends into the follow-up activities' (2021: 23). The first stage in the mediation process is the selection of the picturebook and the planning of the read-aloud session. In this stage, the storyteller evaluates the affordances of the picturebook written and visual texts and peritextual features in relation to the context and the purpose(s) of the read-aloud session. Picturebook selection is an explorative process through which the storyteller identifies salient aspects in the written and visual texts. For what concerns visual elements in picturebooks, the concept of salience refers to Kress and van Leeuwen's definition (2021). It is the degree to which an element draws attention due to its size, its place in the foreground or its overlapping of other elements, its colour, its tonal values, its sharpness of definition; it 'results from a complex interaction, a complex trading-off relationship between a number of factors' (2021: 210) and can create a hierarchy of importance among elements, selecting some as more worthy of attention than others. For what concerns the written text, Stibbe (2021: 160) mentions that 'patterns of linguistic features can come together to form salience patterns which represent particular participants prominently in a text'.

The read-aloud performance is the second stage in the picturebook mediation process; it depends upon the systematic interaction between the storyteller, the children and the picturebook (Häggström 2020: 119), which influence each other, and it includes two main sets of actions: the read-aloud and the read-aloud talk. During the read-aloud performance, the storyteller shares the written and visual text of a picturebook with children telling the story out aloud and combining different semiotic resources in order to allow the audience to enjoy the story, make meaning and participate in the interaction (Masoni 2019). During the read-aloud performance the storyteller decodes and performs the verbal text of the picturebook: s/he uses the punctuation as a guide to know when to pause, give emphasis or change voice intonation; s/he uses graphic devices (such as font and font size) as a guide to modulate voice pitch and voice speed and s/he differentiates between characters' speech and narrative variating the tone of voice and voice pitch. In addition, the storyteller combines semiotic resources such as gestures, gaze, facial expressions, body movements and use of props which are orchestrated to help children make meaning and orient their attention to key elements in the picturebook. During the read-aloud performance the storyteller integrates reading aloud with read-aloud talk. The read-aloud talk enables meaningful interaction among participants through questions, comments, inferences and predictions that are not in the written text of the picturebook. Read-aloud talk is aimed at contemplating, exploring and explicating the picturebook and establishing rapport with the children (Ellis and Mourão 2021). Read-aloud talk orients children's attention to the images, to the props or to key elements in the story, facilitates comprehension of the story and stimulates children's responses. The third stage of picturebook mediation includes the follow-up activities which can stimulate the children to think and reflect upon the story, the characters and the events and to give personal responses to the picturebook (Ellis and Mourão 2021).

During read-aloud sessions in English L2 about nature, the process of picturebook mediation is aimed not only at helping children make meaning of the language but also at scaffolding communication about the environment influencing children's interpretation of events, situations and people raising their sense of belonging to nature. By giving salience to key concepts in the story and orienting children's attention to natural elements, storytellers can help children capture some fundamental ecological principles such as appreciating the interdependence between species and ecosystems; feeling concern, empathy and respect for all living things; and experiencing wonder and awe towards nature (Muthukrishnan 2019).

9.1.2 A multimodal perspective on picturebook mediation

Picturebook mediation is a multimodal, interactive process aimed at making meaning, facilitating children's comprehension of situations and events, orienting children' attention to key elements in the story and stimulating children's responses (Masoni 2019; Ellis and Mourão 2021). Different types of semiotic resources are combined in multimodal ensembles by storytellers in order to make meaning and interact with children. To understand how storytellers and children interact with and through different semiotic resources during read-aloud sessions about nature in English L2, this chapter analyses the picturebook mediation process from a multimodal perspective that considers 'a full range of communicational forms people use – image, gesture, gaze, posture and so on – and the relationships between these' (Jewitt 2017: 15).

Multimodality analyses meaning as it is developed, negotiated and established through organized sets of socially and culturally shaped semiotic resources. Meaning is made through the co-deployment of semiotic resources separately, and at the same time, all semiotic resources contribute jointly to meaning-making as it emerges from a process of interaction, contrast and conjunction of modes (Kress et al. 2014: 1–2): social actors design meaning by selecting and using available semiotic resources at each specific moment in specific contexts (Kress and van Leeuwen 2001: 20). Meaning is constructed both in and in between different semiotic modes, and meaning-making involves the design and production of multimodal wholes in which modes and semiotic resources are interwoven and influence each other (Bezemer and Kress 2016: 28; Jewitt, Bezemer and O'Halloran 2016: 2). The intertwining of modes and semiotic resources used simultaneously by social actors can be defined as a multimodal ensemble. A multimodal ensemble is a 'coherent, integrated, communicational unit' (Bezemer and Kress 2016: 25). Semiotic resources operate in ensembles to serve 'complementary functions' (Bezemer and Kress 2016: 30). Resources are combined by social actors through the process of 'multimodal orchestration' (Lim 2021: 108; Jewitt 2017: 27) which results in the harmonization of corresponding, complementary and dissonant resources in multimodal ensembles (Jewitt 2017: 465). A multimodal perspective on picturebook mediation process allows the researcher to analyse the co-occurrence and interplay of different semiotic resources in multimodal ensembles (Bezemer and Cowan 2021: 20). It also allows the researcher to identify possibilities and constrains offered by semiotic resources in the multimodal orchestration during read-aloud sessions about nature in English L2.

In educational contexts, such as the context of the present study, language is generally considered the most significant mode of communication (Jewitt 2017: 15). It has often been argued that language serves the widest range of communicative functions or that it enables the highest, most complex forms of thinking and is therefore the most important. Multimodality scholars have pointed out that there are differences between modes in terms of possibilities they offer for making meaning but it is not the case that one resource has more or less potential than others (Jewitt, Bezemer and O'Halloran 2016: 3). Multimodal approaches consider semiotic resources as equally important and having meaning potential in multimodal ensembles; such perspective allows the researcher to understand the role of language (speech and writing) within multimodal ensembles and how language is used in combination with other semiotic resources to make meaning. Multimodal approaches offer a new look at the functions of language: as Kress et al. underline, '[w]e feel that in order to newly and properly understand language we need to step outside it and take a satellite view of it' (2014: 10). A 'satellite view' taken by adopting a multimodal approach offers a wider perspective on language in general and on language education in the specific context of the present research study. As Norris points out, '[l]anguage, while being the most researched and well-understood mode, here becomes a (very important) part within the multimodal constellation when people act and interact, illuminating language from a new perspective, allowing us to gain new insights into linguistics' (Norris 2020: 5) and in language education. This might lead to a greater acknowledgement of how learning and using a language must be understood as embedded within broader processes of communication and action (Nelson and Kern 2012: 62). Understanding the implications of embodied communication and interaction in informal contexts provides additional insights and new perspectives on children's language education. In addition, an exploration of the role of semiotic resources used by participants during read-aloud performances can contribute to reflecting on understanding children and storytellers' meaning-making processes to identify key aspects in communication about the environment.

Taking a multimodal perspective on picturebook mediation in read-aloud sessions about nature in English L2, the research questions addressed in this study are: what elements in picturebooks were identified by storytellers as salient aspects for read-aloud sessions about nature and what semiotic resources they used in the read-aloud performances to give salience to key elements about nature?

9.2 The organization of *TALES* initiative

The data discussed in the present study were gathered during four events of the initiative *TALES*[2] organized in July 2021 at the Natural History Museum of Friuli (Museo Friulano di Storia Naturale) in Udine (Italy). The Natural History Museum of Friuli owns important collections of exhibits belonging to different branches of natural sciences, and it aims to promote the awareness of the local and global biodiversity, with a special focus on the environment and the rich natural heritage of the region Friuli Venezia Giulia (Italy) and its surrounding areas across national borders (Austria and Slovenia). The museum staff organizes activities and workshops addressed to a wide audience of visitors including schools and contributes to enriching the educational offer and to promoting a hands-on approach to natural sciences. The events analysed in this chapter were addressed to children from six to nine years old.

In accordance with the museum staff, the first step in the organization of *TALES* was creating a list of picturebooks for read-aloud sessions in English at the museum. I selected sixteen informative picturebooks[3] in English that can help children familiarize with natural aspects and promote a sense of care and belonging towards the environment. The list of selected picturebooks was submitted to the museum experts who checked them for coherence, scientific accuracy of the events presented and terminology used in the story.

Four student teachers (S. P., E. P., I. G. and E. S.) participated in the initiative *TALES* as volunteer storytellers. Each one of them selected a picturebook from the list and gave a read-aloud during the four events at the museum. Due to Covid-19 restrictions, the maximum number of participants who could attend each event was fifteen children. All in all, forty children attended the events of the initiative *TALES*.

The events took place in the outdoors area of the museum. The decision to host the events outdoors allowed children and storytellers to interact keeping social distance but without wearing face masks (in accordance with Covid-19 measures since the events took place during the pandemic). This had a significant impact on the range of semiotic resources that participants could use to make meaning during the events.

9.2.1 Data gathering and methodology for the analysis

The approach of the present study combines ethnographic observations and multimodal analysis of video recordings. The analysis focuses on two steps of the picturebook mediation process: the storyteller's picturebook selection and the read-aloud performance at the museum. The data for the analysis of picturebook selection were gathered through semi-structured interviews with volunteer storytellers conducted before the events at the museum. Each volunteer storyteller of the initiative *TALES* was interviewed. The language used during the interviews was English (an L2 for all participants). The four semi-structured interviews were conducted online via Microsoft Teams, and they were video recorded and transcribed. A first set of questions focused on general information about the picturebook and the elements of the story (settings, characters, plot and theme) that captured the storyteller's attention. Three sets of questions investigated the storyteller's interpretation of the structure and meaning of the verbal text and the illustrations in the picturebook both as separate units and related to each other. A last set of questions focused on the storytellers' planning their performance and the expectations related to the storytelling event. The aim of the interviews was investigating what elements in picturebooks about nature were salient for storytellers and how they meant to give relevance to key elements in the story during their read-aloud performances. The concepts of visual and linguistic salience (Kress and van Leeuwen 2021; Stibbe 2021) are used for the analysis of the storytellers' answers in semi-structured interviews in order to identify what they consider salient aspects in visual (illustrations and peritextual features) and linguistic (written text) elements in the picturebooks; these aspects were fundamental for planning their read-aloud performance.

The second step of the analysis focuses on picturebook read-aloud performances at the museum. The data for the analysis of read-aloud performances were gathered through multimodal annotation of video recordings. I was present during each event at the museum in order to conduct video recordings, observation and take field notes about participants (parents, children, museum staff), setting, camera positioning and contextual factors. The multimodal annotation of video recordings and the analysis of time-aligned annotations allowed me to identify what ensembles of semiotic resources were used by storytellers to give salience to key elements in picturebooks during the read-aloud performance. To annotate the videos I used ELAN (2022), an open access software for video annotation developed by the Max Planck Institute for Psycholinguistics (Nijmegen, the Netherlands). During read-aloud sessions, salient aspects identified by storytellers in the picturebooks were embodied in the performances. Through ELAN I annotated visual, spatial, oral and aural semiotic resources that allowed storytellers to embody the story: verbal language, voice features (such as tone, volume and pitch), gestures, facial expressions, movements in space and use of images and props were time-aligned annotated in multiple tiers. To elaborate ELAN raw data, I used the software TMA (2021) (developed as part of my PhD thesis in collaboration with a computer developer). TMA generates graphs and tables in order to identify and visualize ensembles, correlations and patterns in the data within specific time spans. I used the transcription table generator in TMA (Figure 9.1, Section 9.3.1) that groups together annotations of semiotic resources that co-occur in the same time span. The tool allows us to visualize the ensembles of semiotic resources used by storytellers during the performance and to analyse how storytellers gave salience to key elements about nature in stories through multimodal configurations of semiotic resources.

In this study, my point of view is informed by the direct involvement in the organization of the *TALES* events, the discussion and reflection with storytellers, the observation of the events and the analysis of the data. The research design of the study was in compliance with the ethical guidelines of the University of Udine and the museum privacy requirements for all participants who were present during the events (storytellers, children and parents/caregivers), as I obtained all the necessary informed consents.

Time	Image	Transcriptions
00:02:25.110 00:02:26.908		[Spoken language]: Language of picturebook [Transcription]: Was bright [Voice Intonation]: Statement [Voice Tone]: Surprised [Voice Volume]: Lowers her/his voice [Gaze]: Looks at the children [Gesture]: Iconic [Hands Movement]: Hands movement
00:02:27.000 00:02:30.636		[Gaze]: Looks at the images of the book [Turns the Page]
00:02:30.636 00:02:33.805		[Spoken language]: Language of picturebook [Transcription]: And the stone was loud [Voice Intonation]: Statement [Voice Volume]: Raises her/his voice [Gaze]: Looks at the children [Proxemics: book]: Moves the book closer to children
00:02:33.666 00:02:35.954		[Gaze]: Looks at the children

Figure 9.1 TMA output: transcription of multimodal ensembles in E. S.'s read-aloud performance. Copyright: the author.

9.3 Discussion

In the first stage of the picturebook mediation process (see Section 9.1.1) the storytellers of the initiative *TALES* chose the picturebook for their sessions from the preselected list (see Section 9.2). During the read-aloud sessions, the selected picturebooks became the 'play script' for the storytellers' performances: although the picturebooks did not offer explicit directions for the storytellers to follow, the interplay between the multimodal elements in the picturebook (written text, illustrations, peritextual features and graphic devices) identified by the storytellers influenced the way in which the story was told, the responses of children and the interactions between participants during the performance. The present section analyses and discusses the data gathered through the semi-structured interviews with the volunteer storytellers before the storytelling events and the data gathered through the multimodal annotation of videos of TALES read-aloud performances. In the first part I will briefly present the four picturebooks selected by the storytellers, then I will discuss the storytellers' answers. In the second part I will discuss the configurations of semiotic resources used by storytellers during the read-aloud performances.

9.3.1 Student teachers selecting picturebooks about nature

S. P. was the volunteer storyteller of the first event at the museum; she chose to give the read-aloud of the picturebook *The Beeman* by Laurie Krebs and illustrated by Valeria Cis (Krebs and Cis 2008). In the picturebook, a beekeeper and his grandson take care of a beehive and through the written text and the detailed illustrations the reader/listener can appreciate the slow process of beekeeping and honey production. The aim of the session was stimulating children's curiosity about bees and presenting beekeeping as a caring practice. The second event was conducted by E. P. and it was based on the picturebook *A Forest* by Mark Martin (Martin 2012) that underlines the importance of trees for life and the impact of deforestation on our planet. The sparse text and the illustrations in the picturebook present the sequence of events that gradually lead humans to replace trees with buildings and factories. Deforestation causes storms and flooding that wash away factories and buildings, letting trees repopulate the earth again. *We Love Dinosaurs* by Lucy Volpin (Volpin 2016) was read aloud by I. G. during the third session at the museum. The aim of the session was allowing children to experience the sense of wonder through the observation of unknown creatures. In the picturebook, facts about dinosaurs are presented through bright and colourful illustrations depicted on each double-spread page and through the brief text written in rhymes. In the last session, the storyteller E. S. gave the read-aloud of the picturebook *A Stone Sat Still* by Brendan Wenzel (Wenzel 2019). In this picturebook events are presented through the complementary interplay between the sparse written text and illustrations. The steadiness of a stone, depicted on each page, emphasizes the dynamic interactions taking place with and around it and recalls the multisensory nature of human experience in the environment.

Despite being very different in terms of topic, design features, content of the written text, type of illustrations and narrative structure, the four informational picturebooks have aspects in common which influenced the storytellers' selection. First of all, the structure of the narrative influenced storytellers in the selection of the picturebook. According to the storytellers, the presence of a clear sequence of logically connected events in a linear or circular structure allows children both to follow the unfolding of the narrative and to understand the connections in the lifescape presented in the story.

For instance, the picturebook *A Forest* has a circular structure. As E. P. stated, 'it starts with a graphical representation of a forest' that covers almost the entire double-spread. Then, the number of trees depicted on the page gradually diminishes, page after page, and 'in the central pages of the picturebook the images of trees are completely replaced by the images of buildings'. The central pages of the picturebooks depict a storm that washes away all the buildings and factories leaving space to the illustration of 'one little tree which soon gives rise to a new forest' that covers the entire last double-spread page. E. P. pointed out that the circular structure of the narrative allows children to understand the importance of respecting the balance in human relation with the environment. The presence of repetitions of words and expressions in the written texts of the picturebooks was noticed and taken into consideration by storytellers as an aspect that can give salience to natural elements and orient children's attention to key elements, characters and characters' actions in the story, thus facilitating the comprehension of expressions and events. In the specific context of the initiative *TALES*, the presence of repetitions in the written text of the picturebooks is a feature that not only does it scaffold children's comprehension of expressions and chunks of language, but it also emphasizes and gives salience to the natural elements at the core of the story. Key elements such as tree(s) or the stone are mentioned in the written text on (almost) every double-spread page. As S. P. pointed out during the interview, on every page of the picturebook *The Beeman*, the written text starts with the expression 'Here is/Here are' followed by the names of tools used by the Beeman (the gloves, the smoker, the extractor, etc.) or the name of members of the bee colony (queen bee, drone bees, workers). According to S. P., the repeated expressions 'Here is/Here are' potentially orient children's attention to key elements in the double-spread page. During the interview, she reported that in her performance planning she was considering using various props (as she did) to show children in more detail the characteristics of beekeeping tools mentioned in the written text in order to involve children, stimulate their curiosity and 'make the story more realistic'. S. P. identified another repetition in the written text: each section in a double-spread ends with the noun phrase referring to the protagonist, 'the Beeman', reconnecting the reader/listener with the title and the theme of the picturebook. According to S. P. a repetition at the beginning and at the end of each sequence can 'give a rhythm to the performance' and can help children 'understand the sequence of events and actions in the story' which put bees and humans into close relation.

Design features in the written text of the picturebooks were taken into consideration by storytellers in their selection. S. P. noticed that keywords in the written text of the picturebook *The Beeman* are written in bold and in a large font size. According to her, this can help the reader/listener focus the attention on main elements of the story. The font used for the title on the cover of the picturebook and for the words written in bold in the text is peculiar and captured her attention: swirl lines surround each letter in the keywords (e.g. bee, queen bee, drone bees, gloves, beehive) and recall 'the buzzing of bees around flowers'. Similarly, in *We Love Dinosaurs*, I. G. noticed that different font sizes combine with the meaning of words and illustrations in order to emphasize the dinosaur's actions and characteristics: 'tall' is written in a big font and 'small' is written in a small font concretely depicting the meaning of the adjectives.

Illustrations in the picturebook influenced the storytellers' selection. All the four storytellers in the interviews stated that illustrations are clear and detailed and allow the listeners/readers to observe specific features and characteristics. Referring to the picturebook *A Forest*, E. P. noticed that the illustrations of trees are 'one different from the other' and presenting various features (sizes, colours, shapes) which might be used to invite children to observe, identify and recognize different characteristics in trees (and there were real trees in the courtyard of the museum where the storytelling events took place).

S. P. noticed that in all the pages of *The Beeman* there are references to beekeeping as a practice of care that bonds humans and bees in different ways throughout the seasons of the year. This is made visible through the characters' actions and facial expressions which express positive emotions. As far as the illustrations are concerned, S. P. noticed that the role of the queen bee in the beehive is made salient in the picturebook as an entire double-spread represents her in the honeycomb surrounded by some other bees. In that specific page, the Beeman and his grandson do not appear visually but the written text printed on the page is the Beeman's direct speech that, as a voice-over, states, 'She's the heart of the hive.' S. P. appreciated the authors' choice: according to her, the double-spread entirely focused on the queen bee can help children understand her importance in the colony and the fact that humans should not 'interfere too much with the delicate balance in the beehive'. The illustrations in the picturebook *A Stone Sat Still* had a significant role in E. S.'s selection. She reported that in the book, the landscape changes page after page and different creatures appear but 'the stone is always present': covered in mud, hidden by long wavy grass and immersed in water, the stone is an element of the environment through which life develops and thrives. E. S. stated that this can contribute to focusing children's attention on the key element (the stone) inviting them to spot it in every page and at the same time to observe differences and similarities from one illustration to the other identifying changes in the environment that surrounds the stone. The stone becomes part of the 'lifescape'.

9.3.2 Student teachers giving read-alouds at the museum

The storytellers' use of voice was extremely important during the read-aloud sessions at the museum: stressing words, changing delivery speed and tone of voice gave emphasis to words and expressions and contribute to making meaning clearer. During the performances, the storytellers used both low-volume voice to convey a sense of wonder, magic and mystery and loud voice to capture children's attention and orienting it to specific expressions and elements. The small number of participants for each event and the fact that all children were sitting around the storytellers allowed storytellers to use mainly a quiet voice which contributed to making more evident variations in voice features. For instance, while S. P. was reading aloud the central pages of *The Beeman*, when the Beeman and his grandson are visiting the beehives, she lowered her voice whispering the words in the written text. In this way she gave children the idea that human actions should not disturb the colony of bees and should not interfere with their activities.

Variations in the tone and in the volume of storyteller's voice were frequently used by E. S. while she was reading aloud the picturebook *A Stone Sat Still*.

She combined the use of different voice features (volume and tone) with the language of the picturebook in order to convey the meaning of expressions related to the stone. As can be seen in Figure 9.1 she lowered her voice whispering, 'was bright' referring to the stone lit by the moon. At the same time, she made an iconic gesture moving slowly her hand from right to left in order to convey a sense of magic and wonder. She shifted her gaze from the children to the illustration in the picturebook pausing and staring at the image of the bright stone. Then, she turned the page and she rose significantly the volume of her voice while reading aloud 'And the stone was loud'; she also moved the picturebook closer to the children to show them the image of a pebble hitting the stone.

Similarly, in *We Love Dinosaurs* I. G. used voice features in relation to the different font sizes in the written text: she raised and lowered her voice in relation to the size of words written on the page and the meaning to be conveyed. She combined verbal language, voice features and gestures in order to help children imagine the appearance and the behaviour of dinosaurs creating a feeling of connection with them. During the performance some children mimed I. G.'s actions: they roared and moved their arms pretending to be dinosaurs.

Variations in voice volume, pitch and tone helped storytellers to reproduce effectively onomatopoeic words (e.g. splish-splash, bang, crash, etc.). As mentioned in the previous section, in the picturebook *The Beeman* swirl lines surround the letters in the title of the picturebook. The storyteller associated the font and the design features used by the illustrator to a combination of voice sound and hand/finger movement: she reproduced the sound of a buzzing bee with her voice and with hand and finger movement she reproduced the flight of a bee in the air every time she mentioned 'the Beeman' at the end of a sequence of the story. Repetitive patterns of semiotic resources such as voice features and gestures were used by storytellers to emphasize repetitive expressions in the written text, capture the children's attention and orient it to key elements in the story.

The storytellers also used proxemics to orient children's attention towards the illustrations in the picturebook. After reading aloud the written text on the page, the four storytellers leaned forward and moved the picturebook closer to the children giving them time to observe, generally in silence, the illustrations. After letting the children observe carefully the illustrations, the storytellers, generally without speaking, pointed to the images in order to orient children's attention to some of the image details; for instance, in the case of *A Forest*, E. P. pointed to the different trees depicted on the page.

The storytellers included the use of props in their performances; this expanded and enhanced the story beyond the pages of the picturebook. They let children observe the props (beekeeping tools, the stone, dinosaur toys) during the performance, moving the objects closer to each child and letting children touch them. In the case of the read-aloud session of the picturebook *A Forest*, trees that surrounded the storytelling corner in the museum courtyard became 'props' for E. P.'s performance. He gazed and pointed at trees in the grounds of the museum thus orienting the children's attention to the main elements of the picturebook before starting to read the story. Children interacted with the storyteller by turning their heads and bodies to look at the trees around them. In the read-aloud performance of *The Beeman*, S. P. placed a small beehive, a smoker, gloves, a beekeeping jacket and hood and a piece of honeycomb all around her; in this way she could easily pick them up and show them to the children during the read-aloud session. The use of props was combined with gestures and gaze. S. P. used gaze to orient children's attention to specific elements: they shifted gaze from the picturebook, to the props and to children, and children's gaze followed the storytellers' gaze. Gaze created a connection between storytellers, the audience and the natural elements presented in the story of the picturebook.

Storytellers used repetitive patterns of semiotic resources in their performances: in the first session S. P. read aloud the written text on each double-spread of the picturebook *The Beeman* starting with 'Here is/here are', then she pointed to key elements illustrated on the page and finally she put down the picturebook, took the real object and showed it moving it closer to the children. She repeated the same sequence of actions for each double-spread. The expression 'Here is/Here are' combined with hands gesture and gaze was used by the storyteller to create expectation and orient the children's attention first towards the illustrations in the picturebook and then towards the real objects. A repetitive pattern was used by E. S. during read-aloud talk (see Section 9.1.1) about the picturebook *A Stone Sat Still*. After reading aloud the sequence in every double-spread page, she asked children 'where is the stone?' leaning forward and moving the book closer to the children to focus the children's attention to the main element in the story. The same ensemble was repeatedly used by the storyteller, creating a familiar pattern that children could rely on. The children replied pointing at the image of the stone in the page but in the last pages of the picturebook where the image of the stone is half-hidden in the environment, children pointed at the illustration and exclaimed 'the stone!' before the storyteller asked the question: children had become part of the performance.

9.4 Concluding remarks

The picturebooks selected for this study are econarratives that offer children an insight of how we humans represent the ecosystem we inhabit and belong to and how humans position themselves in the ecosystem and what role we create for ourselves. The availability of a multiplicity of semiotic resources for the realization of meaning and interaction requires the selection of resources suitable for this specific aim (Kress et al. 2014: 41). Information gathered through semi-structured interviews demonstrates that in the selection of the picturebook the storytellers took into account the structure of the narrative, the presence of repetitions of words and expressions in the written text, the illustrations and design features in relation to the context and audience of the read-aloud session about nature.

Salient aspects identified by storytellers during the interviews were embodied in the read-aloud performances of the initiative *TALES*. Key elements in stories about nature were highlighted through various modes such as verbal language, voice features, gestures, gaze and the use of props combined in multimodal ensembles. The multimodal orchestration resulted in a configuration of modes utilized by storytellers to form salient ensembles and focus children's attention to key elements about nature, thus connecting children to the environment. When storytellers give a read-aloud of picturebooks about nature, they select certain aspects of reality and make them salient through the use of semiotic resources: storytellers orient children's attention by pointing to, gazing at and lingering on specific illustrations in the picturebook, to the props or to natural elements in the environment that surrounds the storytelling corner. Read-aloud sessions are an example of positive action for citizenship education through ecological multimodal communication. The mediation of picturebooks about nature integrates multisensory, multimodal and ecological communication in order to strengthen and extend children's connections with nature. Multimodal communicative practices such as informal read-aloud sessions can contribute to creating memories in children which are linked to nature; such memories promote respect for nature we all belong to and eco-sustainable ways of living.

Read-aloud sessions offer student teachers the opportunity to extend their own ecoliteracy through the exploration of environmental narratives in picturebooks. Read-aloud performances with children can raise student teachers' awareness on strategies to give salience to nature through positive multimodal communication about the environment.

Notes

1 The read-aloud sessions were held in English by and for non-native speakers. To acknowledge the 'plural' identity of English in children's and storyteller's linguistic repertoires and to account for very different levels of participants' personal commitment to and experiences with English language, in the present research study the target language used by storytellers and children during read-aloud sessions will be referred to as 'English L2'.
2 https://yell.uniud.it/en/storytelling/tales.
3 https://padlet.com/elisabrtl83/t6jnb3ylfn1ono4r.

References

Allen, S. (2018), 'The Science of Awe', The University of California Berkeley. Available online: https://ggsc.berkeley.edu/images/uploads/GGSC-JTF_White_Paper-Awe_FINAL.pdf (accessed 11 February 2022).

Bezemer, J. and K. Cowan (2021), 'Exploring Reading in Social Semiotics: Theory and Methods', *Education 3-13*, 49 (1): 107–18.

Bezemer, J. and G. Kress (2016), *Multimodality, Learning and Communication*, London: Routledge.

Bruno, R. T. (2020), *Educare al Pensiero Ecologico. Letture, Scritture e Passeggiate per un Mondo Sostenibile*, Milano: Topipittori.

Capra, F. (2007), 'Sustainable Living, Ecological Literacy, and the Breath of Life', *Canadian Journal of Environmental Education*, 12 (1): 9–19.

Colombo, R. (2012), 'Sulla Natura', in Hamelin (ed), *Ad Occhi Aperti. Leggere l'Albo Illustrato*, 227–38, Roma: Donzelli editore.

Eisler, R. (2000), *Tomorrow's Children: A Blueprint for Partnership Education in the 21st Century*, New York: Basic Books.

ELAN (Version 6.3) [Computer Software] (2022), Nijmegen: Max Planck Institute for Psycholinguistics, The Language Archive. Available online: https://archive.mpi.nl/tla/elan.

Ellis, G. and J. Brewster (2014), *Tell it Again: The Storytelling Handbook for Primary English Language Teachers*, British Council. Available online: https://www.teachingenglish.org.uk/sites/teacheng/files/pub_D467_Storytelling_handbook_FINAL_web.pdf (accessed 21 August 2021).

Ellis, G. and S. Mourão (2021), 'Demystifying the Read-Aloud', *English Teaching Professional*, 36: 22–25.

Goga, N., S. Iversen, and A. Teigland (2021), 'Introduction', in N. Goga, S. Iversen, and A. Teigland (eds), *Verbal and Visual Strategies in Nonfiction Picturebooks: Theoretical and Analytical Approaches*, 1–5, Oslo: Scandinavian University Press.

Grilli, G. (2020), 'Introduction', in G. Grilli (ed), *Non-Fiction Picturebooks: Sharing Knowledge as an Aesthetic Experience*, 11–16, Edizioni ETS.
Häggström, M. (2020), 'The Art of Read-Aloud, Body Language and Identity Construction: A Multimodal Interactional Analysis of Interaction Between Parent, Child and Picture Book', *International Journal of Language Studies*, 14 (1): 117–40.
Heeks, P. (1996), 'Information Books', in P. Hunt and S. Ray (eds), *International Companion Encyclopedia of Children's Literature*, 428–37, London: Routledge.
Jewitt, C. (2017), 'An Introduction to Multimodality', in C. Jewitt (ed), *The Routledge Handbook of Multimodal Analysis*, 2nd edn, 15–30, London: Routledge.
Jewitt, C., J. Bezemer, and K. O'Halloran (2016), *Introducing Multimodality*, London: Routledge.
Kiefer, B. and M. Wilson (2011), 'Nonfiction Literature for Children: Old Assumptions and New Directions', in S. Wolf (ed), *Handbook of Research on Children's and Young Adult Literature*, 290–98, London: Routledge.
Krebs, L. and V. Cis (2008), *The Beeman*, London: Barefoot Books.
Kress, G. and T. van Leeuwen (2001), *Multimodal Discourse: The Modes and Media of Contemporary Communication*, London: Arnold.
Kress, G. and T. van Leeuwen (2021), *Reading Images. The Grammar of Visual Design*, 3rd edn, London: Routledge.
Kress, G., C. Jewitt, J. Ogborn, and C. Tsatsarelis (2014), *Multimodal Teaching and Learning: The Rhetorics of the Science Classroom*, London: Bloomsbury Academic.
Lim, V. F. (2021), *Designing Learning with Embodied Teaching: Perspectives from Multimodality*, London: Routledge.
Mallett, M. (2010), *Choosing and Using Fiction and Non-Fiction 3–11: A Comprehensive Guide for Teachers and Student Teachers*, London: Routledge.
Martin, M. (2012), *A Forest*, London: Templar Books.
Masoni, L. (2019), *Tale, Performance, and Culture in EFL Storytelling with Young Learners. Stories Meant to Be Told*, Newcastle upon Tyne: Cambridge Scholars Publishing.
Mourão, S. (2015), 'The Potential of Picturebooks with Young Learners', in J. Bland (ed), *Teaching English to Young Learners: Critical Issues in Language Teaching with 3–12 Year Olds*, 199–218, London: Bloomsbury Academic.
Mourão, S. (2016), 'Picturebooks in the Primary EFL Classroom: Authentic Literature for Authentic Responses: Children's Literature in English Language Education', *CLELE Journal: Children's Literature in English Language Education*, 4 (1): 25–43. Available online: https://clelejournal.org/sh-html/ (accessed 30 January 2022).
Muthukrishnan, R. (2019), 'Using Picture Books to Enhance Ecoliteracy of First-Grade Students', *The International Journal of Early Childhood Environmental Education*, 6 (2): 19.
Nanson, A. (2021), *Storytelling and Ecology: Empathy, Enchantment and Emergence in the Use of Oral Narratives*, London, New York: Bloomsbury.
Nelson, M. and R. Kern (2012), 'Language Teaching and Learning in the Postlinguistic Condition?', in L. Alsagoff, S. McKay, G. Hu, and W. Renandya (eds), *Principles*

and Practices for Teaching English as an International Language, 47–66, London: Routledge.
Nikolajeva, M. and C. Scott (2001), *How Picturebooks Work*, New York: Routledge.
Nodelman, P. (1988), *Words About Pictures: The Narrative Art of Children's Picture Books*, Athens: University of Georgia Press.
Norris, S. (2020), *Multimodal Theory and Methodology for the Analysis of (Inter)action and Identity*, London: Routledge.
Schenetti, M., I. Salvaterra, and B. Rossini (2015), *La Scuola nel Bosco. Pedagogia, Didattica e Natura*, Trento: Erikson.
Sipe, L. (2008), *Storytelling: Young Children's Literary Understanding in the Classroom*, New York: Teachers College Press.
Stibbe, A. (2021), *Ecolinguistics: Language, Ecology and the Stories We Live By*, 2nd edn, London: Routledge.
Terrusi, M. (2014), 'Letteratura per l'Infanzia e Narrazioni Naturali', in R. Fernè and F. Agostini (eds), *Outdoor Education*, 69–74, Roma: Spaggiari.
TMA [Software] (2021), https://yell.uniud.it/risorse/multimodal-communication.
Volpin, L. (2016), *We Love Dinosaurs*, London: Nosy Crow.
Von Merveldt, N. (2018), 'Informational Picturebooks', in B. Kümmerling-Meibauer (ed), *The Routledge Companion to Picturebooks*, 231–45, London: Routledge.
Wenzel, B. (2019), *A Stone Sat Still*, San Francisco: Chronicle Books.

10

Communicating In and About the Ocean through SCUBA Interaction and Ocean Picturebooks

Grit Alter

Introduction

When looking at the table of contents of this volume on *Ecological Communication and Ecoliteracy: Discourses of Awareness and Action for the Lifescape*, readers may be surprised to find a chapter on SCUBA diving. As a sport, SCUBA diving can, by all means, not be labelled as an ecological activity; its level of sustainability and environmental friendliness is certainly disputable as it cannot be denied that SCUBA diving – SCUBA standing for self-contained underwater breathing apparatus – does have an immense impact on the environment. SCUBA diving, recreational as well as scientific, impacts the environment even when researchers are trying to better understand the ocean to save it, and recreational SCUBA divers do not want to see it destroyed either as they like to continuously enjoy the beauty of the underwater world.

So, why include a chapter on an activity not typically known as environmentally friendly and sustainable? As a passionate SCUBA diver, I have been fascinated with two elements of this sport: the first regards how people are able to communicate underwater, that is, how they are able to explicate complex meanings using an intricate system of hand signs. The second regards how the ocean[1] and what lies underneath the surface of the water is perceived, how the ocean as an ecosystem and especially its fragility is communicated to young people. After all, even when certainly unjust, they are the ones who will inevitably need to take care of the ocean and right the wrongs caused by generations before them. This concern with young people and making the complexity of, for example, coral reefs approachable to them stems from my career as a professor of Teaching English as a Foreign Language to primary school learners. While interacting underwater addresses the 'ecological communication' of the title of this volume, the focus on a picturebook for young readers allows us to develop 'ecoliteracy' at the example of ocean literacy (NMEA 2021; UNESCO 2017).

In this contribution, I have the opportunity of combining the two dimensions of SCUBA diving: underwater communication of recreational SCUBA divers, on the one hand, and communicating the intricacies of the ocean ecosystem to young readers, on the other. I aim to analyse these through the lens of ecolinguistic studies. As will be further explored later, the present studies draw on the branch of ecolinguistics that can be understood as investigating the complex relationship between language and environment. Specifically, it is concerned with 'the study of interactions between any given language and its environment' (Fill 1993: 4, 133), between single languages or between speakers, and groups of speakers (cf. Fill 1993: 4). It engages in the 'complex relations occurring between environment, languages and people speaking these languages' (Wendel 2005: 51). In a nutshell, ecolinguistics refers to the 'study of language according to the environment it is used in' (Derni 2008: 22). Hence, it can be applied to communicating *in* an ecosystem and communication *about* an ecosystem.

Embedded in this twofold idea, this chapter investigates some instances of communication above and under water, in and about the ocean. The reason for turning to the ocean is that it is the ecosystem that has gained renewed attention due to its significance for the climate and healthy balance of the Earth. Not only is the ocean a complex ecosystem which it is necessary to communicate *about*, particularly so with regards to its endangerment, but it also constitutes an intriguing environment *in* which humans communicate. It investigates the following research questions: 'How do humans communicate in specific ecosystems?' and 'How do humans communicate about specific ecosystems?' While both questions are explored using the example of the ocean as an ecosystem, the chapter itself consists of two parts, each with its own short theoretical frame.

For the first question, answered in the second part, the ocean presents an interesting case in point because the density of the water naturally limits verbal and voice communication. In view of the specific means of interaction SCUBA divers, for example, needed to create, I interrogate language use *in* this environment by turning to SCUBA dive communication and exemplifying how hand signals allow people to interact underwater. Constituting a hostile environment for humans, they need to develop and rely on alternative life-sustaining interactions (cf. Stibbe 2021: 8). Features such as risk communication (Lies 2015; Renn 1991) and the clarification of linguistic modes on a metalinguistic level allow us to identify a very specific dynamic of ecosystem and language. To answer this question, I will draw on literature on recreational SCUBA diving and explore characteristics of SCUBA diver interaction. This is subsumed under the hypothesis that if demanded by a certain environment, language can be reduced to a minimum and still function to enable communication.

For the second question, the focus remains with ocean but shifts towards ocean-related picturebooks. I use *The Brilliant Deep* (Messner 2018), an ocean picturebook on coral restoration which contextualizes SCUBA diving in marine science and communicates the research results to a wider public, which can help saving the ocean. While SCUBA divers turn to non-verbal communication *in* the ocean, authors and illustrators of picturebooks apply an intricate interplay of verbal and visual text to encode and communicate *about* the ocean. The question thus also touches upon the kind of language and visualizations that are used to inform young readers about the ocean, marine science and corals. This question will be addressed through a close reading of Messner's picturebook that applies Nikolajeva and Scott's (2000) theory on the interplay of verbal and visual text. The reading investigates to what extent the picturebook presents anthropocentric perspectives or pays tribute to the ocean as a complex ecosystem in its own right, disregarding human presence. It follows the hypothesis that picturebooks are highly useful for teaching young people about the ocean, introducing them to the fragility of the ocean and fostering an awareness for how essential it is to protect it. Compared to 'the concern ecolinguists feel about the role of language in the deterioration of the environment' (Fill 2018:1), picturebooks and their language in particular can be promising media to raise young people's awareness of the ocean's fragility.

While both parts present two separate studies, they merge as the respective contents illustrate and exemplify communication and language use with regards 'to the environment it is used in' (Derni 2008: 22). Hence, this chapter considers communicating above, below and about the ocean and takes Derni at her word when it explores these spaces. When interpreting the structure of the *Routledge Handbook of Ecolinguistics* (Fill and Penz 2018b) as a differentiation of different strands of ecolinguistics, albeit closely related and complementary to one another rather than separate, my approach fits into ecolinguistics as referring to 'the role of language concerning the environment' (Fill 2018: 3) and regards SCUBA communication and picturebooks as a medium to educate about the ocean as ecological linguistics.

10.1 Interacting above and under water: Ecolinguistics and SCUBA dive communication

As Stibbe (2021: 8) notes, the term ecolinguistics has been used to refer to various studies that address language(s) and ecosystems. These include, for example,

> studies of texts such as signposts which are outdoors; analysis of texts which happen to be about the environment; studies of how words in a language relate to objects in the local environment; studies of the mix of languages surrounding pupils in multicultural schools; studies of dialects in particular geographical locations. (Stibbe 2021: 8)

This indicates that the academic field of ecolinguistics is not only broad, but that it can be rather challenging to agree on a common understanding of its concept or to set a fixed frame of elements and themes that can be part of the discourse. What scholars seemingly agree on, though, is 'the topical focus on communication and human relations with the environment' (Milstein 2009: 344). An engagement 'with the ways people communicate about the natural world' (Milstein 2009: 344) is foregrounded, because this influences how humans relate to the environment and its current state of crisis. A prominent example of communicating about the natural world – environmental communication – is related to the terms and phrases humans use to refer to current climatic and geophysical processes. Labelling these as 'climate change' or 'climate crisis' mirrors humans' attitude towards and relationship with this process. Whereas the label 'climate change' indicates a natural development, 'climate crisis' implies a more severe account and acknowledges human impact on increasingly extreme climate and weather phenomena such as droughts, floods, fires, rising water temperatures, and melting glaciers.

As mentioned earlier, ecolinguistics addresses the 'study of language according to the environment it is used in' (Derni 2008: 22). This refers to 'questions about adaptation of ways of speaking to specific environmental conditions' (Mühlhäuser 2011: 199). Mühlhäuser's research exemplifies how humans express their relationship to the environment to which they are inextricably linked through the language they use to label it. For instance, the inhabitants of the Pitcairn Island named 'a considerable number of animals and fish [...] after the person who first caught or used them' (Mühlhäuser 2011: 205). An interesting example of adapting language to the environment is non-verbal underwater communication without technological support.

10.2 Communicating *in* the ocean

All human interaction and communication are characterized by situated language use, and this applies to all modes – verbal, visual or deictic – which all influence how communication is carried out. Communication is always ecologically embedded (Mühlhäuser 2011: 198); it depends 'on the natural habitat of language users' (Steffensen and Fill 2014: 9). No communication is only verbal so that the 'whole human body participates in languaging' (Li, Steffensen, and Huang 2020: 5; cf. Ekman and Friesen 1969).[2] Even so, SCUBA divers' communication underwater presents a specific form of and setting for interaction. Communicating underwater is a specific communicative situation in which the very environment presents a natural barrier to voice-based communication. Hence, underwater is an interesting environment to investigate through an ecolinguistics lens. In this context, the following part explores how SCUBA divers interact under water.

When submerging oneself under the water, SCUBA divers enter a complex environment. Underwater, humans experience their limitations first-hand as they are surrounded by an environment for which they are physically not equipped. The very essence of being alive, breathing as well as oral communication need to be enhanced by technology and a different semiotic system to remain healthy and be able to communicate. The self-contained underwater breathing apparatus (short: SCUBA) was invented to allow humans to breathe underwater; its modern version is based on Jacques Cousteau's research (Cousteau's Aqua Lung n.d.). To ensure communication, modes as hand signals, tools as writing slates, and voice communication technology are used. Due to the financial burden, however, voice communication which demands specific equipment and technology is generally only used by professional SCUBA divers.

Recreational SCUBA divers use a specific non-verbal repertoire to interact and communicate in an environment in which the density of the water largely impedes the transmission of sound waves. The most common communication tool recreational SCUBA divers use to interact underwater is an elaborate set of international hand signals (US Navy 2016; Bevan 2011; cf. Ekman and Friesen 1969).[3] While these hand signals are reduced to the essence to transfer essential meaning, their use is still elaborate enough to allow humans to express complex meanings (Prosser and Grey 1990; Behnke 2015). The signals mainly consist of deictic gestures to point at oneself, others, animals, or directions, as well as internationally established and recognized signs for SCUBA-specific content as exemplified in the following figures.

The hand signal in Figure 10.1 depicts the sentence: 'We need to resurface to a depth of 5m to do a 3min safety stop.' It is usually encoded by keeping the ring and little finger of one hand closed to a fist, stretching out the thumb, index finger, and middle finger of the same hand, and covering them with the open outstretched other hand; it looks like a table with three legs.

The hand signal in Figure 10.2 is used to encode that a SCUBA diver has problems equalizing the pressure in their ear. For the sentence 'I have problems with my ear', they point at it with one finger and add the sign for 'not ok' for which they spread out all of the fingers of the same hand and turn it around the axis of their forearm. A direct transcript of this sign is 'ear not ok'.

The hand signal in Figure 10.3 shows the interaction to ask about each other's air supply. This is encoded by one diver tapping two fingers of one hand to the

Figure 10.1 Signal for '*We need to resurface to a depth of 5m to do a 3min safety stop*'. Copyright: the author.

Figure 10.2 Signals for '*I have problems with my ear*'. Copyright: the author.

Figure 10.3 Signal for '*How much air do you have?*' and the answer '*I have 100 bar left*'. The fist indicates 50 bar, each raised finger adds 10 bar. This would sum up to 180 bar. Copyright: the author.

Figure 10.4 Signal for '*Ok*'. Copyright: the author.

palm of the other hand. The other diver decodes this as a question, checks their air supply, and forms a 'T' with both hands to indicate 100 bar, shows a fist for 50 bar, and uses one finger to add 10 bar each. A direct transcript of the hand signal to express this interaction reads 'You – air?' and the response '180'. In a setting in which verbal communication is possible, this interaction would be similar to the following: 'How much air do you have left?' with the other person replying, 'I have 180 bar.'

Each interaction below water, that is, each question and answer, continues until the divers confirm that they have understood the content with the ok sign by touching the thumb to index finger in a circle and extending the other fingers (Behnke 2015: 4; Figure 10.4).

Shared knowledge of clearly structured and contextualized signs ensures divers' safety and supports their enjoyment of the dive. This also means that compared to informal face-to-face oral language, SCUBA language is less flexible and less dynamic because divers need to rely on clear, shared commands and responses. While established hand signals tend to not change their meaning, new symbols can be added. Recently, a 'P' was suggested to indicate that someone found plastic and plans to pick it up. It is formed with one hand vertically straight up, fingers together and the other hand forming a semi-circle with the fingertips touching the fingertips of the first hand and the thumb of the semi-circle touching the top of the palms of this hand (Divernet.com 2019).

Although Ekman and Friesen (1969: 53–4), among others, point out that intentionality is a challenging concept when it comes to human interaction, the specific setting of the underwater world demands that the signals follow a clear communicative intention and need. As fast and uncontrolled hand movements during dives usually indicate stress, nervousness, or that something is wrong, divers need to avoid these gestures and control their non-verbal behaviour to ensure that they do not communicate unintentional meaning. This becomes particularly apparent during night dives when hand signals can only be seen when a torch is correctly and intentionally used. For instance, a quick circular or left-to-right movement catches the other divers' attention. They may then either slowly circle the light around what is interesting to see or encode that something is not ok. To avoid misunderstandings, divers need to hold the torch firmly in their hand so that quick movements do not happen unintended.

Using and understanding these hand signals is vitally important because underwater there is no option for SCUBA divers to clarify their or their partner's intended meaning verbally. Rather, they need to be able to diligently read each other's body language to understand other divers' physical and mental states and the meanings they try to convey. Thus, SCUBA dive communication underwater literally presents 'life-sustaining interactions of humans with other humans, other organisms and the physical environment' (Stibbe 2021: 9).

Similar to many other specific contexts such as free time activities, technical contexts, or subcultures, also SCUBA divers use a specific jargon closely linked to the activity itself. Here, communication on a meta-level is a further feature of the complex design of SCUBA dive communication. Dives are usually framed by the pre-dive briefing which contains the dive plan and potential risks that could occur during the specific dive. Moreover, it outlines the maximum depth and duration of the dive as well as some geographical features and sometimes the animals likely to be seen. At the end of the briefing, the most common hand signals are repeated and clarified with every participant to make sure that divers communicate using the same language when underwater. The meaning and use of these signs are made explicit by showing the sign and adding the respective verbal representation. Such meta-linguistic transductions, namely expressing and transferring meaning across semiotic systems (cf. Bezemer and Kress 2008), ensure that the signs and their meaning are as unambiguous as possible.

The dive briefing is a form of concrete risk communication (Lies 2015; Renn 1991). It directly refers to the risks that are involved in diving, that is, challenging passages, the difficulty that may occur when entering and exiting water, or sections in which divers need to pay special attention. As such, regarding this specific environment, risk communication positions SCUBA divers as guests in the ecosystem they enter and emphasises their subordinate role and the fragile position they have underwater.

Applying the research question of how humans communicate in a specific ecosystem to the underwater world, this exploration showed that by using hand signals to interact underwater, SCUBA divers adapt their ways of 'speaking' to particular environmental conditions (cf. Mühlhäuser 2011: 199). As indicated earlier, being surrounded by water in the depths of the ocean, recreational SCUBA divers need to rely on hand signals for immediate understanding and clarification of meaning. SCUBA hand signals as a means of non-verbal underwater communication and the explicit focus on meta- and risk communication demonstrate the 'complex relations occurring between environment, languages and people speaking these languages' (Wendel 2005: 51). In SCUBA communication, it is essential to clarify the codes people are using to ensure they know as exactly as possible what meaning these convey; the addressee needs a high level of situational awareness. Each interaction underwater is framed by precise openings and closings and is constantly accompanied by verifications.

To secure their safety underwater, SCUBA divers reduce complex expressions to minimal content that remains meaningful and carries all the information necessary in specific situations. Hand signs as well as meta- and risk communication encode the essential elements, the core of what one needs to transport into a language that remains clear and carries significant content. In a way, the design of picturebooks is similar, because the standard picturebook consists of only thirty-two pages (Ommundsen 2018: 229), and hence, the content authors and illustrators aim to convey also needs to be reduced to its core. As my field of research is located within picturebook research, I consider it to be highly interesting to analyse how an ocean-related picturebook communicates *about* this ecosystem. Albeit a very different medium with a very different audience, Kate Messner's *The Brilliant Deep: Rebuilding the World's Coral Reefs: The Story of Ken Nedimyer and the Coral Restoration Foundation* (2018) uses verbal and non-verbal language to educate a young readership about the health of coral reefs, the research for and implementation of which relies on scientific SCUBA diving.

10.3 Communicating about the ocean: Non-fiction picturebooks

On the one hand, SCUBA diving can be problematic because it contributes to the crisis in the ocean. On the other, though, scientists such as Ken Nedimyer have demonstrated that SCUBA diving can also contribute to saving the ocean and to informing a wider public of its beauty, and encourage a desire to protect it.

The present section focuses on the picturebook *The Brilliant Deep*, written by Kate Messner (2018) and illustrated by Matthew Forsythe, and analyses how verbal and visual modes interact to create meaning and can be an exemplification of 'eco-imagistics': Fill and Penz suggest researchers should highlight 'the role of images and particularly of language-image combinations in representing environmental topics and problems' (Fill and Penz 2018a: 440).

In what follows, I will explore how the picturebook *The Brilliant Deep* communicates the need for and process of how coral reefs are restored to young readers. The book introduces the scientist Ken Nedimyer and his discovery that a single coral gamete can grow into a new coral. He observed the spawning of staghorn corals while SCUBA diving. Investigating further, he found that these can be multiplied and regrown by cutting small pieces and attaching the pieces to rocks. The new colonies can then be used to grow even more corals. During their research, Nedimyer and his team replanted these new coral colonies on the limestone of dying reefs, a practice that led to the foundation of the Coral Restoration Foundation. The foundation now engages scientists and volunteers around the world to regrow coral reefs (Coral Restauration Foundation 2020).

As a literary format, picturebooks are particularly accessible as most of these texts narrate content by making use of an intricate interplay of the verbal and visual modes (Ommundsen, Haaland and Kümmerling-Meibauer 2022: 3). Drawing on Nikolajeva and Scott (2000), this interplay, sometimes also referred to as interanimation, can be distinguished as a symmetrical, enhancing, complementary or counterpointing and contradictory relationship of both modes. In the symmetrical relationship, both modes essentially provide similar information and tell the same story, as is the case in Carle's *The Very Hungry Caterpillar* (1969). In enhancing interactions, both modes mutually amplify each other's meaning. A complementary interaction of verbal and visual text is enhancing in essence but the interaction of both modes is more significant than in enhancing interaction. Both 'words and pictures support [. . .] one another by providing additional information that the other lacks, the additional material may be minor, or quite dramatically different' (Nikolajeva and Scott 2000: 229). *The Cloud* (Cumming 2010), for instance, is a picturebook in which complementary interaction can be identified. In counterpointing interaction, the verbal and visual text 'collaborate to communicate meanings beyond the scope of either one alone' (Nikolajeva and Scott 2000: 226); *Rosie's Walk* (Hutchins 1968) is a prime example. In picturebooks that are designed with a contradictory interaction, the verbal and visual text present different kinds of information and oppose one another as is the case in *The Girl in Red* (Frisch and Innocenti 2012, for a more detailed account please see Alter and Merse 2023).

Picturebooks that refer to scientists and their discoveries may contain complex information that can be challenging to understand for young children. Hence, *The Brilliant Deep* (Messner 2018) follows an enhanced and complementary interanimation of verbal and visual text which facilitates comprehension in the main target audience of this book, namely children.

To begin with, I reflect on how the verbal text focuses on the use of technical terms and lexis, how scientific information is provided, and whether it contains references to an anthropocentric vision of the ecosystem. Regarding the visual text, I will take a critical look at how the underwater world is represented in colours, lines, and composition. I argue that the child-friendly design of both verbal and visual text not only offers a realistic depiction of the ocean but also an accessible connection to the underlying scientific concepts. In general, Nedimyer's research as presented in the book illustrates how SCUBA diving can essentially contribute to saving the ocean by creating in young readers a desire to protect it.

Despite the young target audience of the picturebook, Messner does not shy away from using technical lexis to tell Nedimyer's story. This regards terms for ocean animals and plants such as 'angel fish' and 'sea stars' (opening 7),[4] 'sea urchins' and 'algae' (opening 10), 'mollusks, sponges, invertebrates' (opening 11), 'staghorn corals' (opening 12) but also collocations such as 'corals spawn' (opening 2). Young readers are thus familiarized with organisms essential to the health of coral reefs. With the help of realistic drawings, children are also helped in identifying these organisms.

Next to providing young readers with the lexis to label selected ocean organisms, the book offers precise and accurate information about biochemical processes in the ocean. It refers to how the rising of the ocean's water temperature causes the corals to lose their colour and how this leads to fewer fish on the reefs (opening 9). Sea urchins are introduced as the 'gardeners of the reef' who control the growth of algae. When there are less urchins, more algae can grow (opening 11).

Of particular importance to Nedimyer's research are live rocks. As the book emphasizes, these are not really alive, but rocks covered in algae and other organisms. These organisms transform ammonia and nitrates into harmless compounds which in turn make the water healthier for all living beings (opening 12). While such explanations seem to be rather complex and the information may overwhelm young readers, the book follows a slow pace and carefully crafts the science behind the research. This is also supported by the short and comprehensive blocks of written text that can often be found in picturebooks. In one instance, the factual information about how the scientists go about growing the new corals is presented in child-friendly and accessible comparisons, for example, that the 'dab of epoxy' with which the 'volunteers attach the coral colonies' is 'just the size of a Hershey's Kiss' (opening 19). Using a language that is familiar to children, many of whom indeed dab dabs when painting and are likely to have seen and tasted this chocolate candy, invites them to imagine how the respective science is practiced, even when they may not be familiar with epoxy as a specific kind of chemical resin that here functions as glue.

Certainly, it would have been possible that the interdependence of corals losing their colour and fewer fish on the reef, and the threat algae pose to corals, was made more explicit. Even so, *The Brilliant Deep* is a children's book which justifies this kind of reduction of complexity. As to offer more information on these issues, the last opening of the book provides readers with further information on coral reefs, on what is threatening them and on what to do to save them. Here, the book mentions that 'protecting parrotfish and sea urchins might help to save the reefs, since these animals eat the algae that can overwhelm corals if it's not kept in check' (opening 23). Young readers and their guardians can use the information provided to answer questions that may occur while reading the book.

What needs to be highlighted is that *The Brilliant Deep* never explicitly connects the significance of healthy reefs to the well-being of humans. Rather, the book emphasizes that corals need to be restored and that coral reefs need to be healthy for their own sake, not to benefit humans for their enjoyment or survival. This resonates with Fill and Penz's question whether representations in media 'do justice to the life of animals, or [. . .] simply show animals from the human point of view with particular emphasis on their usefulness for humans' (Fill and Penz 2018a: 440). *The Brilliant Deep* adheres to this demand.

Its biocentric perspective also offers a counternarrative to the anthropocentrism Heuberger (2003) identified in dictionaries.

The poetic tone of the verbal text emphasizes the beauty and depth, literal as well as metaphorical, that lies within the delicate intricacy of the ocean. The phrase 'it starts with one' opens the book at the very beginning and is repeated at the very end. When it is first mentioned, it refers to one gamete that can start a new coral reef. At the end of the book, it refers to Ken himself, who as a single person initiated a worldwide movement to protect the ocean. This phrase, hence, frames the book and emphasizes how much of an impact one single organism can have, be it a gamete or a human being. After readers are introduced to the danger the ocean is in and what can be done to help it, this 'one' reappears, this time referring to 'one hopeful dive' and 'one optimistic experiment' (opening 16). By not finishing these sentences, Messner creates suspense as readers do not yet know to what extent the experiments have been successful.

Furthermore, the use of anaphora mirrors the flow of the narration similar to the waves on the ocean and emphasizes the continuity of underwater life circles. The pronoun 'some', for example, at the beginning of sentences that describe the paths gametes take after spawning (opening 3), creates a flow and rhythm in the verbal text that renders the gametes salient. This is continued in the repetition of 'another' (opening 21) gamete that may nest in just the right spot to start a new coral reef. The mere impact, but also the chance by which coral reefs can multiply, is also stressed by the rhetorically impressive contrast of 'one' and 'millions of tiny lives' (opening 2). Here, language not only mirrors the science of coral reproduction but also makes it approachable through sound and specific rhetoric.

To visually illustrate Nedimyer's resistance to the assault on nature, Forsythe selected a rather unusual palette of colours to illustrate the biodiversity in the ocean. The large-scale drawings that simultaneously show soft edges and sharp forms offer an immersive experience of the underwater world. Compared to other picturebooks on coral reefs which are often extremely colourful and in which illustrators use very bright and shining colours (e.g. *Commotion in the Ocean* by Giles Andreae 2002, or *Mister Seahorse* by Eric Carle 2006), *The Brilliant Deep* is illustrated in rather muted tones to create the myriad shapes of animals, plants, and organisms under water. Forsythe's use of colours ranges from fiery red to muddy green, purple and burnished gold. These lend the illustrations more realism as the range and intensity of colours decrease the deeper one dives. Overall, the tone of the drawings seems to be rather serious, which is also mirrored in the mainly straight faces of the protagonists. This, in turn, reflects the seriousness of the topic. If humans do not change their affluent lifestyles, it will not take long until the colours Forsythe uses to depict the deeper parts of the ocean also become reality in the shallows.

As Stibbe and, in a similar way, Fill opine, '[e]colinguistics can explore the more general patterns of language that influence how people both think about, and treat, the world. It can investigate the *stories we live by* – mental models which influence behaviour and lie at the heart of the ecological challenges we are facing' (Stibbe 2021: 1, similar in Fill 1993). The way in which *The Brilliant Deep* offers insights into Nedimyer's life and research, presenting information and technical lexis in a child-friendly narrative, exemplifies how one of the stories we live by can and even needs to be told to foster young people's ocean literacy, their awareness of and sensitivity to circumstances that threaten the ocean and can secure its health (NMEA 2021; UNESCO 2017). As to increase children's awareness of environmental issues, it is necessary to use a multimodal language that is accessible to them, that they understand and that allows them to speak about and name the ecological crisis by which they are surrounded. Through picturebooks, young readers can be empowered to engage with experiences to 'widen [. . .] knowledge, and broaden [. . .] perspectives around ocean science and sustainable development of the ocean and its resources' (UNESCO 2017: 16) and, more importantly, to keep the fragile ecosystem healthy and independent of humans' needs.

10.4 Conclusion

To engage with communication in and about a specific ecosystem, this chapter explored two contexts. While the first part (Section 10.2) offered insights into non-verbal communication underwater as an example of communicating *in* a specific environment, the second (Section 10.3) discussed an ocean-related picturebook as an example of communicating *about* a specific environment. In both parts, SCUBA diving played a decisive role, albeit as a recreational sport in the first and as a means of scientific research in the second.

To interact underwater, SCUBA divers utilize a fixed set of hand signals and engage in intensive meta-communication to clarify their meaning as well as the risks involved in immersing oneself in the ocean. This presents an interesting example of how language is used in a specific environment in which verbal communication is impeded, due to the context itself. Communicating under water, SCUBA divers cannot engage in elaborate processes of clarifying misunderstandings. Hence, static and fixed hand signals need to be as unambiguous as possible and based on shared knowledge of the intended meaning. This is partly achieved through the internationally recognized system of signals which vary only in a few details; these differences, if they become apparent, are clarified during the briefing before the dive.

Although SCUBA divers add to the ocean's precarious situation, scientists like Ken Nedimyer show how research can also benefit from them. His discovery and implementation of coral restoration programmes around the world rely on SCUBA divers who plant new corals which revitalize coral reefs. The picturebook *The Brilliant Deep* narrates this discovery and the scientific processes of coral restoration in a child-friendly way. It invites the target audience to an enjoyable reading (or read-aloud) experience while simultaneously teaching them about the sensitive ecosystem of the ocean. This picturebook achieves this by telling a non-fiction story that contextualizes scientific facts in a language and illustrations that are highly accessible by young and older readers alike.

Undeniably, most environments would thrive best in the absence of humans, and this also holds true for the ocean. This contribution did not focus on a critical evaluation of SCUBA diving as a high-impact sport but on the intricate means of communication this sport has created. '[O]ne can manage only what one knows, and a corollary that one knows that for which one has a linguistic expression' (Mühlhäuser 1996: 125). Hence, humans have to expand their knowledge about the ocean to better understand it and find ways to save it. Humans often care about entities that they appreciate and like, that they admire, and to which they attach meaning and value. SCUBA divers usually appreciate the reefs and want to see them healthy and intact. Communicating about this issue, either while situated in this specific environment or while reading an ocean-themed picturebook, allows humans to build a relationship to this ecosystem and may increase their awareness of its endangerment. Both dimensions can counter an alienation from nature as humans closely engage in and with nature. Human activity certainly and progressively destroys the ecosystems found in the ocean, but it is also through human activity that these can be saved. Being able to communicate and being aware of the intricacies of the ocean as a fragile ecosystem under and above water is one of the first steps towards ecological communication and ecoliteracy.

Notes

1 Following NMEA and Sea Change, the singular is used to address the ocean. This reinforces the critical importance that there is only one ocean as an interconnected body of water that consists of five basins: the Atlantic, Pacific, Indian, Arctic, and Southern (NMEA 2021, n.p., Sea Change 2020, n.p.).
2 This estimation assumes that participants in communication are able to perceive language with all senses. Communicating orally on the telephone or using written language in messaging services limits the role bodies can play during interactions but offers other affordances.
3 Since there are only a few organizations that train SCUBA divers, and as these operate internationally, it is indeed the case that the hand signals are also international. If there are differences, these are only minor and are clarified through meta-communication before dives. Hence, although SCUBA divers may not speak the same verbal language, with a short meta-reflection on the hand signals they use, that is, asking each other with which agency they became SCUBA divers, they will still be able to communicate underwater.
4 Picturebooks are usually not paginated; pages are counted as double-spreads ('openings') beginning with the first page in which the narration starts.

References

Alter, G. and T. Merse (2023), 'Introduction: Positioning Picturebooks in Secondary English Language Teaching', in G. Alter and T. Merse (eds), *Re-thinking Picturebooks for Intermediate and Advanced Learners: Perspectives for Secondary English Language Learners*, 13–29, Tübingen: Narr.

Andreae, G. and D. Wojtowycz (2002), *Commotion in the Ocean*, Westminster: Tiger Tales.

Behnke, L. (2015), *SCUBA Diving Hand Signals: Pocket Companion for Recreational SCUBA Divers*, Create Space.

Bevan, J. (2011), *The Professional Diver's Handbook*, Gosport: Submex Ltd.

Bezemer, J. and G. Kress (2008), 'Writing in Multimodal Texts: A Social Semiotic Account of Designs for Learning', *Written Communication*, 25 (2): 166–95. https://doi.org/10.1177/0741088307313177.

Carle, E. (1969), *The Very Hungry Caterpillar*, Cleveland: World Publishing Company.

Carle, E. (2006), *Mister Seahorse*, London: Puffin.

Coral Restoration Foundation (2020), Coral Restoration Foundation. Available online: http://www.coralrestoration.org (accessed 14 September 2021).

Cousteau's Aqua Lung (n.d.), Available online: https://www.cousteau.org/legacy/technology/aqua-lung/ (accessed 14 September 2021).

Cumming, H. (2010), *The Cloud*, Swindon: Child's Play International.
Derni, A. (2008), 'The Ecolinguistic Paradigm: An Integrationist Trend in Language Study', *The International Journal of Language, Society and Culture*, 24: 21–30.
Divernet.com. (2019), *Signalling P for Plastic*. Available online: https://divernet.com/SCUBA-news/signalling-p-for-plastic/ (accessed 14 September 2021).
Ekman, P. and W. V. Friesen (1969), 'The Repertoire of Non-Verbal Behavior: Categories, Origins, Usage and Coding', *Semiotika*, 1 (1): 49–98.
Fill, A. F. (1993), *Ökolinguistik - Eine Einführung*, Tübingen: Narr.
Fill, A. F. (2018), 'Introduction', in A. F. Fill and H. Penz (eds), *The Routledge Handbook of Ecolinguistics*, 1–7, London: Routledge.
Fill, A. F. and H. Penz (2018a), 'Ecolinguistics in the 21st Century New Orientations and Future Directions', in A. F. Fill and H. Penz (eds), *The Routledge Handbook of Ecolinguistics*, 437–43, London: Routledge.
Fill, A. F. and H. Penz, eds (2018b), *The Routledge Handbook of Ecolinguistics*, London: Routledge.
Frisch, A. and R. Innocenti (2012), *The Girl in Red*, Mankato: Creative Editions & Paperback.
Heuberger, R. (2003), 'Anthropocentrism in Monolingual English Dictionaries: An Ecolinguistic Approach to the Lexicographic Treatment of Faunal Terminology', *AAA: Arbeiten aus Anglistik und Amerikanistik*, 28 (1): 93–105.
Hutchins, P. (1968), *Rosie's Walk*, Oldenburg: Stalling.
Li, J., S. V. Steffensen, and G. Huang (2020), 'Rethinking Ecolinguistics from a Distributed Language Perspective', *Language Sciences*, 80, Article 101277: 1–12. https://doi.org/10.1016/j.langsci.2020.101277.
Lies, J. (2015), *Praxis des PR Managements: Strategien - Instrumente - Anwendung*, Berlin: Springer.
Messner, K. (2018), *The Brilliant Deep: Rebuilding the World's Coral Reefs*, San Francisco: Chronicle Books.
Milstein, T. (2009), '"Somethin" Tells Me It's All Happening at the Zoo': Discourse, Power, and Conservationism', *Environmental Communication: A Journal of Nature and Culture*, 3 (1): 25–48.
Mühlhäuser, P. (1996), 'Linguistic Adaptation to Changes Environmental Conditions: Some Lessons from the Past', in A. F. Fill (ed), *Sprachökologie und Ökolinguistik*, 105–30, Blaufelden: Stauffenburg.
Mühlhäuser, P. (2011), 'Ecolinguistics, Linguistic Diversity, Ecological Diversity', in S. Harding (ed), *The Postcolonial Science and Technology Studies Reader*, 198–210, Durham: Duke University Press.
[NMEA] National Marine Educators Association (2021), 'Ocean Literacy: The Essential Principles and Fundamental Concepts of Ocean Sciences for Learners of All Ages'. Available online: https://static1.squarespace.com/static/5b4cecfde2ccd188cfed8026/t/60b90193ec346816a95717bb/1622737304272/OceanLiteracy_ENG_V3.1_2021.pdf (accessed 14 September 2021).

Nikolajeva, M. and C. Scott (2000), 'The Dynamics of Picturebook Communication', *Children's Literature in Education*, 31 (4): 225–39.

Ommundsen, Å. M. (2018), 'Picturebooks for Adults', in B. Kümmerling-Meibauer (ed), *The Routledge Companion to Picturebooks*, 220–30, London: Routledge.

Ommundsen, Å. M., G. Haaland, and B. Kümmerling-Meibauer, eds (2022), *Exploring Challenging Picturebooks in Education. International Perspectives on Language and Literature Learning*, London: Routledge.

Prosser, J. and H. V. Grey (1990), *Cave Diving Communication*, Washington, DC: National Speleological Society.

Renn, O. (1991), 'Risikokommunikation – Bedingungen und Probleme Eines Rationalen Diskurses über die Akzeptabilität von Risiken', in J. Schneider (ed), *Risiko und Sicherheit Technischer Systeme*, 193–209, Basel: Birkhäuser.

Sea Change (2020), European Marine Board and CoExploration Limited. Available online: http://www.seachangeproject.eu/ (accessed 14 September 2021).

Steffensen, S. V. and A. F. Fill (2014), 'Ecolinguistics: The State of the Art and Future Horizons', *Language Sciences*, 41 (A): 6–25.

Stibbe, A., ed (2021), *Ecolinguistics Language, Ecology and the Stories We Live By*, London: Routledge.

UNESCO (2017), 'Ocean Literacy for All: A Toolkit'. Available online: https://ioc.unesco.org/publications/ocean-literacy-all-toolkit (accessed 12 September 2021).

US Navy (2016), '8 Surface Supplied Diving Operations', in US Navy (ed), *US Navy Diving Manual*, 8–24, Washington, DC: US Naval Sea Systems Command.

Wendel, J. N. (2005), 'Notes on the Ecology of Language', *Bunkyo Gakuin University Academic*, 5: 511–16.

Positive Multimodal Analysis of EU Learning Materials to Promote Ecoliteracy for Young People

Sole Alba Zollo

Introduction: Ecoliteracy and the European Union

Originally, the term literacy was used to refer only to the ability to read and write. Over the years this concept has evolved and its meaning has expanded to include the 'knowledge of a particular subject, or a particular type of knowledge'.[1] As a consequence, it now refers to the ability to understand and make decisions in different contexts and discourses such as science literacy, financial literacy, digital literacy, among others. This term has also been applied to ecology giving birth to three notions: ecological literacy, environmental literacy and ecoliteracy (see McBride et al. 2013 for a definition of these concepts). Given the arbitrary and, sometimes, indiscriminate usage of these three conceptions, in the present study the notion of ecoliteracy is preferred because this term, coined by Capra (1997), focuses on the creation of sustainable communities and this research field adopts the ecosophy (short for ecological philosophy) of sustainable development (Baker 2006). Ecosophy is a philosophy of ecological harmony. For Stibbe (2021: 12) each ecolinguist employs their own philosophical principles, which reflect their own values, but all share the same ideas on the interrelationship among human beings, other living organisms and the physical environment.

The ideology of sustainable development spread in the 1980s with the convening of the World Commission on Environment and Development (WCED) in 1983 which addressed growing worries for the deterioration of the environment and its consequences for social and economic development. In their report 'Our Common Future', the WCED defined sustainable development as 'development that meets the needs of the present without compromising the ability of future generations to meet their own needs' (WCED 1987: 24). Since then, this ideology has become dominant in the education system. Unlike environmental literacy, ecoliteracy highlights the concept of sustainability and introduces a spiritual approach by discussing the role that creativity and spirituality may play in enhancing ecoliteracy: 'An ecoliterate person is prepared to be an effective member of sustainable society, with well-rounded abilities of head, heart, hands, and spirit, comprising an organic understanding of the world and participatory action within and with the environment' (McBride et al. 2013: 14). Through different channels such as education, family, national and international organizations, people acquire ecological knowledge, which enhances their awareness of environmental protection. The dissemination of ecological knowledge among citizens has become a priority for institutions in order to develop people's ecological behaviour and achieve a higher level of ecoliteracy. Over the past decade, the EU has been generating a variety of informative materials in a form that can be easily understood by the young generations, to foster a multidirectional dialogue on the promotion of a sustainable environmental framework.

Following the socio-semiotic strand of multimodal analysis (Kress and van Leeuwen 2021) and research on Positive Discourse Analysis (PDA) (Bartlett 2012, 2018; Stibbe 2017, 2021; Hughes 2018), this study aims to analyse a sample of informative and educational text types taken from the EU's website *Learning Corner*[2] in order to detect the most significant multimodal features that can encourage environmental positive discourses in a class of BA students. Then, an empirical study was conducted with groups of students to verify their response to the EU resources and their capability to propose alternative local green actions.

The following section will deal with the scope of the research, the collected data and methodology. After illustrating the theoretical framework (Section 11.2), Section 11.3 will be devoted to a summary of the analysis and the presentation and discussion of both theoretical and practical results of multimodal ecological communication. Finally, Section 11.4 presents some concluding remarks.

11.1 Aims, data selection and methodology

The *Learning Corner*, one of the EU's websites, offers a variety of informative and didactic resources aimed at explaining some fundamental aspects of the European Union and its policies on topical issues, such as the environment, to students of different age groups. In particular, between 1 and 15 September 2021 the section 'Environment, climate and energy'[3] was explored and a sample of different text types (brochures, leaflets, videos and activity books) was collected; I excluded games, quizzes and maps because of their high level of interactivity and changeability. Then, the data were grouped in four corpora according to the target audience (materials for students up to nine years of age, between nine and twelve, between twelve and fifteen and over fifteen). Since some materials were addressed to two different age groups, two data sets (materials for students up to nine years of age and materials for students from nine to over fifteen) were identified to prevent a duplication of documents. For the first phase of the study a small sample of texts was taken into consideration (Table 11.1), while for the empirical study a larger sample of texts was selected (Appendix B).

The present study is aimed at addressing two key research questions: What is students' response to the EU materials after becoming familiar with some aspects of the Social Semiotics theoretical framework? Can awareness in multimodal communication help students to find alternative ways to protect the 'lifescape' and take positive action?

The focus of this study is mainly twofold. First of all, the analysis is aimed to detect the main verbal and visual discursive strategies of knowledge communication employed by the EU in order to convey aspects of institutional discourse on environmental protection to the young generations and develop eco-friendly awareness. After a preliminary investigation of the collected data, I decided to narrow my analysis and mainly focus on three videos and one activity book (Table 11.1), whose findings are discussed in Subsection 11.3.1.

The second phase of the research took into account the pedagogical implications of the collected data and the types of action they may suggest (see Subsection 11.3.2). A four-month empirical study (from September to December 2021) was conducted in a class of ninety-four undergraduate students (between eighteen and twenty), attending the course 'English for Specific Purposes', within the three-year degree programme in political science at the University of Napoli Federico II (Italy), in order to investigate how these students respond to a sample of the EU resources. After an introduction to some relevant aspects

Table 11.1 Data set

10 Global Climate Facts (1 video) – ages over 15
Green Deal Proposal (1 video) – ages 12–15; over 15
EU for Paris agreement (1 video) – ages 12–15; over 15
52 steps towards a greener city (activity book) – ages 12–15; over 15

of social semiotics at the start of the course and the analysis of the EU materials selected as data set (Table 11.1), students were invited to complete two tasks (see Appendix A) through group work. Firstly, they were asked to choose and collect a sample of various text types from the list of EU materials provided by the teacher (see Appendix B), and after that they were encouraged to identify what they thought are the key multimodal communicative features which conveyed positive messages. Then, they were stimulated to suggest concrete examples of green projects at the local level to contribute to building a more sustainable future and identifying possible and fruitful discursive solutions for taking positive ecological actions.

11.2 Theoretical framework: Positive multimodal discourse analysis and ecolinguistics

The term Positive Discourse Analysis first appeared in 2004 in Martin's work *Positive Discourse Analysis: Solidarity and Change* where the scholar, by analysing two texts encoding two opposite ideologies on the topic of the oppression of the Indigenous Australians, underlines that deconstructive and constructive activities are both necessary to uncover inequalities and redistribute power. PDA is rooted in Critical Discourse Analysis (CDA) that critically looks at how linguistic patterns can be used by dominating groups to maintain their power in society, but it goes beyond it to detect discourses that can be effective in encouraging the change we desire to see. Instead of highlighting injustices, PDA aims at identifying and promoting alternatives: it 'analyses the discourse we like rather than the discourse we wish to criticize' (Macgilchrist 2007: 74).

Several scholars have recognized the potential of PDA in different fields, from politics (Macgilchrist and Van Praet 2013; Su 2016) to education (Rogers and Mosley Wetzel 2013). More recently, Hughes (2018: 198) proposes Progressive Discourse Analysis as an alternative to PDA, since positive discourse is 'concerned with progress toward a better world', by suggesting hopeful, inspiring and healing discourses. Progress is a reconstructive process, a question of design. Progressive (or positive) discourse analysis 'considers how people make the world a better place and designs interventions based on such considerations' (Bartlett 2018: 133). Some CDA analysts argue that also CDA is positive since its critique is fundamental to promote change for the better; Hughes, however, points out that PDA is not an alternative to CDA but a complement to critically analysing discourse and both approaches are aimed at progressive social change.

The alternative term *progressive* may help analysts 'grapple more critically with the question of what constitutes "positive" social change' (Hughes 2018: 198) and (re)construct inspiring and resisting discourses, for example, designing ecological alternative discourses.

Fill and Mühlhäusler (2001) connect ecology to language by identifying the most important strands of ecolinguistic research: ecology as metaphor, language and environment and critical ecolinguistics. Language and ecology are not separate. Language can influence the way we think about environment and how we act, so ecolinguistics can question linguistic patterns that can induce people to destroy, damage or protect nature. It is through language that social practices are shaped and it is through language that they can be resisted. Linguistics tools can help analyse key stories that influence our behaviours, reveal the stories that underlie our culture and question them from an ecological perspective.

Although many studies on the relation between language and environment have been published (Mühlhäusler 2003; Devauld and Green 2010 among others), there are not many studies that have tried to combine a critical approach to challenge common-sense assumptions and a more empirical one to detect practical solutions. In fact, ecolinguistics 'is still limited to the discussion of the relation between language and ecology, often from a critical perspective, rather than designing alternative discourses aimed at promoting more environmentally-conscious practice' (Chen, Bartlett and Peng 2021: 7). Analysing positive discourses can help identify linguistic patterns that can encourage human beings to care about and protect the environment. Stibbe (2017) suggests we should question the current stories that lead to environmental destruction and look for new stories that can offer positive alternatives. The scholar underlines that proposing alternatives is also part of CDA, but the main difference between CDA and PDA and ecolinguistics is in terms of application: the first aims to unveil hidden ideologies and solve problems by removing the negative rather than promoting positive discourses while the latter aims to promote alternative voices and provide new encouraging stories against the damaging dominant discourses.

Given that the data under investigation include various multimodal resources, the socio-economic approach of Multimodal Discourse Analysis (MDA), developed by Kress and van Leeuwen in their seminal book *Reading Images. The Grammar of Visual Design* (1996; 2021), is also applied to the analysis of the EU's texts.

Kress and van Leeuwen (2001) distinguish between medium and mode. Modes are socially shaped and culturally given semiotic resources for making meaning. They are abstract ways of meaning-making which can realize all three Hallidayan meta-functions (ideational, interpersonal and textual) and in materially different media. Since modes are flexible, texts are often characterized by the creation of new modes or the transformation of existing ones to respond to producers' communicative needs. MDA 'explores the meaning-making potential of different communication modes and media and their actual use and dynamic interaction with each other and with the sociocultural context in which they operate' (Djonov and Zhao 2014: 1). Grounded in Halliday's theory of meta-functions, MDA points out that also images can potentially convey three types of meanings: representational, interactive and compositional. As also shown in Section 11.3, '[i]mages construct not only representations of material reality but also the interpersonal interaction of social reality (such as relations between viewers and what is viewed). In addition, images cohere into textual compositions in different ways and so realize semiotic reality' (Unsworth 2008: 3).

11.3 Analysis and discussion

For the first part of the research, I decided to present in class some of the socio-semiotic tools elaborated by Kress and van Leeuwen, focusing on representation of social actors, composition and page layout, modality, typographical features and colour. After introducing some main theoretical concepts, three videos (*10 Global Climate Facts, Green Deal Proposal, EU for Paris agreement*) and one activity book (*52 steps towards a greener city*) were analysed and discussed with the students. The multimodal analysis of the collected data allowed us to detect the way the EU multimodally communicates environmental issues to young people providing positive discursive features as alternative to the mainstream environment discourses, which tend to underline people's inappropriate behaviours and the catastrophic effects of these actions on the natural world. The results of this analysis will be illustrated in Subsection 11.3.1.

Moreover, I decided to conduct an experiment study with groups of students to observe their response to the EU materials and also verify whether these materials can help the young to take positive action. Despite discourse analysts' call for PDA to combine critique and design, it still remains vague how to design new discourses. As Bartlett (2018: 138) points out: '[It] could be claimed that the focus on positive discourses advocated by Martin has pushed ahead while little progress has been made with respect to converting such analysis into

Design or consideration of the specific social conditions affecting the uptake of both dominant and alternative discourses'. This is one of the reasons why Subsection 11.3.2 will present the students' outputs to verify the effectiveness of the multimodal positive discursive features detected in the first phase of the investigation and whether students can design new environmental discourses.

11.3.1 The EU Learning Corner section 'Environment, climate and energy': A Positive Multimodal Discourse Analysis

10 Global Climate Facts[4] is a short video that illustrates ten global climate facts and how climate change is affecting people's lives. The video becomes not only an instrument to persuade the audience there is no time to waste but also a means of self-promotion, since it mentions the measures that the EU is adopting to reduce the consequences of global warming and suggests actions to minimize its effects on communities.

The first six facts include mainstream threatening discourses where ecological awareness is raised through 'moral panic' by a combination of verbal and visual elements. The first five video frames show the catastrophic consequences of unsustainable industrial civilization; in these sections we find images of an arid and dry land, flood, wildfires, a smog-filled urban area, an African child fetching water from a well and endangered animals accompanied with phrases such as 'the warmest years', 'the hottest months', 'increasing of natural disasters', '7 million deaths including over 500,000 children', 'extinction of animals' and 'destruction of habitats'. On the contrary, the following three facts illustrate the attempts of the EU to neutralize gas emissions. By showing images of lush cereal crops, smart cities, green buildings and people working on sustainable solutions, the EU promotes a different 'story', that is, the institution is not obsessed with unlimited economic growth but is now more concerned with ecosystems' preservation and people's well-being. Through positive discourses, the organization 'aims to make Europe the first climate-neutral continent by 2025' and invites everyone to take action and find other 'stories' that can have a less harmful impact on nature. In particular, in the last video frame, through the use of the inclusive pronoun 'we', the audience is not seen as a victim or a passive observer of environment deterioration, but they can collaborate with the EU and be principal actors. This message of active collaboration is reinforced by the following linguistic parallelism: 'The longer we wait before taking action the higher the cost will be'; parallelism is a common rhetorical device that contributes to making the text memorable since it exploits the 'poetic' function of language (Partington and Taylor 2018). The more threatening messages in the first six frames are mitigated not only by sentences that invite viewers to act but also by how modes interplay, since the verbal text is accompanied by beautiful green views and relaxing music. Through verbal, visual and sound features, the EU constructs an emancipatory discourse aimed at offering a message of hope: it is possible to find a balance between people's well-being and ecosystem preservation thanks to social commitment. As stated by Stibbe (2021: 29), 'Resisting a dominant destructive discourse is calling for a decrease in the use of the discourse based on a convincing account of the harm it causes, opening up space for other, potentially more beneficial, alternatives.'

The same message is conveyed by the *Green Deal Proposal*,[5] which is one of the *EU Green Deal* six videos targeting people from twelve years of age. The video[6] mentions the main actions of the *European Green Deal*, that is, Europe's new growth strategy, to transform people's lives and make the EU the world's first climate-neutral continent. Since the EU is now aware that unlimited economic growth will lead to ecological destruction, it is determined to develop a new strategy that protects jobs and preserves people's well-being. This transition to climate neutrality, which means reducing gas emissions and also absorbing more carbon emissions through new regulation on land use and forests, is endorsed by the close-shot images of Ursula Gertrud von der Leyen and sections of her speech delivered in 2019 when presenting the *European Green Deal* before the European Parliament. The sentence 'we have to act now' pronounced by the president of the European Commission resonates throughout the entire video and the 'demand' pictures (Kress and van Leeuwen 2021), that is, images where the represented participants look directly at the viewer, ask for social participation and reinforce her message addressed to European citizens to be activists. The president is seemingly directly looking at the viewers, so an interaction is established between the represented participant in the video (von der Leyen) and the audience. This activism will bring 'real benefits such as zero pollution, affordable secure energy, smarter transport and high-quality food', visually represented by a tree that symbolically turns from brown into green. The video is interspersed with excerpts from Ursula von der Leyen's talk. She moves from the use of 'we' to 'I' ('we have to act now', 'I want Europe to become the first climate-neutral continent in the world by 2050') and returns to the inclusive 'we' in the last sentence 'We Europeans are ready'. Moreover, the fact that the social actors (van Leeuwen 1996) 'we' are here identified as 'Europeans' presupposes that both policymakers and citizens are active participants in the development and promotion of a carbon-neutral strategy across Europe to try and counteract climate change.

The *EU for Paris agreement* video[7] is a clear example of positive discourse that inspires citizens and encourages them to act. It aims to make people become familiar with the agreement which was reached in December 2015 and provided for an action plan to reduce global warming to well below 2°C from 2020 onwards. Each image is accompanied by an imperative verb ('breathe', 'admire', 'respect', 'preserve', 'act', 'protect', 'cherish') which calls the viewer to action. All the verbs acquire a positive connotation since they are superimposed on beautiful nature scenery. Even though according to the politeness theory developed by Brown and Levinson (1987) imperatives may be face-threatening acts, they are often used in promotional discourse to create a connection between the producer and the audience (Zjakic, Han and Liu 2017) or they function as suggestions and recommendations (Pennock-Speck and Fuster-Márquez 2014). In the video under scrutiny the postcard-like natural scenery functions as a mitigating visual device, so the use of imperatives helps engage with viewers and also invites them to act. Nevertheless, the presence of high colour saturation makes these images appear surreal. When images do not appear realistic, they are in 'low modality' (Kress and van Leeuwen 2021). Modality 'refers to the way we communicate as how true or as how real a representation should be taken (i.e. not how true or how real it really is)' (Per and Machin 2020: 63). Since the still images of the video under investigation appear to convey the idea of a utopian world rather than a more sustainable life, they might not inspire actions for a better life.

The booklet *52 steps towards a greener city*[8] contains fifty-two practical suggestions, 'within everyone's reach' (p. 5), on how to support urban biodiversity throughout the year.

Examples of positive discourses can be detected on the first page (Excerpt 1), where the verb 'share' and the sentence 'It forms a delicate web of interconnected living things, and you are part of it' explicitly state that we are equally part of living creatures against the traditional discourse of humans versus animals and plants.

Excerpt 1

From flowering meadows with butterflies and bees to forests sheltering birds and bats, we share our planet with a rich variety of life called biodiversity. It forms a delicate web of interconnected living things, and you are part of it. In fact, it's your job to protect it, and keep it safe. (p. 6)

Among the positive actions suggested, we find becoming a locavore or a member of nature protection organizations (p. 40). Promoting biodiversity by supporting local producers is an example of ecological counter-discourse and the sentence 'Maybe you have a special skill they need!' becomes highly promotional thanks to the pronoun 'you', directly addressing the reader; the evaluative adjective in the noun phrase 'special skill' represents every addressee as unique and valuable. Addressing the reader personally can be a persuasive device, since in Western societies individuality is extremely valued and in public institutions there is a tendency to 'synthetic personalization' (Fairclough 2015: 52); this device gives the impression of treating the reader not as part of a mass audience but as an individual and is reinforced by the positive evaluative adjective 'special'.

Providing a brief analysis of the headings is important as they are the first elements that catch readers' attention and they provide key information to guide readers. Considering the semantic choices of all headings, it is possible to notice that the majority of verb and noun phrases belongs to the semantic sphere of protection ('look after', 'bird-safe', 'protect nature', 'a safe haven', 'protect wildlife', 'care for wetlands'). In other cases, we find the 'NATURE IS A PERSON' metaphor (Stibbe 2021: 66). Welcome and farewell verbs are both used positively, referring to the necessity of embracing nature in our everyday life ('Welcoming wildlife to your garden', p. 28) or getting rid of some bad habits ('Say farewell to food waste', p. 11). By personifying the wildlife, it may be implied that nature has its intrinsic value, so this metaphor places nature as the centre.

The text presents a mixture of registers. We find technical terms ('ecosystems', 'biodiversity', 'predators', 'pollinators', 'native flora') that make the text look scientific, and thus, reliable, and colloquial expressions ('you can do your bit', 'when you are done', 'make the most of it', 'spread the word') to establish solidarity between the author(s) and the readership. The same goal is achieved by some rhetorical figures such as personification 'Nature will thank you for it' and synecdoches such as 'feathered friends' (standing for birds).

Regarding the use of the personal pronouns 'we' and 'you' and the possessive adjectives 'our' and 'your', from the Foreword section ('we can all make the difference'), there is an extensive use of the inclusive 'we', which contributes to creating a sense of solidarity between the institution and readers. Consequently, by referring to their common belonging to the 'web of inter-connected living things' (p. 6), the EU wants to encourage their citizens to play an active role in improving the environmental condition of urban areas. The frequent use of 'you' is linked to the need of directly addressing the readers and underlining that it is their responsibility to change things. Moreover, there are several examples of premodification ('single-use plastics', 'eco-friendly shower gels', 'peat free potting soil'), which contribute to creating very concise and highly descriptive language, and modals of possibility (can and might), underlining the wide range of possible measures to be taken. Multimodally, the pictures present a low degree of modality since they are not realistic; they are often 'offer images', offering suggestions rather than demanding some kind of interaction, and the use of medium long shots widens the distance between the represented participants and the readers (Kress and van Leeuwen 2021: 124–5). Given the instructional nature of the booklet, images with an icon signifier, whose meaning is based on similarity of appearance, have been preferred as they are more immediate and easily understood. On the other hand, as these visuals do not suggest any type of interaction, they reduce identification with the represented participants and green initiatives might result in being too abstract.

Since I also wanted to see students' response to the EU materials on ecology and whether the EU multimodal texts could help students suggest alternative discourses to preserve the environment and take positive action, an ecoliteracy project work comprising two tasks (see Appendix A) was proposed in class during the winter semester 2021. Because of space constraints, the next subsection will be only devoted to the discussion of Task 2 and it will briefly illustrate some of the most original ideas proposed by the students to promote change in everyday actions.

11.3.2 The ecoliteracy project work: Students' outputs

During the first week of the course students were asked to form groups and choose their own team members (between two and five students).[9] For Task 1 they were first invited to select one of the topics listed in Appendix B, then on the basis of some of the MDA areas of analysis presented by Kress and van Leeuwen (2021) and discussed in class during the course (in particular, representation of social actors, composition and page layout, modality, typographical devices and colour), they had to identify key multimodal discursive features. For this activity, at the end of the semester, they had to submit a report in which they commented on the material analysed from a multimodal perspective. For the second task, the different teams were invited to design an ecological project and present it in class by imagining a meeting with the municipal council of their city/town. In order to help students design persuasive projects, a few lessons were devoted to the presentation of key verbal and visual characteristics which are often included in the discourse of advertising. At the end of the course, thirty final projects were presented[10] and ninety-four students[11] took part in the whole project work. Table 11.2 includes the topics of the projects categorized into four categories (EU policies in practice, in-person activities, technological devices and regeneration of abandoned areas/buildings) according to the main semiotic resource categorization (actions, materials and artefacts) used by the students to communicate; several projects present some overlapping elements. Due to space constraints only a small sample will be discussed in this section.[12]

Table 11.2 Main topics of students' projects

EU policies in practice
- *Well-being and Food*
- *Revaluation of mountain territory*
- *Gratifying dumpster*
- *Composting at home – The green and brown alternative*
- *A local circular economy*
- *There is no planet B*
- *Fighting climate change together*
- *Our project for a sustainable and green Casoria*
- *Unplastic your life!*

In-person activities (planting trees, making toys with recycling materials, awareness raising events, activities for schools, ecological competitions)
- *A tree for the future*
- *Why buy it when you can make it?*
- *Ecophilia Fever*
- *Let's turn the city upside down!*
- *Plastic pollution*
- *Ride the green, cycle off the beaten track*
- *Nice to Be Bio*

Technological devices (Apps, QR codes, GPS, machines, interactive maps)
- *#NapoliGreenGum*
- *whatahumanwears.com*
- *Eco-plastic*
- *For a better world we need better citizens*
- *MECO – Motivational Eco-friendly App*
- *Let's make a 'greener' Peninsula!*
- *The future project*
- *Technologically green. Our solutions for your tomorrow*
- *City air purifiers*
- *No more food waste*

Regeneration of abandoned areas/buildings
- *Italsider: from the past to the future*
- *Go-green Bagnoli!*
- *Sustainable refurbishment and reuse of neglected building in Torre del Greco*
- *The Bagnoli Bay Green Project*

As younger generations, particularly Generation Z and millennials, are very familiar with digital media (Mirriahi and Alonzo 2015), several projects include the use of social media, mostly Instagram, and the creation of an app for mobile devices or a real barcode. For instance, a group of students designed an app that allows us to monitor water pollution through detection systems placed along the banks of rivers, lakes and stretches of coastline to reduce environmental and health pollution and create better places to live and grow. If citizens use the application and carry out various environmental activities, they can obtain some benefits: tickets for the purchase of food, reduced waste taxes and university credits for students. Other students were able to combine their technological skills with their artistic ones. For example, inspired by city air purifiers installed in some European metropolitan areas, a group of students drew an original and creative skyscraper-sized air purifier for their own towns, located in an area known as 'Terra dei Fuochi' (literally land of fires) because of toxic waste illegally buried and burned there by organized crime (camorra). Inspired by the Dutch Smog Free Tower, the world's first outdoor air cleaner, a group of students designed a tower which stands atop an enormous glass-roofed greenhouse whose shape resembles the local volcano Mount Vesuvius in the area of Naples.

This is an instance of how most groups explored new semiotic resources and new ways of using existing semiotic resources in digital environments. The concept of ecoliteracy is shaped through their selection and use of those resources explored during the course (see Section 11.3.1). As Price, Jewitt and Brown (2013) mention, since the communicative landscape constantly changes, the development of multimodal resources is connected to social change and people's needs to use new semiotic resources and/or explore new ways of using the traditional ones.

The potentials of digital technologies were also explored by the group *MECO-Motivational Eco-Friendly App*. They introduced their project with the following reflection: 'Let's face the truth, we spend many hours of our day holding a phone, wandering aimlessly on social media, so we wonder: why don't we use that time to look after our world?' Thus, they invented *MECO*, an app based on a set of features (accumulation of point, reminder, no waste, anti-waste recipes) to reduce waste. It allows users to collect points through small daily actions that can help improve their lifestyle and protect the environment. The gained points can be used to purchase eco-sustainable products, such as a pocket ashtray and notebooks made with ornamental stone processing waste. *MECO* also informs users about news and studies related to the environment, and it is equipped with a notification system to remind people to live a more sustainable lifestyle. If the user clicks on the notification, they will receive further information on the benefits of their green

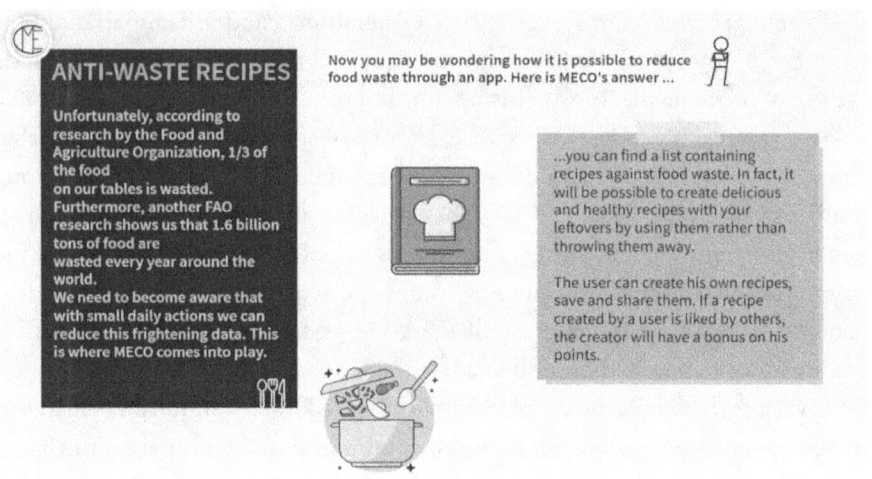

Figure 11.1 *MECO – Motivational Eco-Friendly App.* Copyright: the author.

actions. For example, they will discover that by turning off the tap while brushing their teeth, they will save an average of 30 litres of drinking water per day. App users can also be helped to create recipes with their leftover food (Figure 11.1).

This project is an example of hypertextuality, as the students introduced visual hyperlinks rather than the more traditional verbal forms for hyperlinks, thus enhancing the app interactive aesthetics. By clicking on the two pictures, a pink recipe book and a white pot, the user can find recipes against food waste or how to create their own recipe. Textually the two images appear in a very salient position (in the centre of the screen), and they are made salient even further by the contrast with the yellow background. Interpersonally the written text on the right signals to the reader that the page is connected with other sections. The theme of reusing food scraps and leftovers is present in other projects, and a new way of conceiving the relationship between human beings and food becomes an alternative positive discourse towards sustainability in these texts.

The group *What a human wears* chose to discuss sustainability in fashion. They started their presentation by stating that even though in the Paris Agreement (2015), the Juncker Plan (2017) and the Glasgow Climate Pact (2021), most of the signatory countries promised to cooperate to fight climate change and build a Europe sensitive to environmental exploitation, none of the agreements mentioned the impact of the fashion industry on the environment. The students presented the problem of 'fast fashion' and suggested an alternative: the website *whatahumanwears.com* that provides sustainable fashion tips and a list of local boutiques and retailers of eco-friendly fashion brands.

The group *Sustainable refurbishment and re-use of neglected building* presented a green project for their town, Torre del Greco, located on the Bay of Naples and famous for the production of artefacts made of coral. Since the area has some abandoned buildings, the project is based on the restoration of the former courthouse built in the 1980s and abandoned in 2009. The objective of the group project is to restore this neglected building and increase its value while reducing the impact on the environment and creating new spaces reserved for young people and non-profit associations. Figure 11.2 shows not only students' commitment to the project since they were even able to get the original maps of the building but also their ability to combine their technological skills and creativity. In their map, ideationally, colours clearly serve to identify the different places, as specified in the legend on the right of Figure 11.2. Textually, they create coherence in the map as the different colours distinguish different rooms for different purposes (i.e. purple for study rooms and green for meeting rooms). Given that colour also conveys interpersonal meaning, the choice of pastel colour palette can convey a message of tranquillity and well-being: the students specified that they used purple for the study rooms and green for the meeting rooms because, according to them, these two colours are, respectively, associated to productivity and relax.

The group *Why buy it when you can make it?* decided to organize an event drawing inspiration from the EU's storybook *Tom and Lila*.[13] One of Tom and Lila's ecological adventures is aimed at sensitizing children to use handmade toys: the protagonist, Tom, recycles natural materials, such as pebbles, twigs and logs, and creates a little toy train for his friend Timmy. Since plastic toys are the source of unprecedented pollution, the students planned a voluntary event in their city where the participants could create toys using recycling materials and their old toys. The students also created a brochure (Figure 11.3) and imagined that in 2012 they had founded the association 'Tom and Lila's friends' with the aim of promoting a series of initiatives to safeguard Naples' environmental and cultural heritage. In

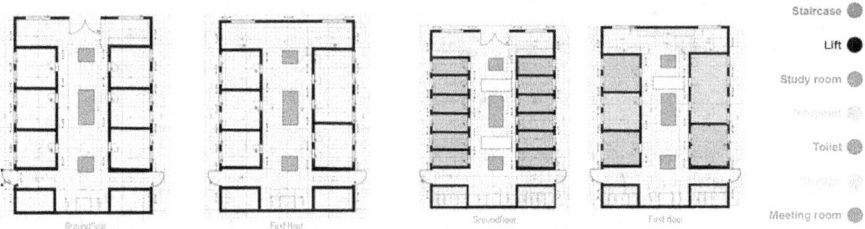

Figure 11.2 Maps, before and after restoration. Copyright: the author.

Figure 11.3 Brochure *Why buy it when you can make it?* Copyright: the author.

terms of composition the brochure is a triptych where both the verbal ('What you should bring') and visual text (Tom, Lila and a basket full of used toys) in the centre connects the other two pages. Moreover, different kinds of letter shapes, fonts and sizes convey different meanings: for example, typographical features (i.e. serif and sans-serif fonts, angularity and curvature) alternate, communicating both functionality/effectiveness, professionalism and merriness/indulgence.

11.4 Concluding remarks

The introduction of Kress and van Leeuwen's theoretical framework (2021) at the beginning of the course was essential to investigate a sample of text types collected from the EU's website *Learning Corner* and identify with students the most significant verbal and visual strategies that can contribute to encouraging positive discourses on ecology. In addition, the class project work allowed us to assess whether the EU materials can help develop eco-friendly consciousness among the younger generations. Project work aimed to encourage students towards ecological critical thinking, and, thanks to the analysis of texts from a Positive Multimodal Discourse Analysis (PMDA) perspective, students were able to suggest ways to make the world a better place and design actions that can be undertaken to pursue that purpose. They clearly showed a sense of ownership over the projects which allowed them to elaborate and hybridize the EU institutional discourses on the environment with the more locally contextualized and less authoritative voices of the local communities. This involved transferring ambitious institutional discourses into localized smaller but maybe more concrete actions. As it can be seen in Table 11.2, only a few projects were directly related to the topics discussed in the EU materials. Not only were most topics an original contribution, but also the local actions proposed by some teams were extremely innovative.

Given the results of the students' outputs, it is possible to conclude that promoting PMDA within ecolinguistics might be helpful to develop new forms of language which inspire people to care about the ecosystems life depends on. That means looking for alternative discourses with a focus on sustainable linguistic and multimodal choices: for instance, discourses which promote well-being rather than happiness, improving rather than changing, reducing rather than eliminating, reversing the course of climate change rather than fighting climate change.

It is still unclear what the 'positive' in PDA and ecolinguistics means in practice. This study can be considered positive since the case study presented aims to elicit social activism among the young. Thanks to the ecoliteracy project I investigated and interpreted student-generated data focusing on the extent to which they used their own agency in their collective projects. The ecoliteracy project provided students the tools to position themselves not as passive recipients of positive ecological messages but as agents of social change. By imagining local ecological initiatives, students became aware of what they could accomplish and start to work towards the design (Kress 2000) of future good practice.

Notes

1. *Cambridge Dictionary*, s.v. 'literacy (n.)', accessed 20 September 2022, https://dictionary.cambridge.org/dictionary/english/literacy.
2. *Learning Corner*, accessed 20 September 2022, https://europa.eu/learning-corner/home_en.
3. 'Environment, climate and energy', *Learning Corner*, accessed 20 September 2022, https://learning-corner.learning.europa.eu/learning-corner/learning-materials_en?f%5B0%5D=topics_topics%3A11.
4. *10 Global Climate Facts*, accessed 20 September 2022, https://audiovisual.ec.europa.eu/en/video/I-211936?lg=EN&sublg=en.
5. *Green Deal Proposal*, accessed 20 September 2022, https://audiovisual.ec.europa.eu/en/video/I-181464.
6. Given the enormous impact the present Russia–Ukraine war is having on the EU policies, it is important to clarify that this video was released on 11 December 2019.
7. *EU for Paris agreement*, accessed 20 September 2022, https://learning-corner.learning.europa.eu/learning-corner/learning-materials/eu-paris-agreement_en.
8. *52 steps towards a greener city*, accessed 20 September 2022, https://op.europa.eu/it/publication-detail/-/publication/080dffa8-49c5-11e8-be1d-01aa75ed71a1/language-en/format-PDF.
9. The students have provided permission to use their material for research purposes.
10. Most students preferred to use PowerPoint slides to illustrate their work.
11. I am grateful to all the students for their collaboration and enthusiasm in taking part in the project.
12. The written content given by the students is shown in their original version without any revision.
13. *Tom and Lila*, accessed 20 September 2022, https://learning-corner.learning.europa.eu/learning-materials/tom-and-lila_en.

References

Baker, S. (2006), *Sustainable Development*, London: Routledge.
Bartlett, T. (2012), *Hybrid Voices and Collaborative Change: Contextualising Positive Discourse Analysis*, New York: Routledge.

Bartlett, T. (2018), 'Positive Discourse Analysis', in J. Richardson and J. Flowerdew (eds), *The Routledge Handbook of Critical Discourse Studies*, 133–47, London: Routledge.

Brown, P. and S. Levinson (1987), *Politeness*, Cambridge: Cambridge University Press.

Capra, F. (1997), *The Web of Life*, London: Harper Collins.

Chen, W., T. Bartlett, and H. Peng (2021), 'The Erasure of Nature in the Discourse of Oil Production: Part I of an Enhanced Eco-Discourse Analysis', *Pragmatics and Society*, 12 (1): 6–32.

Devauld, C. and L. Green (2010), '"Don't Throw Anything Away!" Greenwashing in Public Relations', in *Proceedings of ANZCA: Media, Democracy and Change*, 1–12, Canberra: Australia and New Zealand Communication Association.

Djonov, E. and S. Zhao, eds (2014), *Critical Multimodal Studies of Popular Discourse*, New York: Routledge.

Fairclough, N. (2015), *Language and Power*, London, New York: Routledge.

Fill, A. and P. Mühlhäusler eds (2001), *The Ecolinguistics Reader: Language, Ecology, and Environment*, London: Continuum.

Hughes, J. M. F. (2018), 'Progressing Positive Discourse Analysis and/in Critical Discourse Studies: Reconstructing Resistance through Progressive Discourse Analysis', *Review of Communication*, 18 (3): 193–211.

Kress, G. (2000), 'Design and Transformation: New Theories of Meaning', in B. Cope and M. Kalantzis (eds), *Multiliteracies: Literacy Learning and the Design of Social Futures*, 153–61, London: Routledge.

Kress, G. and T. van Leeuwen (2001), *Multimodal Discourse. The Modes and Media of Contemporary Communication*, London: Arnold.

Kress, G. and T. van Leeuwen (2021 [1996]), *Reading Images: The Grammar of Visual Design*, 3rd edn, London: Routledge.

Macgilchrist, F. (2007), 'Positive Discourse Analysis: Contesting Dominant Discourses by Reframing the Issues', *Critical Approaches to Discourse Analysis Across Disciplines*, 1 (1): 74–94.

Macgilchrist, F. and E. Van Praet (2013), 'Writing the History of the Victors? Discourse, Social Change and (Radical) Democracy', *Journal of Language & Politics*, 12 (4): 626–51.

Martin, J. R. (2004), 'Positive Discourse Analysis: Solidarity and Change', *Revista Canaria Estudios Ingleses*, 49: 179–200.

McBride, B. B., C. A. Brewer, A. R. Berkowitz, and W. T. Borrie (2013), 'Environmental Literacy, Ecological Literacy, Ecoliteracy: What Do We Mean and How Did We Get Here?', *Ecosphere*, 4 (5): 67.

Mirriahi, N. and D. Alonzo (2015), 'Shedding Light on Students' Technology Preferences: Implications for Academic Development', *Journal of University Teaching and Learning Practice*, 12 (1): 1–16.

Mühlhäusler, P. (2003), *Language of Environment, Environment of Language: A Course in Ecolinguistics*, London: Battlebridge.

Partington, A. and C. Taylor (2018), *The Language of Persuasion in Politics: An Introduction*, London, New York: Routledge.
Pennock-Speck, B. and M. Fuster-Márquez (2014), 'Imperatives in Voice-Overs in British TV Commercials: Get This, Buy That, Taste the Other', *Discourse and Communication*, 8 (4): 411–26.
Per, L. and D. Machin (2020), *Introduction to Multimodal Analysis*, 2nd edn, London: Bloomsbury Publishing Plc.
Price, S., C. Jewitt, and B. Brown (2013), *The SAGE Handbook of Digital Technology Research*, London: SAGE Publications Ltd.
Rogers, R. and M. Mosley Wetzel (2013), 'Studying Agency in Literacy Teacher Education: A Layered Approach to Positive Discourse Analysis', *Critical Inquiry in Language Studies*, 10 (1): 62–92.
Stibbe, A. (2017), 'Positive Discourse Analysis. Rethinking Human Ecological Relationships', in A. F. Fill and H. Penz (eds), *The Routledge Handbook of Ecolinguistics*, 309–35, London: Routledge.
Stibbe, A. (2021), *Ecolinguistics: Language, Ecology and the Stories We Live By*, Abingdon: Routledge.
Su, T. (2016), 'Positive Discourse Analysis of Xi Jinping's Speech at the National University of Singapore Under Appraisal Theory', *Journal of Language Teaching and Research*, 7 (4): 796–801.
Unsworth, L., ed (2008), *Multimodal Semiotics: Functional Analysis in Contexts of Education*, London, New York: Continuum.
van Leeuwen, T. (1996), 'The Representation of Social Actors', in C. R. Caldas-Coulthard and M. Coulthard (eds), *Texts and Practices: Readings in Critical Discourse Analysis*, 32–69, London, New York: Routledge.
WCED (1987), *Report of the World Commission on Environment and Development*. Available online: file:///C:/Users/Dell/Downloads/A_42_427-EN.pdf (accessed 20 September 2022).
Zjakic, H., C. Han, and X. Liu (2017), 'Get Fit! The Use of Imperatives in Australian English Gym Advertisements on Facebook', *Discourse, Context and Media*, 16: 12–21.

Appendix A

TASKS for the ecoliteracy project work

1. By critically analysing and deconstructing the selected materials, try to identify the most significant multimodal communicative strategies which convey positive messages. Write a comment (between 1,500 to 2,000 words) and send it to your teacher by 31 December 2021.

2. Please suggest concrete examples of green projects at the local level to contribute to building a more sustainable future and identify possible and fruitful discursive solutions for taking positive ecological actions. Present your project to the class (via PPT presentation, video or speech) at the end of the course (9, 13 and 15 December 2021).

Appendix B

List of the EU materials and guidelines for Task 1

Environment, Climate, and Energy – Learning materials (https://europa.eu/learning-corner/learning-materials_en?topic=89)

Each group is invited to select a topic from the following list and collect the text types from the websites provided. Please, choose the topic according to the number of students specified in square brackets.

1. *Our planet, our future* (website and brochure) – ages nine to twelve; twelve to fifteen
Brochure (thirty-two pages)
[number of students: 2/3]

2. *Ready for the Green Challenge?* (slides, teaching kit) – ages twelve to fifteen; fifteen and over
[number of students: 2/3]

3. *EU Climate Action* (twenty-six videos) – ages twelve to fifteen; fifteen and over
[number of students: 4/5]

4. *EU Energy Policy* (five videos) – ages twelve to fifteen; fifteen and over
[number of students: 2/3]

5. *Fighting climate change together* (seventeen videos) – ages twelve to fifteen
[number of students: 3/4]

6. *52 steps towards a greener city* (activity book) – ages twelve to fifteen; fifteen and over
[number of students: 2]

7. *Climate Adaptation Strategy* (two videos) – ages fifteen and over
EU for Paris agreement (one video) – ages twelve to fifteen; fifteen and over
[number of students: 2]

8. *EU Green Deal* (six videos) – ages twelve to fifteen; fifteen and over
[number of students: 2/3]

9. *EU invests in the planet* (brochure – forty pages) – ages fifteen and over
[number of students: 2/3]

10. *Paneuropa versus Smog* (comics – twenty-three pages) – ages fifteen and over
[number of students: two]

11. *The flight of the cranes* (brochure – twenty-nine pages; teaching notes – two pages; five videos) – ages nine to twelve
[number of students: three]

12. *Tom and Lila* (story book – nine texts) – up to nine years
[number of students: 4/5]

Conclusion

A Closing and an Opening for Action-Taking through Communication

Maria Bortoluzzi and Elisabetta Zurru

The contributions to this volume create a rich tapestry of complementary threads and themes; they offer theoretical and applied advances to conceptualise, through verbal and non-verbal communication, values, beliefs and actions about and for the lifescape(s).[1]

The volume opens with two context-setting contributions which anticipate themes, approaches and suggestions offered in Parts II and III, respectively. The reflection by Alwin Frank Fill on the concept of 'tension' in verbal and non-verbal communication offers insights into the potential and drawbacks of this complex notion that can also be interpreted as a metaphor for our times. The instability of tension, Fill argues, can result in devastating consequences (such as environmental degradation and wars) as well as in renewing relations and connections between humans and the con-vironment. Fill's chapter also introduces the relevance of reaching out beyond verbal communication, which will be investigated in Part II.

Instability, in the sense of diachronic change, is the focus of Robert Poole's contribution. Through corpus-assisted discourse analysis, Poole offers clear evidence of diachronic development in language usage regarding climate factors, issues or weather events. This powerful and evidence-based methodology to identify discoursal trends which instantiate our relationship with ecosystems can be used for citizen advocacy, policymaking and education, among other areas. Poole's contribution also introduces the main theme of Part III: corpus-assisted eco-pedagogy can offer a learner-centred, discovery-based methodology for language study in relation to how we conceptualise the con-vironment. We believe that the knowledge and involvement derived from eco-pedagogy supports not only language education and awareness but also citizen education and social action.

Part II opens up to multimodal discourse and moves towards different strands of what we call ecomultimodality. Investigating a variety of text typologies and practices, the studies in Part II show the potential of multimodal studies to identify ensembles of verbal and non-verbal interactions, conventions and repertoires which orchestrate communication instantiating lifescapes. M. Cristina Caimotto demonstrates how communicative practices based on 'automentality' tend to be normalised and virtually go unquestioned. On the other hand, she analyses multimodal texts promoting sustainable mobility (as an alternative to 'fossil lifestyle') and draws the conclusion that these texts would benefit from being better aligned with deep principles of positive change and eco-sustainable citizen life. Elisabetta Zurru also reflects on how positive change can be actively promoted (or potentially prevented) by verbal, visual and multimodal metaphors used for representing the impending situation of the global climate crisis in its urgency. The 'ticking clock' can become an inescapable doomsday scenario contributing to paralysing hopelessness or be refrained to support and sustain a positive call to action. Time is also an underlying theme in Emilio Amideo's study: in discussing the complex clusters of interrelated and overlapping texts in one of Kara Walker's art installation, the author cogently demonstrates how art works can intersect our lives interacting with our bodies and actions. While the installation is made to melt and, in time, disappear, it contributes to individual and collective 'social-ecological memory' of a hegemonic colonial past which is still evident in the exploitative mindset towards the 'other' (human and more-than-human).

The last two contributions of Part II foreground the more-than-human. Gavin Lamb's work investigates the concept of 'hospitality' in multispecies encounters showing how conservation discourses become ineffective due to an unequal power relation between species (in this case the encounter between pinnipeds and humans). Media and social media coverage gives evidence of the problematic (and ultimately lethal) conceptualisation of 'hospitality'. Maria Bortoluzzi expands multispecies to encompass plants and explores the representation of plant identity as instantiated in institutional and promotional texts advocating for the protection of plants and ecosystems. Identity categorization is discussed and problematised due to the radical change in perspective offered by plants in relation with lifescapes.

In the contributions of Part III, research meets educational advances through ecoliteracy as enhanced by linguistic and multimodal education addressed to different communities of learners. In the chapter introducing the section, Andrea Sabine Sedlaczek complements Peirce's semiotic theory with ecolinguistics and multimodal studies. Thus, she proposes a flexible and holistic framework of analysis to promote and enhance ecoliteracy practices addressed to (young) adult learners. In the following chapter, Elisa Bertoldi focuses on university students who will become teachers of young learners. The study investigates the multimodal interaction of student teachers as storytellers and groups of children during picturebook narration in English as L2. The purpose of the events is involving children in econarratives that give salience to beliefs and practices respectful of the con-vironment. Grit Alter's chapter investigates SCUBA diving communication conventions as representative of the extreme fragility of humans in underwater conditions; this is complemented by the analysis of a children picturebook about ocean studies to raise awareness on the delicate and endangered balance of the ocean ecosystems. The study is a reflection on complementarity of ecoliteracy for adults and children. In the last chapter of the volume, Sole Alba Zollo uses the analysis of promotional strategies in EU resources for young adult learners to engage university students in a learning-by-doing educational task: planning eco-sustainable initiatives for a local community of their choice and writing promotional multimodal texts to inform and involve citizens. Ecoliteracy is carried out through student-centred learning by design.

The tapestry of the volume has been collectively woven in its threads, colours, patterns and materials; its stories have been told. As the contributors were developing them, in their different theoretical and applied areas, other questions surfaced, new issues appeared and unexpected perspectives opened. Ecolinguistics, ecoliteracy and ecomultimodality are areas that live and thrive interdisciplinarily and transdisciplinarily and can expand in multiple research directions. To remain within the scope of this volume, we believe that multimodal studies (in their different strands) have a lot to contribute to ecological communication towards what we call ecomultimodality, namely multimodal studies with a caring view and ethically informed attitude towards the lifescape and climate justice. A great number of multimodal studies have done that already, and several ecolinguistics studies have also dealt with multimodal aspects. We believe in the potential of these fast-expanding research areas, which will offer precious insights for positive ecological communication and action.

Similarly, we think that ecoliteracy can profit from being informed by studies about language and other semiotic systems. This is not a novel concept, since some scholars have already expanded ecoliteracy through ecolinguistics (or other strands of discourse studies); however, we need to underline the extraordinary potential of this complementarity. We also think that ecoliteracy would profit from cross-fertilising with multiliteracies studies which include reflections on a variety of semiotic practices and affordances.

Contributors have underlined the well-known limits of verbal and semiotic methodologies based on human language, body and perception to describe what is other-than-us (their *Umwelt*), and we can hardly imagine. Research needs to adopt and develop innovative methodologies, inevitably human, but also more flexible, inclusive of and reaching out to the more-than-us in the web of life.

We would like to end by mentioning fundamental human voices who have not been included in the volume, even though some contributions evoked them. Their resilient existence shows that humans are able to establish deep contact with the con-vironment and lifescapes. On the one hand, literary and creative works of art allow us to explore the limits of human language and its anthropocentrism and give us insights into what is 'beyond' human limitations. On the other, we want to mention the voices of the native peoples whose cultures are still able to narrate the lifescapes, including humans, rather than depicting their human exceptionalism. These peoples and their more-than-human surroundings are among the most affected by the current climate imbalance and lack of global climate justice. Their stories and voices are the way forward to mediate the lifescape, and learn it again.

Note

1 This contribution was jointly written and edited by both authors.

Index

Abasnnouga, G.   128 n.13
action   1, 46, 50, 56, 118, 157, 169, 183, 185, 198, 203, 209, 212, 241, 251, 258
   of 'breathing life'   169
   climate action   90, 97, 98, 101
   collective action   92, 136
   courses of action   139
   ecological action   90, 92, 255
   environmental action   90, 100
   and facial expressions   210
   green action   247–8
   human action   162, 164, 210
   Involved in action   158
   participatory action   236
   plant action and agentivity   170
   positive action   3, 10, 167, 184, 240, 244, 245
   read-aloud talk   201
   reciprocal action   39
   of 'restoring life to the land'   165
   social action   7, 154, 155, 159
   transformative actions   5, 8
   types of   237
activation   155, 158
activism   90, 242, 251
actor-network theory   155
Adami, E.   7
adjective collocates   58
   of hurricane   49–53
   of wildfire   54, 55
advocacy   56, 67–84, 257
The 2030 Agenda for Sustainable Development   158–60
agentive stances   138–9
Aldred, D.   70, 78
Alexander, R.   5, 45
Alfred: A Masque (Thomson)   112, 127 n.1
Allewaert, M.   115
Amor vittorioso (Gastoldi)   30, 40
Analysis of a Net Zero 2030 Target for Greater London report   81

animal(s)   26, 27, 48, 140, 152, 170, 227
   human animal   10, 134
   idioms and stereotypes   28–9
   more-than-human animal(s)   2, 7, 11, 46, 126, 260
   non-human animal(s)   46–8, 59, 153, 155, 157–60, 164, 165, 168, 190
   welfare   141, 142
Anthropocene   3, 71, 88, 132–50, 170, 186, 190, 192
anthropocentric mentality   4
anthropocentrism   10, 154, 229, 260
anticipatory discourse   138, 139, 142, 149
anti-ecological discourse   10
artivism   90, 91, 130
Attenborough, D.   157, 166, 167
An Audience (Walker)   114, 119, 123, 124
automentality   13, 69, 72, 77, 258
automobility   70, 72, 74, 77, 78
awareness   1, 7, 8, 10, 36, 39, 89, 90, 97, 101, 114, 118, 124, 166, 186, 200, 204, 219, 257, 259
   children's awareness   16, 230
   critical language awareness (CLA)   55
   ecocritical language awareness   45, 49, 57, 60
   eco-friendly awareness   237
   ecoliterate awareness   188, 191
   ecological awareness   15, 59, 179, 184, 194, 241
   environmental awareness   157
   of environmental protection   236
   historical awareness   116
   public awareness   44
   rhetorical awareness   56
   self-awareness   199
   situational awareness   225
   social awareness   48, 116
   students' awareness   12
   student teachers' awareness   213
   young people's awareness   219

Baartman, S. 128 n.11
Baker, P.C. 70
Bakke-Jensen, F. 141, 142
Baldry, A. 158
Balkmar, D. 78
Baluška, F. 153
Barlow, Z. 9
Bartlett, T. 240
The Beeman (Krebs) 207–12
Bellewes, E. 170 n.1, 171 n.5
Beloved (Morrison) 121
Bennett, L. 9
Bevitori, C. 47
binary theory of phenomena 41
Black diaspora 115
Bonnefille, S. 47
Borrell, J. 73, 74, 83
Bortoluzzi, M. 7, 258
Boyd, A. 97
Bradley, R.S. 89
The Brilliant Deep 16, 219, 226–31
Brønn, P.S. 142
Brown, B. 247
Brown, P. 243
Brubacker, R. 154
Buckley, P. 9
Bühler, K. 25
Bush, G.W. 47
business communication 47

Caimotto, M.C. 7, 13, 258
Candea, M. 148
Cape Town water clock 99–100
Capra, F. 8, 9, 29, 40, 169, 235
carbon footprints 4, 92
Carle, E. 226
catastrophic convergence 71
Cauzzo, B. 170 n.1
CDA. *see* critical discourse analysis (CDA)
CDS. *see* critical discourse studies (CDS)
Center for Ecoliteracy 9, 29, 40
children 79, 127 n.8, 227, 228, 241, 249
    The Brilliant Deep 16, 228
    children's awareness 16, 230
    ecological communication 16
    Picturebook Mediation 197–214
    picturebook narration 259
children's awareness 16, 230
Christianity 114

Chutel, L. 100
citizenship education 5, 198. *see also* ecoliteracy
climate change 14, 37, 41, 45, 56, 71, 89, 93, 95, 137, 140, 143, 163, 220, 248, 251
    10 Global Climate Facts 241
    anthropocenic-caused climate change 88
    consequences of 60, 103
    discourse 46, 47, 88, 103
    and geopolitics 73
    and global warming 46, 57, 58
    human-influenced climate change 3
    Intergovernmental Panel on Climate Change (IPCC) 44, 72, 89
    public awareness of 44
    social awareness of 48
    social evidence of 49, 52
    ticking clock metaphor 103
Climate Clock 97, 100
climate crisis 3, 44, 48, 49, 53–7, 67, 68, 71, 83, 167, 169, 220, 258
clock is ticking metaphor 98–102
The Cloud (Cumming) 227
'Coal consumption affecting climate' 3
Code, J.M. 179
collocation 50, 160, 161, 227
collocational pairing 50
colonial history 113
colonialism 114–16, 127 n.3
comic effects 33–4
communication 2
    about the ocean 226–30
    business communication 47
    ecological communication 213, 218, 231, 236, 259
    environmental communication 91, 93, 94, 103, 220
    human communication 6, 116
    knowledge communication 237
    meta-communication 230, 232 n.3
    metaphorical communication 95
    multimodal communication 7, 152, 213, 237
    non-verbal communication 1, 3, 9, 11–13, 95, 152, 219, 220, 230, 257
    in the ocean 221–5

personal communication 36
Positive Discourse Analysis
  approach 103
risk communication 219, 225
SCUBA communication 219–20
'situated' communication 6
underwater communication 217, 218, 220, 221, 224, 225
verbal communication 1, 3, 9, 11–13, 95, 152, 218, 231, 257
visual communication 89, 116
visuality and multimodality 94
voice communication 218
communication underwater 217, 218, 220, 221, 224, 225
conflict 12, 13, 30, 34–8, 40, 67, 79, 80, 82, 141
controversy mapping 136
con-vironment 1, 4, 5, 10, 12, 14, 28, 40, 113, 116, 118, 257, 259, 260
Cooper, F. 154
the Cooperative Principle 35
coral restoration 16, 219, 231
Coral Restoration Foundation 226
corpus-assisted discourse studies 136, 257
corpus-assisted ecolinguistics 12, 45–9
corpus-assisted ecopedagogy 12, 55–60, 257
Corpus Linguistics for English Teachers 57
Corpus of Contemporary American English (COCA) 50
Covid-19 pandemic 1, 67, 68, 93
Cowan, J. 99
critical discourse analysis (CDA) 2, 14, 15, 178, 184, 238, 239. *see also* critical discourse studies (CDS)
critical discourse studies (CDS) 2, 3, 68, 69, 152, 170, 184. *see also* critical discourse analysis (CDA)
critical fabulation 122, 128 n.9
critical language awareness (CLA) 55, 56
critical multimodal studies 169
Crutzen, P.J. 88
cycling 13, 68–74, 76–80, 82

Daggett, C. 71, 77
Dahrendorf, R. 35

Dancygier, B. 7, 103, 104, 105 n.19, 108 n.19
Das Ende der Großen (Kohr) 38
data-driven approach 56, 159
deep ecology 5, 7, 11
deforestation 114, 163, 166, 207
degree of abstraction 59
Demuth, B. 138
Derrida, J. 133, 134
de Saint-George, I. 138, 139
Diamantopoulou, S. 7
Dickinson, J.L. 103
Diehl, C. 125
Die Kunst des Streitens (Rother) 35
discourse 5, 7, 67–84, 103, 104, 116, 117, 122, 136, 152, 153, 155, 157, 170, 181, 235, 238, 241, 242
  anticipatory discourse 138, 139, 142, 149
  anti-ecological discourse 10
  climate change discourse 46, 47, 88, 103
  ecological discourse 46, 59, 103
  environmental discourse 89, 90, 95, 132
  EU institutional discourses 251
  'gathering up' discourses 143
  of hospitality 132, 133, 136, 140
  institutional discourse 157, 169, 237
  interactional 'footings' 139
  media discourse 132, 135
  multimodal discourse 13
  of 'non-hospitality' 133
  on non-human animals 155
  policymaking discourses 13
  political discourse 47
  positive discourses 3, 239, 243, 248
  pseudoscientific discourse 115, 128 n.11
  public discourse 44, 133, 240
  retrospective discourses 142, 144–6, 149
  US discourse 46
  verbal and visual discourses 13
  verbal discourse 2
  Walker's counter-discourse 123
  Western patriarchal discourses 124
distancing 26, 39
dive briefing 225

Division of Conservation and Resources Management (DOCARE)   144, 146, 148
Dixon, M.   127 n.3
Doomsday Clock   99
Döring, M.   5
dys-tension   35–6

earth is a dying living being metaphor   98, 99
ecocritical language awareness   45, 49, 57, 60
eco-fascism   90
eco-friendly awareness   237
ecolinguistics   69–72, 78, 103, 133, 136, 155, 168, 169, 182–5, 218, 219, 251, 259
   corpus-assisted ecolinguistics   12, 44–60
   definition of   5
   positive multimodal discourse analysis   238–40
   and SCUBA dive communication   220
   seminal studies in   7
ecoliteracy   29–30
   for adults   259
   for children   197–214
   in essayistic media texts   177–94
   for young people   235–52
ecoliterate awareness   188, 191
ecological action   90, 92, 103, 238, 255
ecological awareness   15, 59, 179, 184, 194, 241
ecological communication   213, 218, 231, 236, 259
ecological crisis   1, 88, 90, 93, 180, 230
ecological discourse   46, 59, 103
ecological intelligence   9
ecology (of communication)   3, 39, 169, 235, 239
ecomultimodality/multimodal studies   2, 7, 155, 169, 258, 259
econarrative   213, 259
The Economist   132
eco-pedagogy   12, 44–60, 257
ecosystem restoration   161
ecosystems   1, 2, 4–6, 8–11, 13, 14, 16, 29, 88, 90, 93, 113, 137, 138, 152, 156, 159, 160, 161, 163–9, 180, 183, 184, 201, 213, 217–20, 225, 227, 230, 231, 241, 251, 258, 259
Ekman, P.   224
Eliasson, O.   96
elitism   71
Ellis, G.   200
The End of Nature (McKibben)   44
English L2   197–214
English language teaching (ELT)   44–60
environmental alarmism   89, 90
environmental awareness   157
environmental communication   91, 93, 94, 103, 220
environmental discourse   89, 90, 95, 132, 241
environmental education   179, 197, 198
environmental hypocognition   13, 69
environmental videos
   The Green Planet   157, 166–9
   Nature Now   157, 166–9
epistemic stances   138, 139
essayistic media text   15, 177–94
essays   118, 135, 177, 178, 186, 188, 190–4, 195 n.3
EU for Paris agreement   243, 248, 252 n.7
EU institutional discourses   251
EU Learning Corner   236, 241–5, 251
   EU materials and guidelines   255–6
   TASKS for ecoliteracy project work   254–5
euphemisms   27, 40
European Green Deal   242
European Union (EU)   16, 74, 259
   learning materials   235–52
Europe Beyond Coal campaign   74
EU's 'REPowerEU plan'   73
eu-tension   35–6
event-based corpora   135

Fevyer, D.   70, 78
field-specific literacy   179, 180
Fill, A.F.   5–7, 12, 32, 35, 94, 170 n.1, 226, 228, 230, 239, 257
Flusberg, S.J.   103
Fons Americanus (Walker)   113, 126
A Forest (Martin)   207–9, 211, 212
fossil fuels   13, 44, 68, 69, 71–4, 77, 83, 92, 93

4L-4R collocational window 50
Foust, C.R. 102
frames of consistency 46
framing 49, 74, 79, 92, 95, 98, 100, 103, 140, 163, 188
Frayne, C. 47, 48
#FridaysForFuture online protest 1, 100, 101
Friesen, W.V. 224
Furness, Z. 71
Fusari, S. 47, 48

'Gaia' hypothesis 10
Gastoldi, G. 30, 40
'gathering up' discourses 143
Gersie, A. 184
The Girl in Red (Frisch and Innocenti) 227
Glasgow Climate Pact 248
global warming 37, 44, 46, 57, 58, 89, 92, 97, 241, 243
Goatly, A. 46
Goddard, T. 70
Golan, G. 97
Goleman, D. 9
Gössling, S. 71
Grant, W.J. 48, 49
grassroots discourse 68, 74–6
grassroots movements 74–6
The Great Chain of Being 4
Green, J. 177, 185–8, 190–2
Green Deal Proposal 242
The Green Planet (Attenborough) 157, 166–9
greenspeak 46
Gricean maxims 35
Grilli, G. 199
growthism 4, 37–8, 41, 89
Grundmann, R. 46
A Guide to Using Corpora for English Language Learners 57
Gulsrud, N.M. 78–80, 83

Haeckel, E. 39
Hall, S. 118
Halliday, M.A.K. 4, 5, 25, 26, 37, 39, 68, 116, 117
Hamlet (Shakespeare) 38
Hansen, A. 7

Hansen, J. 44
Hartman, S. 128 n.9
Heeks, P. 199
Henderson, J. 78–80, 83
Hendricks, R.K. 95
heritage forests carbon sinks 161
Heuberger, R. 27, 229
historical awareness 116
Hofman-Bergholm, M. 184
Horowitz, J. 141
hospitality 14, 132–50, 258
Hughes, M.K. 89
human-animal interaction 134
human communication 6, 116
human-nonhuman relation 4
Hyland, K. 188
hypocognition 72–4, 83, 93
   environmental hypocognition 13, 69

Ice Watch 96, 101
informational picturebooks 199, 208
Ingersoll, K.A. 147
institutional discourse 157, 169, 237
institutional reports 14, 160
interactional meanings 118, 119
Intergovernmental Panel on Climate Change (IPCC) 44. *see also* IPCC AR6 WGIII
intermediality 30
intermedial tension 30–3
International Environmental Agency (IEA) 75
international hand signals 221–4
IPCC AR6 WGIII 81–3. *see also* Intergovernmental Panel on Climate Change (IPCC)

Jakobson, R. 25
Jewitt, C. 6, 247
Jones, D. 145
Juncker Plan 248

'The Kaua'i 'ō'ō' 191–3
Kees, J. 71
Kendall's Tau correlation coefficient 45, 50, 54
Kincaid, J. 127 n.3
Kohr, L. 38
Krakovska, S. 72, 73

Krebs, L.   207
Kress, G.   6, 7, 117, 158
Krishnamurthy, R.   46
Kumaran, R.   158

Lakoff, G.   72–4, 80, 83, 94, 97
#Lancsbox corpus tools   160
language proficiency tests   57
learning   3, 7, 8, 10, 15, 16, 55–7, 193, 194, 197, 203, 259
   active learning   9
   environmental learning   184
   EU learning materials   235–52
   language learning   58, 60
   literacy learning   181
Ledin, P.   117
Levinson, S.   243
lifescape(s)   1–11, 13, 15, 16, 152–71, 210, 237, 257–60
lifestyle   45, 68, 71, 72, 77, 83, 88, 177, 186, 247
Lim, F.V.   7
linguistic interaction   33–6
linguistic parallelism   241
Litman, T.   71
The Living Mountain (Shepherd)   11
London Cycling Campaign (LCC)   82
Lovelock, J.E.   10
Luna, H.   9

Machin, D.   7, 116, 117, 128 n.13
Mahlman, J.   88
Mancuso, S.   153
Mann, M.E.   89, 92, 94
Margulis, L.M.   10
Martin, J.R.   3, 59, 238, 240
Matlock, T.   103
Matthiessen, C.M.I.M.   25
McBride, B.B.   8, 179, 180
McFall-Johnsen, M.   99
McKibben, B.   44
MECO-Motivational Eco-Friendly App   247, 248
media discourse   132, 135
Messner, K.   219, 225–7, 229
meta-communication   230, 232 n.3
meta-functions of language   25
metaphor
   conceptual metaphor   98, 103, 104 n.1

multimodal metaphor   98, 102, 104 n.1, 258
non-verbal metaphor   88–104
verbal metaphor   99–102, 167
visual metaphor   88–90, 99, 101
metaphorical communication   95
metaphtonymy   96, 97, 101
Meyer, M.A.   147
mobility   13, 68–70, 72, 74, 82, 83, 258
   active mobility   13, 68, 69, 78–83
   green mobility   80
   mobility justice   69–72, 75, 80
   mobility politics   79
   "quasi-private" mobility   70
mobility justice   69–72, 75, 80
Mobility Justice (Sheller)   70
Molena, F.   4
Monbiot, G.   166, 167
Montreal Protocol   90, 92, 100
monumental installation. *see A Subtlety* (Walker)
more-than-human
   animal   2, 7, 11, 46, 126, 260
   identities   7
Morrison, T.   121
Mourão, S.   200
Mühlhäusler, P.   5, 7, 29, 45, 97, 239
multiliteracies pedagogies   8
multiliteracies studies   10, 178, 180, 181, 260
multimodal communication   7, 213
multimodal critical discourse analysis (MCDA)   114, 116–18. *see also* critical multimodal studies
multimodal discourse   13
multimodal discourse analysis (MDA)   239, 240, 245
multimodality   6, 7, 94, 95, 116, 156, 181, 202, 203
multimodal studies   1, 2, 7, 155, 169, 258, 259
multispecies   2, 258
   hospitality   132–50
multispecies discourse analysis   143, 145
Murphy, W.   102
The Musicalization of Fiction (Wolf)   30
Musk, E.   89

Næss, A.   5, 11

Nanson, A.   184, 190
Natural Climate Solutions (NCS)   166, 167
Nature Now   157, 166–9
Nedimyer, K.   226–31
neoliberalism   79
New Literacy Studies (NLS)   178, 180, 181, 183
news media analysis   135, 139
nexus analysis   136
Nikolajeva, M.   219, 226
Nixon, R.   115
non-fiction picturebooks   199, 226–30
non-verbal communication   1, 3, 9, 11–13, 95, 152, 219, 220, 230, 257
non-verbal metaphors   88–104
non-verbal underwater communication   220, 225
Norton, P.D.   77
Norwegian Biodiversity Information Centre   137
Nyong'o, T.   122, 125

ocean picturebooks   217–31
organizational meanings   118, 121
Orr, D.   8, 29
O'Toole, M.   117
'Our Planet, Our Health'   93

Paganism   114
participant roles   164, 203
passivation   155, 158
PDA. *see* positive discourse analysis (PDA)
Peabody, R.   122
Peirce, C.S.   15, 178, 181–4, 194 n.1
Peirce's semiotic theory   182, 258
Penguins of Madagascar (POM) (Green)   188–91
Penz, H.   7, 226, 228
personal communication   36
petro-masculinity   67–84
picturebook mediation   16, 197–213
   informational picturebooks   208
   multimodal perspective   202–3
   picturebooks about nature   207–10
   read-aloud sessions   197–8, 200, 201, 207, 210–12

   stages of   200, 201
   Telling And Listening to Eco-Sustainable Stories (TALES) initiative   204–6
picturebook(s)   16, 197–200, 218, 219, 225–31, 232 n.4, 259
pinniped corpora   136, 137
plant representation   152, 153, 155–8, 166, 168–70
plant(s)   14, 15, 152–70, 199, 258
plurimedial tension   30–3
policymaking discourses   13
political discourse   47
Poole, R.   12, 136, 257
Poppenheimer, L.   127 n.8
positive discourse analysis (PDA)   3, 16, 103, 236, 238
Positive Discourse Analysis: Solidarity and Change (Martin)   238
positive discourses   3, 239, 243, 248
positive multimodal discourse analysis   235–52
power   2, 10, 12, 36, 37, 51, 52, 55, 67–84, 116, 119, 125, 145, 148, 149, 153, 165, 166, 168, 169, 190, 192, 238
Price, S.   247
pseudo-realism   154
pseudoscientific discourse   115, 128 n.11
public awareness   44
public discourse   44, 133, 240
pure Bambi effect   140

quarrel   33–6, 40

Radcliffe-Brown, A.R.   34
Ralph, K.   70
read-aloud sessions   16, 197–8, 200–5, 207, 210, 212, 213, 214 n.1
recycling   125, 249
#ReframeCovid initiative   95
Reisigl, M.   156
representational meanings   117–19, 123
Restoring Life to the Land (RLL2021)   160–5, 169
retrospective discourses   142, 144–6, 149
rhetorical awareness   56
Right/Conservative discourse   79, 80

The Role of Sustainable Land Management in Ecosystem Restoration 160
Rosie's Walk (Hutchins) 227
The Rumpus 192
Rune Aae 138, 139, 141

Schieffelin, E. 184
Schumacher, E.F. 38
Scientist rebellion 93
Scott, C. 219, 226
SCUBA interaction 217–31
   SCUBA communication 219–20
sculptures 90, 113, 114, 116–19, 122, 124, 125
Sedlaczek, A.S. 7, 15
self-awareness 199
semiotic resources 116, 117, 125, 198, 201–3, 205–7, 213, 239, 246, 247
Sheller, M. 70, 75, 80, 81, 83
Shepherd, N. 11
Shiva, V. 11
Sinha, B. 99, 100
'situated' communication 6
situational awareness 225
Sketch Engine 135
slave trade 113, 115, 120, 127 n.3
Small Is Beautiful (Schumacher) 38
Smith, Z. 126
Sobrino, P. 96
Social Actor Theory 158
social awareness 48, 116
social-ecological memory 14, 112–27, 258
socio-semiotic approach 152, 158
Solnit, R. 92
Standard Average European (SAE) languages 38
Steffensen, S.V. 5–7
Stibbe, A. 5–7, 9, 38, 45, 69, 78, 149, 155, 170, 200, 220, 230, 235, 239, 242
Stoermer, E.F. 88
A Stone Sat Still (Wenzel) 208, 210, 212
Støre, J.G. 142
storytelling 184, 205, 207, 212, 213
Streiten Verbindet (Bach and Wyden) 35
students' awareness 12
student teachers' awareness 213
A Subtlety (Walker) 118–25, 127 n.2
sugar 113, 114, 118, 119, 121, 122, 124, 125

Surinderpal, K. 158
suspense 26, 30, 229
sustainable discourse(s) 251
sustainable land management 161, 165
syntactic functions of language 25

Tafirenyika, M. 99, 100
teacher education 16, 198
Teaching English with Corpora: A Resource Book 57
Telling and Listening to Eco-Sustainable Stories (TALES) initiative 15, 197, 198, 204–6
tension 12, 140, 167–169, 257
   in ecological communication 25–41
   between humans and their natural environment 26–30
   intermedial tension 30–3
   in linguistic interaction 33–6
   plurimedial tension 30–3
   between text and music 30–1
   between text and picture 31–3
The Anthropocene Reviewed (TAR) (Green) 177–94
Thibault, P. 158
Thibodeau, P.H. 103
Thunberg, G. 166
ticking clock metaphor
   in news reports 99–100
   in social media 100–2
   in visual arts 96–9
time is a resource metaphor 98, 103, 104
time is running out metaphor 97–9, 101, 102
Trampe, W. 27
Trömel-Plötz, S. 34

unconditional hospitality 133
underwater communication 217, 218, 220, 221, 224, 225
United Nations Convention to Combat Desertification (UNCCD) 160
unreliable narrator 122
Urry, J. 70
US discourse 46

Valvason, E. 159
van Dooren, T. 134, 143, 145, 149

van Leeuwen, T.   6, 7, 116, 117, 154, 155, 158, 200, 239, 240, 245, 251
Van Lier, L.   9
verbal communication   1, 3, 9, 11–13, 95, 152, 218, 231, 257
verbal discourse   2
verbal literacy   8
The Very Hungry Caterpillar (Carle)   226
visual communication   89, 116
visual discourses   13
visuality and multimodality   94
visual metaphor   88–90, 99
Volpin, L.   207

Walker, K.   14, 112–27, 258
Walker's counter-discourse   123
Walks, A.   72
Walsh, E.   48, 49
Walsh, M.   90
Wardi, A.J.   115
war monuments   128 n.13
The Web of Life (Capra)   8

We Love Dinosaurs (Volpin)   207, 209, 211
Wenzel, B.   208
Western patriarchal discourses   124
White, L. Jr.   114
White Wilderness   190
Whorf, B.L.   38
wilderness   58
Wodak, R.   2, 156
World Commission on Environment and Development (WCED)   235
World Heritage Forests (WHF2021)   160, 163–6, 169
World Overview of Conservation Approaches and Technologies (WOCAT)   160

young people's awareness   219
Ytteborg, C.   149, 150

Zhdanava, A.   158
Zurru, E.   7, 13, 258

www.ingramcontent.com/pod-product-compliance
Lightning Source LLC
Chambersburg PA
CBHW071810300426
44116CB00009B/1262